# Lecture Notes in Computer Science 6368

*Commenced Publication in 1973*
Founding and Former Series Editors:
Gerhard Goos, Juris Hartmanis, and Jan van Leeuwen

More information about this series at http://www.springer.com/series/7409

Ella Roubtsova · Ashley McNeile
Ekkart Kindler · Christian Gerth (Eds.)

# Behavior Modeling – Foundations and Applications

International Workshops, BM-FA 2009–2014
Revised Selected Papers

 Springer

*Editors*
Ella Roubtsova
Open University of the Netherlands
Heerlen
The Netherlands

Ashley McNeile
Metamaxim
London
UK

Ekkart Kindler
Technical University of Denmark
Kgs. Lyngby
Denmark

Christian Gerth
Osnabrück University of Applied Sciences
Osnabrück
Germany

ISSN 0302-9743          ISSN 1611-3349   (electronic)
Lecture Notes in Computer Science
ISBN 978-3-319-21911-0        ISBN 978-3-319-21912-7   (eBook)
DOI 10.1007/978-3-319-21912-7

Library of Congress Control Number: 2015944149

LNCS Sublibrary: SL3 – Information Systems and Applications, incl. Internet/Web, and HCI

Springer Cham Heidelberg New York Dordrecht London
© Springer International Publishing Switzerland 2015

Printed on acid-free paper

Springer International Publishing AG Switzerland is part of Springer Science+Business Media
(www.springer.com)

# Preface

This book contains revised selected papers of six annual International Workshops on Behaviour Modelling - Foundations and Applications, which were held from 2009 to 2014 [1–6].

Behaviour modelling is about describing a system in terms of its states and its transitions from one state to another. The transitions may be initiated by the system itself or by the systems environment, including the system's users and other systems. Behaviour models capture system requirements forming the basis of their precision and completeness. They may have execution semantics, and, therefore, they are related to system simulation techniques.

Over the last decade, models have played an ever increasing role in software engineering, driven and dominated by the UML (Unified Modeling Language) and the MDA (Model Driven Architecture) standards. Today, it is possible that major parts of software systems can be generated from models fully automatically.

However, most of today's code generators work mainly from class diagram models and only address structural parts of the software. The code that implements behavioural business rules and governs the protocols of interaction between the user and the environment has to be added using traditional coding techniques. It seems that we have not been as successful in leveraging the power of modelling to raise the level of abstraction and eliminate low level coding in the behavioural realm as we have in the structural realm. Nor have we managed to properly exploit the potential of behaviour models to enable formal analysis and reasoning about behaviour, and thereby assure the quality of the final software.

This was the starting point of the series of workshops on Behaviour Modelling - Foundations and Applications (BM-FA). The objective was to raise awareness of the unrealised potential of behaviour modelling, to identify factors that have contributed to this, and ultimately to propose new ideas that overcome these barriers. We wanted to find better ways for modelling behaviour, for speeding up the software development process, better understanding its behaviour and guaranteeing its correctness.

This volume gives an overview of the ideas, problems, and solutions that were presented and discussed over the course of these six BM-FA workshops. The workshop papers and discussions explored the philosophy and practice of modelling, described the experience and problems with existing notations, and proposed new concepts for modelling behaviour and for combining existing modelling languages in new ways.

# Modelling Practices

This volume starts with the paper written by Haim Kilov, a former academic (Stevens Institute of Technology, USA), who works as an adviser for businesses applying modelling. This paper combines and expresses the opinions of modellers working in different domains and using different modelling techniques, and represents the essence of the contributions of industrial participants of our workshop series. They all talked of the need to recognise and accumulate patterns and abstractions, and of the importance of ensuring that definitions are easily understandable by users. H. Kilov gives a historical example of specifications of insurance business showing that a complex specification is not a quality specification. The author calls on modellers to think clearly, separate essentials from specifics, avoid complexity and eschew tacit assumptions.

# Standards in Behaviour Modelling

After this general introduction of modelling, the volume presents an example of using notations from standard UML for modelling behaviour.

The paper by Martin Gogolla, Lars Hamann, Frank Hilken, and Matthias Sedlmeier presents the evolution of a UML- and OCL–based (Object Constraint Language) tool for modelling. The group has been developing the tool USE (UML-based Specification Environment) for about 15 years. While it started as a tool for structural modelling with OCL constraints, it now addresses behaviour too. The paper illustrates the use of the tool for analysis of a system described structurally with a class diagram, including class invariants; and behaviourally with operation pre- and post-conditions, operation implementations, and statecharts. The paper shows that even for relatively small models, the validation of the structural models by behavioural views is needed, and is a non-trivial task. The authors talk of the need to work further to investigate how such tools would be used in the context of business systems development.

In the next paper, Gefei Zhang and Matthias M. Hölzl state that one of the barriers to widespread adoption of UML behaviour modelling languages is in the complexity of the models. The authors propose metrics of complexity of the UML statechart models arising from different kinds of non-locality for the current behaviour of a model being spread over several model elements instead of being locally available.

To illustrate the application of UML-based approaches for modelling embedded systems, we have chosen the paper by Karolina Zurowska and Juergen Dingel. They note that the execution semantics of UML behavioural models is not uniquely defined by the standard, and various different semantics have been proposed. They explore the possibility of a customisable execution engine that can be adapted to variations of the execution semantics, giving greater flexibility for developers to align their tooling to the task at hand.

# New Ways of Behaviour Modelling: Events in Modelling

The next six papers of this volume present fresh ideas and concepts in modelling behaviour itself and for integrating it with classical modelling and programming mechanisms. We hope that these papers will inspire the modelling community to have a closer look at the potential of behaviour modelling and use them as a glue between the requirements descriptions and system implementations.

The contribution made by David Harel and Shani Nitzan exploits the application of the approach of Behaviour Programming that aligns the software development with descriptions of scenarios. The approach is applied to the domain of programs with animation. Behaviour Programming was proposed by the group led by David Harel. The basis of the approach is the language of Live Sequence Charts (LCS). LSCs extend Message Sequence Charts (MSC) with modalities in order to support the specification of liveness and safety properties and forbidden behaviours. The presented paper uses the ideas of Behaviour Programming in Java for the development of hybrid systems that combine discrete behaviour and continuous animation. The proposed approach integrates the local rules between various objects with the behavioural programming principles. As in hybrid automata, the states are governed by differential equations, enabling continuous behaviours between discrete state changes. The approach has a lot of application potential in modelling and simulation of interactive behaviour as its combines the analogous behaviour with easy changeable rule abstractions to switch such behaviour.

The paper by Jesper Jepsen and Ekkart Kindler proposes the Event Coordination Notation (ECNO) for modelling the desired behaviour of a software system on top of any object-oriented software. The authors emphasise the fact that the mechanism of method invocation built in the foundation of the modelbased development is quite different from the way of the observed object communication captured by behaviour models. Therefore, the authors build their own notation, ECNO, that allows one to model the behaviour of a system on top of structural models such as class diagrams. ECNO is based on the basic coordination mechanisms proposed by Hoare and Milner for defining interactions involving larger parts of a system. One of the main features of ECNO is that it allows modelling behaviour on top of existing object-oriented systems, and this way integrates with classical programming.

# New Ways of Behaviour Modelling: Protocol Modelling

One of the core concepts used in the two papers above is that events are made a first class modelling concept. Once defined, events can be used to coordinate the behaviour of different components of the system. This idea is also a cornerstone of the Protocol Modelling approach proposed by Ashley McNeile, which represents behaviour using event-driven machines, called "protocol machines", composed in the manner of Hoare's CSP. The interest in Protocol Modelling at the workshops is evidenced by the fact that 14 contributions to the workshops made use of Protocol Modelling ideas; and the editors have chosen three papers that illustrate different applications of these ideas. In order to make this book self-contained, we reprint the paper by Ashley McNeile and Nick Simons that introduces Protocol Modelling.

The paper by Marco Konersmann and Michael Goedicke highlights the features of the domain of modern information systems that usually do not use behaviour models and do not enjoy the benefits of reasoning about the behaviour and the ability to model small, interacting behavioural components. The authors predict, however, the need of models for future information systems and propose a framework, which imposes a low barrier for integration of models. The paper presents a new way of programming with protocol models integrated with source code. The protocol models replace the parts that are not implemented yet. The protocol models are executable and can be used for system debugging and testing at earlier design stages. A combination of models and the implemented code in one framework may give rise to a flexible system development approach.

The paper by Serguei Roubtsov and Ella Roubtsova investigates a particular way of system modularisation separating the most changeable parts of systems. The authors call them decision modules, and show how decision modules are expressed in requirements and behaviour models. Decision modules are formalised as protocol machines built using the event-based abstraction and possessing the unidirectional dependency with protocol machines. The paper presents an analysis of different Java implementation techniques (object composition, reflection, the publisher-subscriber design pattern, interceptors, and aspects) aimed at establishing the possibility of implementing decision modules having an event-based abstraction level and unidirectional dependency with other modules. The paper also discusses the functionality of a generic library that was developed by the authors for adopting the new style of modularisation of locally changeable implementations with separated decision modules.

In the paper contributed by the research group led by Jörg Kienzle (Wisam Al Abed, Matthias Schöttle, Abir Ayed, Jörg Kienzle), this compositional approach is used for aspect-oriented concern separation, and built into their tool Concern-Oriented REuse (CORE). CORE contains many other views traditionally used for the UML-based models. Classes statically define what functionality they offer. The message views show how instances of these classes interact with each other and with objects of other concerns to achieve this functionality. The state view complements the message views by using protocol machines to specify the order in which an object's operations should be called. CSP parallel composition is used to synchronise operation invocations. As the main purpose of CORE is model validation and documentation, CORE can combine different state views and generate new logically related protocol views useful for validation and documentation. The team developing CORE continues to experiment with the incorporation of Protocol Modelling ideas into model driven software development.

## Conclusion

The contributions of this volume show that behaviour models can play a significant part in software development. These models can be on a high level of abstraction and very close to domain modelling and requirements modelling; still, they can be used for automatically executing them, for discussing and reasoning with them, and for verifying the correctness of the developed system. With increased tool support, this could lead to the development of implementation platforms which also make use of behaviour models. However, there is still some way to go to exploit the full potential of behaviour modelling — and we need to keep challenging existing notations and concepts, when they do not adequately serve the needs and purposes, so that eventually we will have distilled those concepts and notations that best serve their purpose.

Papers were contributed to the workshops by both European and American researchers, so the key terms: behaviour (behavior) and modelling (modeling) will appear in this volume both in British and American spelling.

The editors would like to thank:

- All the participants of the six international workshops for their contributions and sharing ideas during the workshops
- The invited speakers, Prof. Dr. Gregor Engels (University of Padderborn, Germany) and Michael Poulin (Head of Enterprise Architecture at Clingstone, Ltd. Bromley, UK)
- The authors of this volume
- The reviewers of the Reviewing Committee for their quality reviews and strong interest in the topic

In particular, we wish to thank the publisher, Springer, for making this publication proceedings possible.

June 2015                                                                           Ella Roubtsova
Ashley McNeile
Ekkart Kindler
Christian Gerth

## References

1. BM-MDA 2009: Proceedings of the First International Workshop on Behaviour Modelling in Model-Driven Architecture. ACM, New York (2009). ISBN 978-1-60558-503-1
2. BM-FA 2010: Proceedings of the Second International Workshop on Behaviour Modelling: Foundation and Applications. ACM, New York (2010). ISBN 978-1-60558-961-9
3. BM-FA 2011: Proceedings of the Third Workshop on Behavioural Modelling. ACM, New York (2011). ISBN 978-1-4503-0617-1
4. BM-FA 2012: Proceedings of the Fourth Workshop on Behaviour Modelling - Foundations and Applications. ACM, New York (2012). ISBN 978-1-4503-1187-8

5. BMFA 2013: Proceedings of the 5th ACM SIGCHI Annual International Workshop on Behaviour Modelling - Foundations and Applications ACM, New York (2013). ISBN 978-1-4503-1989-8

6. BM-FA 2014: Proceedings of the 2014 Workshop on Behaviour Modelling-Foundations and Applications. ACM, New York (2014). ISBN 978-1-4503-2791-6

# Reviewing Committee

# Contents

# Modelling Practices

# Business Modelling: Understandable Patterns, Practices, and Tools

Haim Kilov[⊠]

Independent Consultant, Millington, USA
haimk@acm.org

**Abstract.** The paper discusses the key role of abstraction and explicitness in modelling, and argues that abstract, precise, and explicit business domain and process models based on a small system of concepts described in the work of classics of systems thinking, economics, and computing science make possible successful communications between business and IT stakeholders, and thus lead to successful projects. The simple and elegant business models substantially use a system of reusable patterns (relationships), from fundamental (applicable to all models) to business-generic and business-specific. The stable invariants of the business domain are clearly separated from the volatile business processes and especially from the IT-imposed requirements (often restrictions). Modelling practices including the need for human decision often forgotten in modelling, the barriers to adoption of formal modelling, and the overly complex or otherwise inadequate tools used by or imposed on modellers are also described.

"One of my major complaints about the computer field is that whereas Newton could say, 'If I have seen a little farther than others it is because I have stood on the shoulders of giants,' I am forced to say, 'Today we stand on each other's feet.' Perhaps the central problem we face in all of computer science is how we are to get to the situation where we build on top of the work of others rather than redoing so much of it in a trivially different way."

R.W. Hamming, Turing Award Lecture, 1968

When an artefact is to be designed and manufactured, it is necessary to determine what it is, where it is, and what it does. To do that, a specification of semantics, both of the artefact and of the appropriate fragment of the environment, is essential. This specification – at an appropriate abstraction level and from an appropriate viewpoint – should be understandable not only to the designers and manufacturers of the artefact but also, and more importantly, to its users and to those who will pay for it. This has been a rule in any engineering discipline and should have been a rule in software engineering. More often than not, this did not happen.

## 1 Abstraction and Reusable Patterns

"None of it is new; but sensible old ideas need to be repeated or silly new ones will get all the attention."

Leslie Lamport [60]

© Springer International Publishing Switzerland 2015
E. Roubtsova et al. (Eds.): BM-FA 2009-2014, LNCS 6368, pp. 3–27, 2015.
DOI: 10.1007/978-3-319-21912-7_1

Software engineering is complex. Dealing with complexity requires abstraction ("The process of suppressing irrelevant detail to establish a simplified model, or the result of that process" [1]) – a concept that has been known for millennia. In programming, to quote C.A.R. Hoare, "only abstraction enables a manager or a chief programmer to exert real technical control". The same considerations apply to understanding and modelling any complex phenomena including businesses: as noted by F.A. Hayek, the purpose of a (high-level) model of a complex domain is to "bring about an abstract order—a system of abstract relations—concrete manifestations of which will depend on a great variety of particular circumstances which no one can know in their entirety" [2].

The emphasis is on *relations* rather than on relation participants because neither things nor actions exist in isolation. Almost always there is no need to reinvent: important reusable patterns – fundamental, business-generic, and business-specific – have been known and described for a long time. In particular, such fundamental patterns as composition ("aggregation") and supertyping ("generalisation") have been successfully used for decades (or more). Aggregation and generalisation patterns in the context of general systems have been exactified and rigorously defined in [1, 3], and elsewhere; for a short overview, see [4]. These definitions are abstract and such irrelevant details as relation elements are suppressed: to quote F.A. Hayek again, in a recurring pattern "the same... structure may be formed by any elements... of a very different individual character... capable of entering the same relations to each other." [5]. (Observe that both things and actions may serve as relation elements, so that the same relations may be used in "structural" and "behavioural" modelling.)

Recognising a pattern is not trivial and cannot be automated. Discovering and defining a pattern is even more difficult. For patterns to be understandable to their (potential) users, these activities require abstraction. As E.W. Dijkstra noted in his Turing Award Lecture in 1972, the purpose of abstracting is not to be vague, but to create a new semantic level in which one can be absolutely precise. As a consequence, abstraction reduces reasoning to a doable amount (Dijkstra). Abstraction is probably the most important activity of a good mathematician, a good programmer, or a good modeller (systems thinker).

Y. Manin, an outstanding 20th (and 21st) century mathematician, described discovering a new pattern as follows [6]: after acquiring a general vision of the vast territory and focussing on a part of it, a mathematician tries to recognise "what is there" and "what has already been seen by other people"; and finally starts "discerning something nobody has seen". This activity is very familiar to systems thinkers including business modellers. As Manin observes, in the culture of definitions developed by mathematicians, "many efforts are invested into clarification of ... semantics of basic abstract notions and ... of their inter-relations, whereas the choice of words ... and notations for these notions is a secondary matter". This observation is valid for any kind of modelling: unclear semantics, such as using concepts "without the slightest whiff of a definition because 'everybody knows it'", leads to failures, from relatively trivial to life-threatening.

# 2   Where Do the Patterns Come from?

"[w]hen a number of drawings are made after one pattern, though they may all miss it in some respects, yet they will all resemble it more than they resemble one another; the general character of the pattern will run through them all; the most singular and odd will be those which are most wide of it; and though very few will copy it exactly, yet the most accurate delineations will bear a greater resemblance to the most careless, than the careless ones will bear to one another."

Adam Smith. The Theory of Moral Sentiments. 1759

In order to create information management systems that serve the needs of complex, non-trivial and rapidly changing businesses, effective communication between business and IT organizations is imperative. In order to communicate effectively, a small system of understandable concepts and constructs with clearly defined semantics is essential. These concepts and constructs – basic patterns of reasoning – facilitate understanding and, in particular, bridge the proverbial gap between business and IT. They ought to be used as a basis of all kinds of specifications, both of traditional businesses ("problem world") and of IT artefacts ("machines").

Such a small system of fundamental elegant concepts and patterns has been around in programming and modelling for decades. Some have been used for centuries and even millennia in other areas of human endeavour, like engineering, business and law. The semantics of this system of concepts was exactified in a very short (18 pages) international standard, the Reference Model of Open Distributed Processing (RM-ODP) [1]. In this standard everything was explicitly defined, especially the terms "everyone knows" the meaning of (such as "system", "abstraction", or "behaviour"). The fundamental patterns of composition (both of objects and of actions) and super-typing (of objects, actions, and various other relation participants) mentioned above were also precisely defined there. The system of concepts defined in RM-ODP has been successfully used in modelling of many, and varied, non-trivial businesses and IT systems (see, for example, [7–11, 29, 33, 59, 61], and many references there).

Many business-generic and business-specific patterns have also been described in literature. For example, the business-generic pattern of a contract was described by Francis Hutcheson [12] and by the US Uniform Commercial Code, exactified (for example, in [11]) as a composite in the composition of parties, subject matter and consideration, and refined, for example, as a business-specific pattern of a simple financial contract (in [11], partially also based on [16] where invariants were explicitly specified!) or as a business-specific pattern of a trade contractual element [8]. The business-specific pattern of an annuity was described in [13] and, earlier, in [14]. Thus, precise and abstract pattern descriptions have been around for centuries, and their exactification based on these descriptions has been rather straightforward.

Clarity and understandability in general is also essential in economics which, "like logic and mathematics, is a display of abstract reasoning... The economist does not need an expensive apparatus for the conduct of his studies. What he needs is the power to think clearly and to discern in the wilderness of events what is essential from what is merely accidental" [15]. This is an excellent definition of abstraction along the same lines as in [1]!

More recently, for example, accountability requirements in sociotechnical systems were clearly and succinctly specified (and represented in one simple UML diagram)

[46] using the same three types of fundamental patterns (generic relationships) – (non-binary) subtyping, (non-binary) composition, and reference – as those that were successfully used in business modelling for "more traditional" businesses such as insurance and finance.

The classical banking and financial models were based on such reusable patterns, were short (several dozen pages at most, see e.g. the banking model in [16], the life insurance model in [13], and the financial models in [17]) and understandable both to insiders and to intelligent outsiders without any tacit assumptions. Details were often omitted but could be easily explained, as and when needed, on the basis of these abstract models. These are the most important characteristics of abstraction essential in successful business (behaviour) modelling.

The exactifications of these simple and elegant pattern descriptions have been obviously understandable to all stakeholders – from business experts to information technologists. They may be and have been successfully used for communications between business and IT experts (especially those business experts who are unable or, more often, unwilling to become acquainted with the often threatening complexities of the IT-specific methodologies and tools) [7, 8, 10, 18, 29, 33, 38, 58]. Regretfully, too many "modern" business specifications include a lot of irrelevant details (such as screen-based descriptions) and, even if these details are not IT-specific, do not include appropriate abstract overviews. Such modern specifications (sometimes known as "8.5 by 11 by 11" specifications (the name is due to DeMarco?) – literally boxes of documents) are almost useless: they contain everything except a roadmap through their thousands of pages. This clutter of complexity ought to be drastically (orders of magnitude) reduced by using abstraction; and more often than not it means starting the modelling activity from scratch.

As an example of dealing with "modern" models, consider the context of a large insurance company where the project participants insisted that a simple business model was impossible because the amount of materials was huge, and therefore it would be extremely difficult to clarify what was going on and what was supposed to go on in the future. Something was needed to convince the stakeholders that drastic simplifications by means of abstracting out the business essentials were nevertheless possible. Fortunately, the modellers found, then and there, in a local antiquarian bookstore, a 40-page booklet published in 1835 [13]. This small booklet contained a complete, elegant, and non-threatening description of the business of life insurance annuities including relevant regulations, parameterisable business rules, contract forms, tables to be used, and so on. The booklet was demonstrated to the stakeholders who were somewhat astonished (especially since this "ancient" description was non-threatening) but immediately convinced ("serendipity in action"). The same booklet was later demonstrated to stakeholders of other insurance companies, and also of financial companies, with the same excellent results.

The essentials of such complex phenomena as modern financial derivative products are still based on, and built upon, the classical basics, resulting in elegant understandable models. For example, a precise high-level model of mortgage-based securities was presented in Object Management Group in the mid-1990s on a couple of pages; however, as observed by Kevin Tyson in his OOPSLA2000 keynote [18], information technologists in the target audience of that model were (mildly speaking) less than interested in it, probably because it was about the business without any reference to computer-based information technology.

Semiotic pollution [19] – information overload due to complexity – provides a well-known counterexample. Such pollution harms our intellectual environment in the same manner as physical pollution harms our physical environment. After complexity has been introduced into a business or IT system, it is usually too late for a clean-up: only trivial changes can be "reliably" made to that system unless a complete redesign is accomplished. Even apparently local changes may lead to grave consequences if the locality assumption, often unstated, will appear to be mistaken. Examples abound – from 40000-page regulations for which it is not possible to determine whether they are or are not satisfied in a realistic business situation, to information systems with (tens of) thousands of acknowledged errors. For a recent apparently simpler example, Lex's observation – "If the crucial point appears on page 423 [of the annual report], it is concealed. And the company is accountable for that." (Lex, *Financial Times*, 13 November 2014) – is applicable not only to annual reports.

What to do about thousands of business rules? This question was asked by a business subject matter expert in a large company where only "600" out of the "2400" business rules were allegedly implemented in an IT system several weeks before the deadline. The best way to deal with such issues is to recall a quote from H.A. Kinslow [20]: [There are two classes of system designers:] "The first, if given five problems, will solve them one at a time. The second will come back and announce that these aren't the real problems, and will eventually propose a solution to the single problem which underlies the original five". 2400 business rules mean 2400 problems, and, following Kinslow, it would be not just desirable but essential to discover a few, perhaps a few dozen, but much less than 480 (2400 divided by 5), problems which underline the original ones. This approach leads to the need to "think first, program later" – a well-known maxim often forgotten in the WISCA ("Why Isn't Sam Coding Anything?")-compliant worlds of immediate code delivery.

## 3  Structure Over Content

"The fact is that in studies of complex phenomena the general patterns are all that is characteristic of those persistent wholes which are the main object of our interest, because a number of enduring structures have this general pattern in common and nothing else."

F.A. Hayek [62]

The rules defining a relationship ("structure") are generally independent of the identity and nature ("content") of the relationship participants. ("The structure of a system is the set of all the relations among its components, particularly those that hold the system together" [32]). These rules include, at least, the invariant that defines the relationship, and also pre- and postconditions that define operations applicable to the relationship and its participants. The same kind of relationships (such as composition; or contract) when instantiated using different parameters describes the similar properties of similarly related collections of quite different participants (such as things or actions). For example, the invariant of a composition relationship states that the existence of an instance of this relationship implies the existence of exactly one participant in the composite role and one or more participants in the component role, that at least one ("emergent") property of the composite participant is such that it depends upon properties of the components, and that at least the identity of the composite participant is independent of the existence or properties of the components (see e.g. [1, 58, 61, 65, 66]). For a simple example of a composition, in accordance with the Uniform Commercial Code, we may consider a contract (legal agreement) as a composition of parties, subject matter, and consideration; and we can instantiate this composition for various legal or financial agreements. This approach to specifying relationship properties characterizes not only fundamental generic relationships such as composition or subtyping, but also more complex relationships "of the same kind" from the same or different business environments. It represents a basis for reuse of similar, but not identical, constructs. As an example, consider various instantiations of a contract – such as buying a house, getting a mortgage, getting an unsecured (credit card) loan, opening a chequeing account, and so on. At this abstraction level, all such contracts are similar. And at a lower, more detailed, abstraction level, for example, all real estate purchase-and-sale contracts are similar; but they are not similar to other types of contracts such as contracts for credit card loans. The idea of discovering and formulating common structural – rather than individual – properties is well-known in science ("laws of physics"), mathematics ([31, 41] and other writings by E.W. Dijkstra, and especially in category theory [53, 63]), programming, linguistics (grammar), and exact philosophy [32]. We do that in programming when we discuss, for example, while statements having the structure *while expression do statement* without paying too much attention to what the specific *expression* and *statement* are, and independently of the particular programming language used. And we do the same in discussing, for example, trade contracts, or more specific business patterns such as options trade contracts [8]. Emphasis on "attributes and their values" all too often encountered in business modelling has to be avoided by all means because it contributes to excessive complexity and hides the fact that things, components, and operations are not isolated.

These considerations apply not only to creating and reusing specifications, but also to changes to a specification. Changes are inevitable for various reasons: due to better understanding of the business by the business experts or by business analysts; due to business experts changing their mind; due to changes in the environment such as new laws; and for other reasons. (Abstraction may and often does help to anticipate changes.) When we have to make a change, firstly we have to find a place or places where to make it, and secondly we have to actually make it. Changeability is made possible by clarity: it is easy to find a fragment of the specification to be changed if the specification has a simple and elegant structure. Often, it may be possible to determine, with the help of the business experts, which fragments of the business specification are of high, medium, and low stability. Fortunately, in most cases the basic structure of the specification remains the same when changes are made, so that the changes are of a local nature. Specifically, this was observed in non-trivial financial [8, 59] and insurance [10] specifications.

Emphasis on structure over content clearly helps a lot in business modelling. When business analysts, together with business subject matter experts, try to discover and formulate the model of a particular business domain, they ask questions in terms of invariants of patterns – both of generic relationships and of other, more specific, business patterns. Thus it becomes possible to structure business information in an appropriate manner and abstract out the essentials. Often it helps to formulate a question as a proposition – "observable fact or state of affairs involving one or more entities, of which it is possible to assert or deny that it holds for these entities" [1] – so that the early incomplete versions of a business model may be precise but incorrect and therefore serve as questions to business experts. Indeed, as observed by Joseph Goguen, "a precise definition that is somewhat wrong is better than a description so vague that no one can tell if it's wrong" [63]. (Obviously, "precise" is not the same as "detailed".)

## 4   Purposeful Behaviour

"Human action is purposeful behaviour."

Ludwig von Mises [15]

Abstraction is needed to specify the essentials, like when using an appropriate road-map; however, a business process like driving requires human decisions within this framework. Thus, one should distinguish between patterns and specifics ("particular circumstances", Hayek). If behavioural semantics is specified explicitly, with articulated tacit assumptions, then it becomes possible to determine what aspects of behaviour can be automated (using an IT system), and what specifics could or should be based on human decision. However, recognising what details are irrelevant, and in what circumstances, may not be trivial: for example, in investing Richard Oldfield [21] urges the reader to focus on "things which matter – information minimalism," rather than on "idiotic distraction and waste of time" when "staring … mesmerized … at [any] machine which tells one stock prices" and which "impels people to do all sorts of things which are better left undone".

The concept of purposeful behaviour – see also [5] and [15] – is used to specify, in the context of [1], voluntary choices made by people or legal entities ("parties") and directed towards some anticipated future state chosen from a set of possible future states as a result of evaluation by the parties. Different objects fulfilling the same party roles, or the same objects fulfilling these roles in different epochs, may direct purposeful behaviour towards different anticipated future states. The realization of purposeful behaviour may lead to a result different from that anticipated future state. Purposeful behaviour is not predictable, i.e., it cannot be determined from the specification whether an action of purposeful behaviour will or will not occur in a given state. The anticipated future state and the objective toward which purposeful behaviour is directed may be left unspecified in the model.

Most actions in which a party participates are purposeful because the set of possible future states usually includes more than one element (for example, due to possible violations of prescribed behaviour). This contrasts with actions in which only non-parties participate. Therefore the modeller, together with the owner of the model, has to decide which of these party actions are of interest to be explicitly included in the model as elements of purposeful behaviour.

An example of purposeful behaviour of interest to the modeller may include the offer, counteroffer and acceptance of an agreement that may be modelled as a contract. Another example may include the change by a party of the result of a valuation performed by a credit assessment algorithm. Still another example may include explicit modelling of regulatory violations by financial institution employees. Thus, "in the field of finance [...] psychology and free will are added to the difficulties of modelling" [56].

When a party delegates a purposeful behaviour to an information system, that system will choose from a predetermined set of future states according to predetermined criteria. (When the information system is able to generate new behaviours or new choice criteria, the set of all those behaviours and choice criteria is predetermined in the specification of the system.)

There ought to be a possibility for humans to override an IT-based decision. Thus, such behaviour of an IT-based financial system as the recent rejection of Bernanke's mortgage refinancing application would become less likely ("The root of the problems lies in the cultural preference in North America in favour of concrete facts, algorithms and what is imagined to be replicability, and against making judgments based on personal assessment. A personal assessment would disclose that Mr. Bernanke, although without a steady job and perhaps also with an irregular stream of income from speeches and consultation, nevertheless is a very, very good risk." [55]).

In a similar manner, credit and interest decisions made by humans led to substantial success and popularity with customers of UK branches of a Swedish bank (Handelsbanken) where these decisions are made by branch managers rather than in a centralized manner [22]. The banking patterns have remained the same for centuries – see, for example, Adam Smith's observation that in banking "all the operations are capable of being reduced to what is called a Routine, or to such a uniformity of method as admits of little or no variation" [47] – but the specifics are different for different banks under different circumstances; and Handelsbanken succeeded because its branch managers could make their own decisions based on the local state of the market. This is as it should be: as von Mises emphasised, "the specific entrepreneurial profits and losses [...] depend on the adjustment of output to the most urgent wants of the consumers. What produces them is the extent to which the entrepreneur has succeeded or failed in anticipating the future – necessary uncertain – state of the market" [15]. Attempts to completely automate such decisions often fail or, at best, lead to less than optimal results.

## 5   The Stable Basics: The Business Domain

"In contrast with other types of engineers, 'software engineers [generally] do not know how to model the domain in which their software operates' (Dines Bjørner). If only those who are mesmerized by their employees' C++ skills would finally understand this!"

George Hacken [23]

The problems of specification complexity are exacerbated by the desire to do the work faster, and as a result specifications are often started "in the middle" instead of starting with a solid and stable foundation – the basics of the business domain "as it is". These basics are also known as ontology that describes the structure and content of "what is there" in the domain of interest. The classical presentations of various businesses such as finance, insurance, banking, and other areas of human endeavour, always started with clear and understandable domain descriptions. Starting in the middle – either with IT system requirements that may change in a rapid or unexpected manner (or may not even be discovered and formulated without understanding of the stable basics), or with the descriptions of business examples (even if they have fashionable names such as "use cases" [24]) – may cause serious disappointments leading to software systems chasing the existing products [8], to various kinds of hacking, dignified or otherwise, and ultimately to more failures.

Relying only on (volatile) business processes (actions) while ignoring the domain leads to serious problems not specific to information technology. Let us consider the need to drive from "here" to "there." When describing only the business process of driving, we may ask for directions (such as "drive 11.5 miles on Route 22 and then turn right and then at the third traffic light turn left, and…"). Such directions may be useful, provided that there is no road construction work, that the odometer in the car is perfect (and that we remember to look at it), that there are still exactly three functioning traffic lights referred to in the directions, and so on. In real life, we know a better way: use a roadmap. This non-trivial concept is based on the Hellenistic mathematical geography known to us through Ptolemy's Geography. It is a typical scientific theory using a model of the surface of the Earth on a spherical surface with two spherical coordinates and using projections in order to represent the spherical surface on plane charts [25]. After this scientific basis was established, it became possible to apply it in all kinds of technology including that of using roadmaps for getting from here to there.

In any "traditional" branch of engineering, "for each system the developers must investigate and analyse the properties of the problem world domains and of their interactions with each other and with the machine to be built: they must devise a machine whose interactions with the domain to which it is directly connected will ensure that the system requirements – the purposes of the system – are satisfied" [26]. In most branches of traditional engineering, the problem world domains, the system, and the most important aspects of the machine are well known and explicitly described, leading to successful specialisation of engineers where, as Jackson observed, handbooks and well-established approaches are taken for granted, and learning from failures is considered to be normal. In software engineering, more often than not, this is not the case (although at least some concepts may be well-known to many in the research community).

Not everything in software engineering is completely bleak. Business models based on stable business domain specifications have been successfully created and used for better understanding of the business, for making business decisions based on that understanding, for education and training of new employees, and for improving and automation of various business processes [7, 8, 10, 27, 28].

The structure of a business domain is defined using relationships between business things. Each of these business-specific relationships is a refinement of such fundamental generic relationships as "subtyping", "composition", and "reference", defined in international standards [1, 58, 65] and elsewhere. These relationships may be considered as "elementary molecules" encountered in modelling of all businesses (and IT systems!). Models expressed in the terms of these relationships are compact and readable by all stakeholders. Obviously, it is possible and desirable to define and reuse "non-elementary molecules" – business-specific patterns – such as "notification", "joint ownership" [29], "contract", "real estate purchase and sale contract", "trade", "purchase on margin/short sale" [66], "banking clearing house" [66], "settlement of securities transactions" [66], "initial public offering" [66], "roles in organisation" [38], etc. Observe that these business-specific patterns were formulated on the basis of excellent clear and precise decades-old economics texts such as [15–17]. Thus, business modelling never starts with a blank sheet of paper – the elementary molecules are always there for reuse, and in most situations, non-elementary molecules already exist or can be defined and reused.

The same kinds of relationships – business patterns – that define the structure of a business domain can be used, in a similar manner, to define the structure of business processes (relationships between actions – steps within business processes), as well as to define the structure of information technology systems and infrastructure. Indeed, as defined in [1], behaviour is a collection of actions with a set of constraints on when they may occur; and such fundamental relationships as composition and subtyping are defined in [1] not only for objects but also for actions and other kinds of relationship participants. For a simple example, opening a chequeing account is an ordered composition of the following steps: assessing customer needs; choosing a template of an account; offering the template to the customer and getting customer's acceptance; and instantiating the chequeing account contract template. Pre- and postconditions are used to model individual business processes (actions), and process modelling provides important feedback for the domain model showing where the latter ought to be refined.

Starting with the business domain model is not a panacea. Compare two approaches used in different financial companies. In one company, business modelling activities started with defining a trade (in its context) as the most important artefact. This definition was far from trivial and took several weeks of effort, in particular, because it was essential to discover and articulate tacit assumptions of different stakeholders who used the term "trade" to mean somewhat different things, especially for complex trades. The non-triviality of defining a trade started to be understood when the business analysts tried to formulate, together with the business experts, a clear definition of such a "trivial" concept as trade confirmation. After a trade has been defined, to the satisfaction of all business stakeholders and analysts, the rest of the business modelling activities went very smoothly [8]. Contrariwise, in a different financial company business domain modelling was performed along the lines of agile development in which the hard problem of defining a trade was put aside because the stakeholders could not agree on a definition, and as a result some less interesting fragments of the model were successfully demonstrated to the management, but the modelling activity itself had not succeeded.

Relying on tacit assumptions (different for different business stakeholders) may lead to very serious problems and even to disasters. Explicit specification of business semantics is often simple and helps to avoid such problems. As another trade-related example, consider problems with reconciling of trade valuations with counterparties: "if [a company] had been regularly reconciling... it would have discovered much sooner that its counterparties valued those trades completely differently: [reconciliation is a] "simple but extraordinarily efficient way of managing risk" [30]. An explicitly articulated **abstract** business model of trade confirmation with precisely specified semantics was either absent or not demonstrated in an understandable manner to all stakeholders because "everyone knows" what "trade confirmation" means. Per Sjöberg's company, TriOptima, was able to discover these problems, specify them explicitly, including description in a newspaper (*Financial Times*), and provide appropriate solutions for "1200 institutions worldwide" [30]. Thus, understanding and correctly formulating problems leads to (relatively) easy solutions.

Successful business modelling experience suggests that domain (and process) modelling should be done (or, at the very least, led) by good abstractionists. As Bjørner stressed, "Is it really the idea that computing scientist cum software engineers cum knowledge engineers should be the ones who create domain models? Well, for the time being, yes! In collaboration [...] with domain stakeholders. But we foresee that gradually professionals of respective domains will have learned basic techniques of abstraction and modelling as part of their domain specific academic education, but in courses that basically propagate computing science concepts and techniques" [27]. Indeed, best results in business modelling were achieved when those business subject matter experts who were good systems thinkers became interested in modelling to such an extent that they themselves (with some minimal help) created important non-trivial fragments of the model [8].

As an example [8], in a rather complex area of exotic options, the amount of modelling work done within a short timeframe was very substantial: in a few weeks it was possible to create a reasonably complete top-level preliminary business domain model (several dozen pages in length), and start process modelling. This became possible due to the dedication of the business stakeholders, both from the front office and from the back office, who actively participated in all modelling sessions. The IT stakeholders also participated in these sessions. (Changing the mindset of participants from starting with process to starting with domain modelling was the most important aspect (took 3–6 sessions).) The resulting business model was general and used a shared set of concepts and business patterns, both business-generic and business-specific, thus avoiding the distinction between front, middle and back offices which was needed only at more detailed levels of the model. The business stakeholders observed that each of them had his own understanding of the meaning of a trade, a settlement, etc., and understood – among other things – how difficult it was to communicate to business analysts and then to developers the concepts each of them understood somewhat differently. Probably for the first time the front and back office stake-holders were together in one room during some important modelling sessions. It was very instructive to look at changes in individuals' and managers' mindsets. The things they did have value far beyond building IT systems: to quote a leading business stakeholder, "having a business model makes the organization ten times better".

## 6   Modelling Practices

"There is no justification for renouncing the basic engineering technique of specifying what you are going to do, in writing, and at appropriate level of detail, before you do it."

Bertrand Meyer [24]

During the course of the information system development process three kinds of models are produced: business models, platform-*independent* IT solution models, and platform-*dependent* IT solution models.

Different people and organizations use different terms to denote these three kinds of model. Also, in many IT shops there is no analog to the business model, but there are notions of platform-independent and platform-dependent IT solution models. Sometimes the platform-independent and platform-dependent IT solution models are referred to as "analysis" and "design" models respectively. Alternatively, they can be referred to as "design" and "implementation" models respectively, with business models referred to as "analysis" models. Although these three model kinds are very different (due to separation of concerns), at the same time the structure of these models is similar because it is based on the same underlying concepts and constructs (a.k.a patterns).

A business model rigorously and explicitly defines the business entities ("things" such as trades, options, etc.), business processes (such as a trade confirmation process), and the relationships among them. By describing the business as an abstract – realization-independent – model, it establishes a formal system of concepts that can be used to express the business requirements.

A business model consists of a business domain model and a business operation (a.k.a. process) model. The business domain model defines things and relationships of interest, with an emphasis on relationships, and provides the explicit context for all process specifications. It is relatively stable and shows the most important business invariants that remain the same no matter what processes and services are, were, or will be used. Of course, in some cases these invariants will change, but these changes are substantially less frequent than changes in business processes or services.

A business model is independent of whether the business processes will be realized by humans or IT systems (or by a human-computer system interaction). The appropriate realization decisions, including the decisions about stages in realizing IT systems, are to be made explicitly, based on the explicit and precise business models.

The same fundamental relationships that define the structure of a business domain model are used, in a similar manner, to define the structure of a business operation model (business processes, workflow, etc.), as well as to define the structure of IT models. The definition of a mathematical structure as "a set of (indefinable!) objects (or several sets of objects of different natures, distinguished by the titles conditionally conferred upon them) with a given system of relationships between the elements of the sets" [31], together with the general definition of a structure of a system as "the set of all the relations among its components, particularly those that hold the system together" [32] emphasise relationship semantics that is all too often completely or partially ignored in "traditional" approaches to modelling.

The constructs used for a business model are not restricted by any infrastructure (and, of course, by any tool). There should be no code generation from a business model: it serves different purposes (understanding), and it should not be restricted by methodologies or tools.

A business model specifies semantics. Therefore semantic-free artefacts, such as box-and-line diagrams (with "default semantics" of the lines), "named lines" (with names as "is related to" or "is linked"), and "meaningful names" of things (don't forget that a thing may have several context-dependent names also known as synonyms) must be excluded from such models and replaced with relationship specifications with clear semantics based on generic relationships. Then it becomes clear that apparently different relationships have the same kind of invariant (with different actual parameters), and therefore are of the same type ("shape") [33].

As a typical example, when a large architectural "box-and-line" drawing was presented at an important meeting, one of the decision makers was very pleased with his apparent understanding of the architecture and decided to formulate it based on the drawing. However, his understanding was wrong: the authors of the architecture meant something totally different from what this architecture user read from several essential fragments of the drawing. These authors relied on defaults and "common knowledge", and did not articulate what they meant in a precise and explicit manner. Already in 1968, Alan Perlis emphasized that people "use phrases like 'communicate across modules by going up and then down' — all of the vague administratese which in a sense must cover up a native and total incompetence" [20].

Such tacit assumptions as "meaningful names" usually mean substantially or – worse! – somewhat different things for different stakeholders. A name has a meaning only in context ("only in the context of a proposition has a name meaning", Wittgenstein). In particular, business things, relationships, and actions are not the same as IT things, relationships, and actions: for a well-known example, a patient is not the same as a patient record; and a patient may and usually does correspond to several database records, perhaps in different databases (and probably also to something not represented in any database at all) There is no 1:1 correspondence there, even though the "meaningful names" are often the same.

A business model must be understandable without the expert around. In particular, it means that all tacit assumptions must be articulated and made explicit. Regretfully, too often modellers and even model users forget that the purpose of the business model is to "demonstrate that answers [to questions about the model] can be given entirely in terms of the model. If such answers can not be found then the model is inadequate" [34].

Most business systems we currently deal with are open, that is, external relationships between components of these systems and their environment ("changing ecosystem") change in often unpredictable ways. Striving for simplicity is essential for decision making in the context of open systems where the inevitable changes can be understood only when there is something stable (and as simple as possible!) to rely upon. For example, some business systems are resilient so that essential characteristics of their invariants tend to be preserved under changes in their environments. Marriage or mortgage are examples. For a more specific example, when (inevitable) changes were to be introduced in business requirements for an accounting model in a large financial company, it was very easy to localise and implement them due to the clear and understandable business domain specification [59].

Simplicity is essential for clarity and understandability of any model, not just a model of an open system. With respect to (presumably) closed systems of consumer electronics, it is very instructive to refer to Elke den Ouden's thesis at the Technical University of Eindhoven [35, 67]. She concluded that half of all supposedly malfunctioning products returned to stores were in reality in full working order, but just perceived as too complex to be operated successfully, and also noted that the average U.S. consumer would spend a maximum of about 20 min trying to get a newly acquired electronics device to work before giving up. Something was wrong in modelling of behavioural semantics for these products; perhaps it was never properly done in business terms.

Thus, clarity and understandability to various audiences (business subject matter experts, analysts, managers, developers, etc.) is essential for successful and therefore usable business models. Therefore the representations used, including graphical ones, should not be threatening or overwhelming and should be explainable to a non-expert; formal or even graphical representations should be translatable into a structured natural language ("legalese") narrative. Precise specifications must be provided for each used representational artefact. A *business model should be not a burden to read*, although writing it may well be far from trivial. Abstraction levels and viewpoints should be used for understandability.

In creating and discussing a business model, precision is much more important than correctness. Indeed, a precise but incorrect model may be justifiably disagreed with by the model users and correspondingly corrected, while an imprecise model is too vague to be agreed or disagreed with.

Good business modellers generally do not need to know the specifics of an application area before creating a business model: it is much easier for a modeller ignorant (or claiming ignorance) of these specifics (P. Burkinshaw [20]) to discover, articulate and thus make explicit different tacit assumptions of different business (and perhaps IT) experts. In this context, we may refer to Gerald Weinberg's observation that "the student trained in general systems thinking can move quickly into entirely new areas and begin speaking the language competently within a week or so" [36].

We may note another important Weinberg's observation that mastery of one's native (plus at least one non-native) language together with mathematical maturity (as opposed to knowledge of specific areas of mathematics) are essential for success in general systems thinking, while, in Dijkstra's independent opinion, these are the only two necessary prerequisites of a competent programmer. For a somewhat unexpected example, the inability of some "modern" modellers to detect and clarify *grammatically* ambiguous (with more than one parse tree) statements in documents provided by business customers leads to misinterpretations and wrong implementations that may be detected too late if at all. (Regretfully, teaching grammar in secondary schools is not fashionable anymore: "An education that drills children in the structure of a language will produce adults who are able to teach themselves how to send emails in an hour, or to speak an unfamiliar language in three months. One that aims only to teach them to learn how to surf the Web is going to produce an ignorant underclass" [51]).

At the beginning, a model is usually sketchy and short. Still, it has to be precise and explicit: high quality must be maintained from the beginning, and additional incremental functionality may be added afterwards. Early versions of the model may serve as excellent sources of questions to the business experts. The same approach, concepts and constructs should be used in all kinds of models (business, IT system, technological infrastructure, etc.). Explicit division of labour should exist between different models (e.g., between a business problem and an IT solution), as well as between specification and implementation. In particular – and this is very important – there should never be a requirements specification in terms of solutions (e.g., "screens").

More generally, user interface specifications should be clearly separated from business specifications, unless the business is about user interfaces.

The importance of separating a business model from technology was mentioned, for the financial environment, as early as in 1930: "The casual visitor to the Stock Exchange is apt to come away much impressed with the mechanical appliances on the floor … but rather oblivious to its much more important human mechanism. For the securities market is able to function only through the highly specialized work of the several different types of brokers and dealers who go to compose it. Indeed, the day was when the only mechanical appliance in the New York stock market was the old buttonwood tree" [17]. (For an earlier clear and understandable specification of the semantics of English financial institutions, see, for example, a 63-page book [14].)

Creative composition of well-known and successfully used concepts and patterns with "open-mindedness about where those components can be found" – rather than starting from scratch and reinventing (possibly square) wheels – often leads to non-trivial innovation and success [37, 38] in modelling and realisation of the models.

Elucidating the semantics may be difficult for a traditional business (although in most cases possible, often referring to classical books about that business), but, regretfully, is often almost impossible for an existing IT artefact (for procurement and evaluation). The specification of the semantics of the latter is all too often vague and incomplete, leading to the conclusion that it "does what it does".

Finally, and more technically, in behavioural modelling we need to distinguish between an invariant for a collection of objects ("entities", "things") that constitutes the overall model and the fragment of the invariant that is used in a specific action (what remains unchanged but used (referred to) vs. what is not even used). The latter is often much simpler than the former ("abstraction in action").

## 7    Barriers to Adoption

"Almost anything in software can be implemented, sold, and even used given enough deter-mination. There is nothing a mere scientist can say that will stand against the flood of a hundred million dollars. But there is one quality that cannot be purchased in this way – and that is reliability. The price of reliability is the pursuit of the utmost simplicity."

C A R Hoare, Turing Award Lecture, 1980

"…the DP Manager… swiveled round in his chair to face a huge flowchart stuck to the wall: about 50 large sheets of paper, maybe 200 symbols, 500 connecting lines. 'Fred did that. It's the build-up of gross pay for weekly payroll. Noone else but Fred understands it.' his voice dropped to a reverent hush. 'Fred tells me he's not sure he understands it himself.' "

Michael Jackson [39]

One of the most important barriers to successful use of business modelling in general and behaviour modelling in particular is the rushing to code where too often the emphasis is on details and specifics rather than on concepts and essentials. The insistence on immediate gratification, on the "agile, let's-just-do-what-we-need-now" general approaches are "some of the most absurd and damaging contributions of agile methods" that may lead to "historical catastrophes that caused billions of dollars of wasteful efforts [like] the MS-DOS 640 K memory limit, the Y2K mess, the initial size of IP addresses" [24]. Like in the work of a foreign language translator or interpreter, "word-for-word" translation or interpreting without understanding of the business context leads to disasters ("machine translation" is just another example of the above). Developers who are proud to "know the business better than the business people do" and thus try to automate all human decisions – such as on risk management in finance – are a similar example of this barrier.

A somewhat related barrier is that of replacing the business semantics with signatures of operations with "obvious defaults" that are implemented in the code. Let's consider an almost trivial example of a contract specified in this manner using only a signature (since "everyone knows what the domain is about"):

$$contract(house1, person1, person2, money)$$

The semantics of this contract may be any of the following:

- Person1 buys house1 from person2 paying money
- Person1 rents house1 from person2 for money per year
- Person1 babysits for person2 at house1 getting money per hour
- Person2 builds house1 for person1 getting paid money
- ...

Behavioural semantics (e.g., specified by means of pre- and post conditions in the context of the explicitly specified domain invariants) defines (the top level of) what this contract is about. Demonstrating an example like this to business experts has substantially contributed to better communication between business and IT stakeholders.

Another important barrier is that of complexity. This was mentioned by C.A.R. Hoare as early as in 1977: "…the fatal attraction is the very complexity… which totally beggars the comprehension of both user and designer… which would revolt the instincts of any engineer, but which, to the clever programmer, masquerades as power and sophistication. He may even have less creditable motives…" [40] Complex, and sometimes artificially complex, modelling approaches, methodologies, and tools often imposed on modellers lead to complex models perceived as threatening by business experts – the most important target audience of these models (only the business experts can determine whether the models are correct). In such environments, communication between business and IT experts fails miserably.

Complexity sells well not only in industry but also in academia. As E.W. Dijkstra made explicit some time ago, "[h]e who regularly addresses Western academic audiences quickly discovers that, on the average, his audience is impressed to the extent it has not understood him: by a perfectly understandable lecture many people in the audience feel somewhat cheated, and they leave the lecture hall afterwards, complaining to each other 'Well, that was all rather trivial, wasn't it?'. As a result, most audiences exert on most speakers a pressure – subconscious at both sides – to be occasionally unnecessarily obscure" [41]. Similarly, simplicity has to be explicitly taught and promoted in computer science courses, but this is too often not done, and effective thinking is not taught. Many current textbooks and courses emphasise tools and (sometimes buzzword-compliant) methodologies as opposed to concepts.

Computing classics promoting simplicity and elegance are frequently not even mentioned. For example, dozens of students who relatively recently graduated with a BS in computer science have never heard about Dijkstra, Hoare, or Wirth (or such classics as [20]), and have also never heard about the more pragmatic Gerald Weinberg whose text [42] was successfully used as a college textbook in the 1970s. All these classical works have served as sources of inspiration for business modellers.

Attempts to reduce the complex phenomena in business behaviour to computer-based models, together with the use of algorithms instead of – when needed – human decisions is another serious barrier to success and perhaps adoption of business modelling by business experts. All too often, customer service representatives tell users that "the computer does not let me do that", to the detriment both of users and of these representatives. Behavioural semantics cannot always be specified in an algorithmic manner – people are not automata.

Reduction to algorithms cannot and does not work in business modelling – otherwise human decisions would not have been needed. In particular, using statistics in financial models that rely on "the false assumption that market returns follow a normal distribution" is misleading, as emphasised by Hayek [62] decades ago and as recently noted in *Financial Times* [64] with respect to formulating regulations and managing asset allocation by investors. Relationship semantics must be used instead. Hayek discusses the impotence of statistics in dealing with complex systems because statistics eliminates the essential complexity and ignores semantics of relationships between individuals with different attributes: "The statistical method is… of use only where we either deliberately ignore, or are ignorant of, the relations between the individual elements with different attributes, i.e., where we ignore or are ignorant of any structure into which they are organized" [62].

In addition to overemphasis on complex tools and methods, textbooks and often papers on business (behaviour) modelling often ignore the complexity of real businesses. Not only textbooks but also academic papers almost always use toy examples with neat and often trivial problem domains (the "disdain for the inconveniently messy real world" in software engineering textbooks was observed, for example, by Michael Jackson). Such papers are obviously considered irrelevant by those few practitioners who take the trouble to read them. Contrariwise, Dines Bjørner specifically and explicitly emphasised the need to model all kinds of complex and often unpleasant behaviour: "In the real world, i.e., in the domain, all is possible: Diligent staff will indeed follow-up on inquiries, orders, payments, etc. Loyal consumers will indeed respond likewise. But sloppy such people may not. And outright criminals may wish to cheat, say on payments or rejects. And we shall model them all" [27].

Unreadable business models are obviously a serious barrier to adoption. A graphical representation of a business model several square meters in size is useless because nobody can understand it, even if only a small projection of it is shown at a time. In a more traditional business, for example, of using roadmaps, the concept of abstraction, specifically, of using different levels of detail (and perhaps different viewpoints) on different maps, has been successfully used for centuries if not millennia; regretfully, business models are too often represented without any regard for abstraction and thus for human readability. Business stakeholders often just ignore such documents.

Quite a few failed business domain models were developed with the laudable goal of being demonstrated to and agreed upon by business stakeholders. These failures happened not only because the models were too detailed ("many square meters") without an abstract overview, but also because quite often they included fragments of code for those aspects of the model that could not be presented graphically by the tool. More often than not, there was no distinction between the business modelling artefacts (things, relationships and actions), and IT system modelling artefacts (things, relationships and actions – different from but often having the same names as their business counterparts), thus adding to the confusion.

"Speaking different languages" is another well-publicised barrier to adoption. If business and IT stakeholders indeed "speak different languages" then proper translation is essential. For an excellent precise description of translation as a creative act, and of the need for a context-dependent approach to meaning and translation, see Yuri Lotman's book [52] (a very terse and nice overview is provided, for example, in [54]). The "length of context" (Gasparov) essential for understanding and therefore for translation is certainly non-zero and is often substantial, even within the same business ("trade" means different things for different people even in the trading environment, depending on the context), and especially between stakeholders with very different backgrounds. At the same time, generic patterns are the same for (almost) all businesses including the business of software, and using these patterns makes the translation substantially easier.

Finally, buzzwords and catch phrases instead of clear arguments represent an important barrier to adoption of modelling approaches based on solid (classical) foundations. The epigraph to this paper is an illustration observed almost half a century ago and still valid now. In order to understand and specify a business problem and possible solutions, buzzwords like "business logic", "business functions", "business rules" (which are often only in the code), "business objects", "architecture", etc. should be replaced with semantic definitions in context. These definitions ought to be understandable to all stakeholders, especially to business experts. Excellent examples of defining all terms used, especially those that "everyone knows", are provided by [1] and, independently, by exact philosophy [32]. In this manner, for example, a business rule may be defined without using buzzwords – as a proposition about business things, the relationships between them, and the operations applied to them.

# 8  Tools

"The tool should be charming, it should be elegant, it should be worthy of our love. This is no joke, I am terribly serious about this... The greatest virtues a program can show: Elegance and Beauty."

E.W. Dijkstra, 1962 [50]

"Using PL/I must be like flying a plane with 7000 buttons, switches, and handles to manipulate in the cockpit. I absolutely fail to see how we can keep our growing programs firmly within our intellectual grip when by its sheer baroqueness the programming language – our basic tool, mind you! – already escapes our intellectual control. And if I have to describe the influence PL/I can have on its users, the closest metaphor that comes to my mind is that of a drug."

E.W. Dijkstra, 1972 (Turing Award Lecture)

In addition to the intrinsic complexity of business and IT systems, we often impose (artificially) complex notations on those brave people who dare to create, read, and use the models of those systems. The semantics of important constructs of these notations is often not clear. The purpose of a business model is understanding of the business and people-to-people communication. Contrariwise, the purpose of many (most?) tools imposed on business modellers is to create code rather than to represent business semantics in a manner understandable to the stakeholders.

Dines Bjørner [28] clearly demonstrates that effective ("pleasing, elegant, expressive, and revealing") models of all kinds clearly emphasise semantics rather than the syntactic details of "powerful" modelling languages, in the same manner as observed by E.W. Dijkstra decades ago with respect to "powerful" programming languages. Using many if not most "CASE tools" to represent models ought to be done with caution for the reasons eloquently noted by Dijkstra with respect to PL/I. (Some currently popular programming languages are even worse: they impose a very low abstraction level on the programmer and program readers.) Modelling languages have additional problems. Firstly, as noted above, often the semantics of important constructs used there is undefined or badly defined. Secondly, the target audience of a programming language consists of programmers who may be at least somewhat used to artificial complexity introduced by languages and tools, while business stakeholders in the target audience of a business modelling language have no desire to learn a totally unfamiliar language explained in several hundred pages. Too many language and tool vendors (and quite a few users) make "the common mistake of thinking that 'throwing' more syntax at an issue will improve the semantics" [43]. Nevertheless, it is possible to succeed in modelling by using very restricted subsets of modelling languages enhanced by precisely specified semantics of such essential constructs as generic relationships [58, 61, 65, 66] – in the same manner as it was possible to succeed in programming by using very restricted subsets of such languages as PL/I [57].

It is possible to use graphics for business model representation, provided that the notation is explained on the back of the proverbial – perhaps business-size – envelope ("The ease with which ["back-of-the-envelope" sketching] is done, and done so that the result is pleasing, has utility, and is fit for purpose, is the hallmark of a great software engineer, or respectively of a great architect." ([28], Vol. 1, p. 413). If the notation is not explained in this manner then the ultimate users (and approvers!) of business models – the business experts – become disinterested. As a typical example, consider a typical request from a head trader: "tell me about UML in 15 min". This head trader became interested in business modelling and enjoying the process and results after being shown and explained an apparently simple example: two mutually independent subtyping hierarchies (gender-related and function-related – technical or managerial) for the same supertype ("employee") in which an employee satisfies exactly one subtype in the gender-related hierarchy and at least one subtype in the function-related hierarchy [58, Fig. 2-2]. By using only the "bare bones" of UML class diagrams with the emphasis on relationships [58, 61] it was possible to achieve excellent understanding of the business models ("a pleasure to read") by the business experts of several large financial firms (see, for example, [8, 33]). The only difficulty was with respect to UML treatment of icons for relationships: the business experts invariably could not remember, for example, whether the triangle was an icon for subtyping or for composition (UML aggregation), although they very clearly distinguished between the concepts themselves (the experts wanted words or lexical abbreviations rather than icons, or at the very least labelled icons). The complete business models represented using these "bare bones" of UML were usually short: for example, the top level of the secondary mortgage market model took two slide-size pictures to present, while the much more complex and more detailed business model of exotic options took several dozen pages.

The proliferation of ontology languages apparently to be used for business modelling is, as observed by K. Baclawski, a symptom of a more serious problem – the rush to produce tools and languages without any clear [business] purpose. He further properly observed that, rather than tools being constructed to support methodologies, many methodologies are created for the sake of understanding how to use the tools. As a result, in particular, interoperability becomes (almost) impossible.

The (anti-)pattern of replacing concepts with tools discussed by Dijkstra, Wirth and other authors exists not only in software engineering. In economics, replacement of concepts with tools of quantitative economics and econometrics – harshly criticised, in particular, by Hayek and von Mises – resulted in loss of understanding and thus in grave consequences (see, for example, the warnings presented by Hayek in his Nobel lecture [44]). S. R. H. Jones (Letter to the Editor, *Financial Times*, 21 November 2014, p. 8) recently reminded us about the warning of Alfred Marshall in 1901 (!) that, given the complex relationship between economic facts that can't be quantified to those that can, the application of exact mathematical methods to those that can "is nearly always a waste of time". Regretfully, this warning has long been forgotten, and, more than a century later, this replacement of concepts with tools often leads to distrust of all economic theory and very serious social consequences, both in economics and (manifested e.g. as project failures) in software engineering.

Regretfully, many tools available to or imposed on (business) modellers do not support even the fundamental patterns or support them only with serious restrictions (such as support for only binary relationships; no support for mutually orthogonal subtyping or composition hierarchies). When using such tools, there is a mismatch between the layer of abstraction at which business modellers work and that of the representation where information is encoded, which is particularly harmful. As early as in 1978, William Kent observed: "… much of [the user's] learning is really a struggle to contrive some way of fitting his problem to a tool: changing the way he thinks about his information, experimenting with different ways of representing it, and perhaps even abandoning some parts of his intended application because his tool won't handle it" [45]. For a rather typical example, in a large pharmaceutical company the possibility of mutually orthogonal subtyping hierarchies was not even considered by an otherwise excellent business modelling team because the tool imposed on them made such constructs impossible; the problem they tried to solve for a few weeks was solved in less than an hour after this artificial restriction was lifted.

# 9   Conclusions and Future Work

"[A] horrified… manager reacted upon a suggestion of mine with: 'But that would require people to think!'. It was as if I had made an indecent proposal. (The very common reaction to look immediately for 'a tool' as soon as a problem emerges could very well be a symptom of that same attitude.)"

E.W. Dijkstra [48]

Abstraction and precision in modelling are essential: the former is needed for understanding by humans and for being able to communicate at all ("complex phenomena", F.A. Hayek), while the latter (required by mathematics) is needed for discovering – together with the stakeholders – whether a model is correct or not. While some business models satisfy this requirement, (too) many do not.

To finish on a more optimistic note, quite a few good models understandable to all stakeholders have been created based on *a small, conceptually clear, and elegant system of concepts and reusable patterns*, so that the modellers and business stakeholders could concentrate on the business domain and problem at hand, abstract away the irrelevant details, and avoid the complexities of fashionable buzzword-compliant representation mechanisms. (The Oxford English Dictionary defines elegant in our context as "pleasing by ingenious simplicity and effectiveness".)

Classical books and papers by great thinkers – in computing, mathematics, philosophy, economics, and systems thinking – provide us with fresh air needed to make our thinking more lucid, more explicit, and more expressive. These works, some of which are listed as references, present concepts and patterns that help us to understand and formulate the *semantics of deep commonalities* between apparently very different domains or systems.

One of the most important lessons (to be) learned is the need for time to think and to contemplate without the demand to satisfy immediate "practical" needs and to solve immediate short-term problems. To quote Adam Smith again: "Wonder, therefore, and not any expectation of advantage from its discoveries, is the first principle which prompts mankind to the study of philosophy, of that science which pretends to lay open the concealed connections that unite the various appearances of nature; and they pursue this study for its own sake, as an original pleasure or good in itself, without regarding its tendency to procure them the means of many other pleasures… Philosophy, by representing the invisible chains which bind together all these disjointed objects, endeavours to introduce order into this chaos of jarring and discording appearances, to allay this tumult of the imagination, and to restore it, when it surveys the great revolutions of the universe, to that tone of tranquility and composure, which is both most agreeable in itself and most suitable to its nature" [49].

This lesson ought to be learned both in industry and in academia, and especially in teaching (current and) future modellers. My experience in teaching professionals in a university environment suggests that many students at first looked at the work of Adam Smith, of Hoare, and especially of Dijkstra with scepticism ("Is Adam Smith still relevant?", "Dijkstra could not possibly be very serious, could he?"). However, they very quickly understood and gave many examples of concepts and situations discussed by these authors that have been around in the students' professional (including failed and "almost successful" projects), learning, and often personal lives. Quite a few of the students became much better systems thinkers and successfully used these concepts in their and their colleagues' current projects.

A better and more profound theoretical foundation is very desirable for future work. There may be some uneasiness in working with the fundamental relationship patterns described in this paper, despite the very positive gut feeling of analysts, designers, and, perhaps more importantly, business stakeholders. A respectable mathematical foundation for this gut feeling will permit better elucidation of the underlying system of concepts and patterns, and, therefore, its well-justified reuse in various contexts. Category theory (CT) is such a mathematical foundation. The excellent book [53] provides an introduction to the structure of complex systems based on CT, explained in a manner accessible to an audience having mathematical (and systems thinking) maturity, but not necessarily having any knowledge of CT, and includes a wealth of interesting examples from biological and social systems including business enterprises (for a flavour of the relevant CT concepts, see [43]). CT emphasises relations and (emergent) collective state and behaviour essential for understanding and explanation of any complex system. (Regretfully, existing tools used for modelling do not deal with emergent properties, although this concept is explicitly included in the definition of composition in such international standards as [1, 58], and [65].)

Libraries of precisely and explicitly specified reusable business-specific patterns would be a very welcome goal and result of future work. Patterns for mortgage-based securities, and, more generally, for loan-based securities (including peer-to-peer) provide a nice example in a business area extensively discussed in business literature.

Finally, as an interesting and promising direction of future work, it would be desirable to provide an explicit model of all aspects of business modelling, with an emphasis on semantics. This includes an explicit model of the stakeholders and their influence on decision making. Articulation is essential here, although it may lead to (politically or socially) unpleasant consequences; only some contributors were brave enough to be that explicit (Dijkstra, Parnas, Meyer, Hayek, von Mises,...). A top-level specification (business-specific patterns rather than details) appears to be sufficient, reusing concepts and constructs from von Mises and Hayek, perhaps along the lines of [38].

# References

1. ISO/IEC. Open Distributed Processing — Reference Model: Part 2: Foundations (ITU-T Recommendation X.902 | ISO/IEC 10746-2)
2. Hayek, F.A.: New Studies in Philosophy, Politics, Economics and the History of Ideas. Routledge and Kegan Paul, London (1985)
3. Bunge, M.: Emergence and Convergence: Qualitative Novelty and the Unity of Knowledge. University of Toronto Press, Toronto (2004)
4. Kilov, H.: Review of [3]. SIGMOD Rec. **33**(4), 88–90 (2004)
5. Hayek, F.A.: The Sensory Order. Routledge & Kegan Paul, London (1952)
6. Manin, Y.: Mathematics as Metaphor. American Mathematical Society, Providence (2007)
7. Kilov, H., Sack, I.: Mechanisms for communication between business and IT experts. Comput. Stand. Interfaces **31**(1), 98–109 (2009)

8. Garrison, J.S.: Business specifications: using UML to specify the trading of foreign exchange options. In: Baclawski, K., Kilov, H. (eds.) Proceedings of the 10th OOPSLA Workshop on Behavioural Semantics (Back to Basics), pp. 79–84. Northeastern University, Boston (2001)
9. Kilov, H., Linington, P.F., Romero, J.R., Tanaka, A., Vallecillo, A.: The reference model of open distributed processing: foundations, experience and applications. Comput. Stand. Interfaces **35**, 247–256 (2013)
10. Kilov, H., Mogill, H., Simmonds, I.: Invariants in the Trenches. In: Kilov, H., Harvey, W. (eds.) Object-Oriented Behavioural Specifications, pp. 77–100. Kluwer Academic Publishers, Norwell (1996)
11. Kilov, H.: Business Models. Prentice-Hall, Upper Saddle River (2002)
12. Hutcheson, F.: A System of Moral Philosophy. Foulis, Glasgow & Millar (1755)
13. Proposals of the Massachusetts Hospital Life Insurance Company, to Make Insurance on Lives, to Grant Annuities on Lives and in Trust, and Endowments for Children. Printed by James Loring (1835)
14. Hales, C.: The Bank Mirror; or, A Guide to the Funds. In Which is Given, a Clear and Full Explanation of The Process of Buying and Selling Stock in the Bank of England; so that any Person May Become Thoroughly Acquainted with it in a Few Hours, Without Consulting a Broker. Together with an Account of Government and Other Securities, of the Supplies of Government, and Other Important Articles; Compiled Under the Following Heads: Funds, Banks, Credit, Traffic, Money, Stock, Company, Transfer, Dividends, Letters of Attorney, Government Supplies, Taxes, Sinking Fund, Exchequer Bills, Navy Bills, India Bonds, Bills of Exchange, Jobbing in the Funds, South Sea Annuities, India Annuities, Wills, Testaments, Assurances on Lives, Assurances on Property, Including a Sketch of the Rise, Progress, and Revolutions of Commerce, From its Cultivation Under the Asiatic and Grecian Empires, Till Its Present State of Grandeur and Importance … J. Adlard, London (1796)
15. von Mises, L.: Human Action: A Treatise on Economics. Yale University Press, New Haven (1949)
16. Dunbar, C.F.: Chapters on the Theory and History of Banking. G.P. Putnams Sons, New York (1901). Second edition, enlarged and edited by O.M.W. Sprague
17. Meeker, J.E.: The Work of the Stock Exchange, Revised edn. The Ronald Press Company, New York (1930)
18. Tyson, K.: Information Technology and Business in the Post-.COM World (Keynote at OOPSLA 2000). www.oopsla.org/2000/postconf/Tyson.pdf
19. Posner, R.: Semiotic Pollution: Deliberations Towards Ecology of Signs. Sign Syst. Stud. **28**, 290–308 (2000). Tartu University Press, Tartu, Estonia
20. Naur, P., Randell, B. (eds.) Software Engineering: Report on a Conference Sponsored by the NATO Science Committee, Garmisch, Germany, 7–11 October 1968 (1969)
21. Oldfield, R.: Simple but not Easy: an Autobiographical and Biased Book about Investing. Doddington Publishing, United Kingdom (2007)
22. Arnold, M.: UK Account Holders Flock to Swedish Bank's Church Spire. Financial Times, 25 August 2014
23. Hacken, G.: Review of Boca, P., Bowen, J., Siddiqi, J. (eds.): Formal Methods: State of the Art and New Directions. Springer, New York (2009). Computing Reviews, Review No. CR139235 (1202-0120) (2012)
24. Meyer, B.: Agile!: The Good, the Hype, and the Ugly. Springer, Switzerland (2014)
25. Russo, L.: The Forgotten Revolution: How Science Was Born in 300 BC and Why it Had to Be Reborn. Springer, Heidelberg (2004)
26. Nuseibeh, B., Zave, P. (eds.): Software Requirements and Design. The Work of Michael Jackson. Good Friends Publishing Company, Chatham (2010)

27. Bjørner, D.: Domain models of the market — in preparation for e-transaction systems. In: Kilov, H., Baclawski, K. (eds.) Practical Foundations of Business System Specifications, pp. 111–144. Kluwer Academic Publishers, Norwell (2003)

28. Bjørner, D.: Software Engineering, vol. 1–3. Texts in Theoretical Computer Science, the EATCS Series. Springer, New York (2006)

29. Kilov, H., Simmonds, I.D.: Business Patterns: Reusable Abstract Constructs for Business Specifications. In: Humphreys, P., et al. (eds.) Implementing Systems for Supporting Management Decisions: Concepts, Methods and Experiences, pp. 225–248. Chapman and Hall, London (1996)

30. Sjöberg, P.: A Simple but Highly Efficient Approach to Managing Risk. (Interview with Philip Stafford). Financial Times, 5 November 2014

31. Yaglom, I.M.: Mathematical Structures and Mathematical Modelling. Gordon and Breach Science Publishers, New York (1986)

32. Bunge, M.: Philosophical Dictionary. Enlarged edition. Prometeus Books, Amherst, NY (2003)

33. Bernet, O., Kilov, H.: From Box-and-Line Drawings to Precise Specifications: Using RM-ODP and GRM to Specify Semantics. In: Kilov, H., Baclawski, K. (eds.) Practical Foundations of Business System Specifications, pp. 99–110. Kluwer Academic Publishers, Norwell (2003)

34. Mac an Airchinnigh, M., Belsnes, D., O'Regan, G.: Formal Methods & Service Specification. In: Kugler, H.J., Mullery, A., Niebert, N. (eds.) Towards a Pan-European Telecommunication Service Infra-structure. LNCS, vol. 851, pp. 563–572. Springer, Heidelberg (1994)

35. Scientist: Complexity Causes 50 % of Product Returns. ComputerWorld, 6 March 2006

36. Weinberg, G.M.: Rethinking Systems Analysis and Design. Little, Brown and Company, Boston (1982)

37. Hill, A.: Innovation that Succeeds by Exploiting the Past Creatively. Financial Times, 25 November 2014

38. Kilov, H.: Finding work: an IT expert as an entrepreneur. In: Kilov, H., Baclawski, K. (eds.) Proceedings of the OOPSLA 2002 Workshop on Behavioural Semantics (Serving the Customer), pp. 108–120. Northeastern University, Boston (2002)

39. Jackson, M.: Software Specifications and Requirements: a Lexicon of Practice, Principles and Prejudices. Addison-Wesley, Reading (1995)

40. Hoare, C.A.R.: Software Engineering: A Polemical Prologue. In: Perrott, R.H. (ed.) Software Engineering. Proceedings of a Symposium Held at The Queen's University of Belfast 1976, pp. 1–4. Academic Press (1977)

41. Dijkstra, E.W.: Essays on the nature and role of mathematical elegance. http://www.cs.utexas.edu/users/EWD/ewd06xx/EWD619.PDF

42. Weinberg, G.: The Psychology of Computer Programming. Van Nostrand Reinhold, New York (1971)

43. Ehresmann, A.C., Paton, R.C., Vanbremeersch, J.-P.: Mathematical Metaphors and Models Based on Graphs and Categories. http://ehres.pagesperso-orange.fr

44. Hayek, F.A.: The Pretense of Knowledge. Lecture to the memory of Alfred Nobel. nobelprize.org/nobel_prizes/economics/laureates/1974/hayeklecture.html

45. Kent, W.: Data and Reality. North-Holland, Los Altos (1978)

46. Chopra, A.K.: Interaction-Oriented Software Engineering. http://www.lancaster.ac.uk/staff/chopraak/mine/presentations/iose-london-dec-2014.pdf

47. Smith, A.: An Inquiry into the Nature and Causes of the Wealth of Nations. Printed for W. Strahan; and T. Cadell, London (1776)

48. Dijkstra, E.W.: American Programming's Plight. ACM Softw. Eng. Notes 6(1), 5 (1981)

49. Smith, A.: Essays on Philosophical Subjects. London. Printed for T. Cadell Jun. and W. Davies (Successors to Mr. Cadell) in the Strand; and W. Creech, Edinburgh (1795)
50. Dijkstra, E.W.: Some meditations on advanced programming. In: Poppewell, C.M. (ed.) Proceedings of the IFIP Congress 1962, pp. 535–538. North Holland (1963)
51. Hensher, P.: What Do They Know of English. The Spectator, 17 February 2001
52. Lotman, Y.: Universe of the Mind. Indiana University Press, Bloomimgton (1990)
53. Ehresmann, A., Vanbremeersch, J.P.: Memory Evolutive Systems: Hierarchy, Emergence, Cognition. Elsevier, New York (2007)
54. Kull, K.: Semiosis included incompatibility: on the relation between semiotics and mathematics. In: Bockarove, M., Danesi, M., Nunez, R. (eds.) Semiotic and Cognitive Science Essays on the Nature of Mathematics, pp. 330–339. LINCOM EUROPA, München (2012)
55. Geiger, P.: Why Bernanke May Not Have Ticked All the Boxes. Financial Times, 15 October 2014
56. Hacken, G.: Review of Deuflhard, P. et al.: MATHEON: Mathematics for key technologies. Computing Reviews, Review No. 143186 (2015)
57. Kilov, H.: PL/I Subset. University of Latvia, Riga (1974)
58. Object Management Group. UML Profile for Relationships. http://www.omg.org/cgi-bin/doc?formal/2004-02-07
59. Kilov, H., Ash, A.: How to ask questions: handling complexity in a business specification. In: Kilov, H., Rumpe, B., Simmonds, I. (eds.) Proceedings of the OOPSLA 1997 Workshop on Object-Oriented Behavioral Semantics, Atlanta, pp. 99–104. Munich, University of Technology, TUM-I9737, 6 October 1997
60. Lamport, L.: Who builds a house without drawing blueprints? Commun. ACM 58(4), 38–41 (2015)
61. Kilov, H.: Representing business specifications in UML. In: Baclawski, K., Kilov, H. (eds.) Proceedings of the 9th OOPSLA Workshop on Behavioral Semantics, pp. 102–111. Northeastern University, Boston (2000)
62. Hayek, F.A.: The Theory of Complex Phenomena. In: Bunge, M. (ed.) The Critical Approach to Science and Philosophy (In Honor of Karl R. Popper), pp. 332–349. The Free Press of Glencoe, London (1964)
63. Goguen, J.: An introduction to algebraic semiotics, with application to user interface design. In: Nehaniv, C.L. (ed.) CMAA 1998. LNCS (LNAI), vol. 1562, pp. 242–291. Springer, Heidelberg (1999)
64. Mackintosh, J.: Short View. Financial Times, 10 April 2015
65. ISO/IEC 10165-7. Information Technology. Open Systems Interconnection – Management Information Services – Structure of Management Information – Part 7: General Relationship Model (1995)
66. Kilov, H.: Business specifications. Prentice-Hall, Upper Saddle River (1999)
67. den Ouden, E.: Development of a Design Analysis Model for Consumer Complaints Revealing a New Class of Quality Failures. Thesis at the Technical University of Eindhoven in the Netherlands (2006)

# Standards in Behaviour Modelling

# Modeling Behavior with Interaction Diagrams in a UML and OCL Tool

Martin Gogolla[✉], Lars Hamann, Frank Hilken,
and Matthias Sedlmeier

Database Systems Group, University of Bremen,
Bremen, Germany
{gogolla,lhamann,fhilken,ms}@informatik.uni-bremen.de

**Abstract.** This paper discusses system modeling with UML behavior diagrams. We consider statecharts and both kinds of interaction diagrams, i.e., sequence and communication diagrams. We present new implementation features in a UML and OCL modeling tool: (1) Sequence diagram lifelines are extended with states from statecharts, and (2) communication diagrams are introduced as an alternative to sequence diagrams. We assess the introduced features and propose selection mechanisms which should be available in both kinds of interaction diagrams. We emphasize the role that OCL can play for such selection mechanisms.

**Keywords:** UML · OCL · Model behavior · Statechart diagram · Interaction diagram · Sequence diagram · Communication diagram · Model validation · Diagram view

## 1 Introduction

In the last years the Unified Modeling Language (UML) has become a de-facto standard for the graphical design of IT systems. UML [18,20] comprises language features for structural and behavioral modeling. The textual Object Constraint Language (OCL) as part of UML adds precision in form of class invariants for restricting structural aspects and pre- and postconditions for constraining behavioral ones, among other uses of OCL [19,22] within UML.

This contribution puts emphasis on UML interaction diagrams which are syntactically presented in form of sequence and communication diagrams. Interactions describe sequences of messages exchanged among parts of a system. We use interactions for the analysis of a system which has been described structurally with a class diagram including class invariants and behaviorally with operation pre- and postconditions, operation implementations, and statecharts. In general, behavioral diagrams have become more important in the modeling of systems. The specification of interactions using the respective behavior diagrams is more understandable, which is one of the goals of the UML. In addition, the specification of actions is more intuitive using diagrams instead of textual OCL pre- and postconditions, which is widely used for, e.g., business services.

© Springer International Publishing Switzerland 2015
E. Roubtsova et al. (Eds.): BM-FA 2009-2014, LNCS 6368, pp. 31–58, 2015.
DOI: 10.1007/978-3-319-21912-7_2

We introduce new features for interactions in a UML tool and discuss how the two interaction diagrams could be handled in a uniform way.

Our group is developing the UML and OCL tool USE (UML-based Specification Environment) since about 15 years. USE [7,10] originally started as a kind of OCL interpreter with class, object and sequence diagrams available in the tool from the beginning. Other behavioral diagrams have been added over the last years, namely statechart diagrams in form of protocol state machines and most recently communication diagrams. USE claims to be useful for validation and verification of UML and OCL models. USE has been employed successfully in national and international projects (see, for example, [1,6] among other projects).

The rest of this paper is structured as follows. Section 2 introduces a running example. After having set with the example the context of our work, we discuss in Sect. 3 some general issues concerning behavioral modeling: 'abstraction', 'best practices', and 'tool support'. Section 4 explains in more details how our system USE contributes to system validation and verification. Section 5 shows the UML metamodel for interactions and sets the context for the interaction diagram implementation within USE. Section 6 presents new features in sequence diagrams, and Sect. 7 discusses established and new features in communication diagrams. In Sect. 8 a direct comparison between the two interaction diagrams is shown. Section 9 proposes systematic selection mechanisms that could be available in both interaction diagrams. Section 10 compares our approach to related papers. The contribution is closed in Sect. 11 with concluding remarks and future work.

## 2   Running Example

This section explains a running example which is used throughout the paper. In Fig. 1, a small, abstract version of Toll Collect[1] is shown. Toll Collect is a tolling system for trucks on German motorways. In the figure, the following USE features are employed: (a) a class diagram with two classes, (b) two statecharts (two protocol state machines) for each of the classes, (c) one object diagram, (d) one list of commands representing a scenario (test case), and the evaluation of (e) the class invariants and (f) a stated OCL query expression in the system state that is reached by executing the command list. The reached system state is characterized by the object diagram.

The class diagram consists of a part responsible for building up the motorway connections (basically `Point`, `Connection`, `northConnect(Point)`, `southConnect(Point)`) and a part for managing trucks and journeys (basically `Truck`, `Current`, `enter(Point)`, `move(Point)`, `pay(Integer)`). The model includes three OCL class invariants (restricting system structure) and a number of OCL operation contracts in form of pre- and postconditions (restricting system behavior). Apart from the above used standard UML descriptions, the

---

[1] http://www.toll-collect.de/en/home.html.

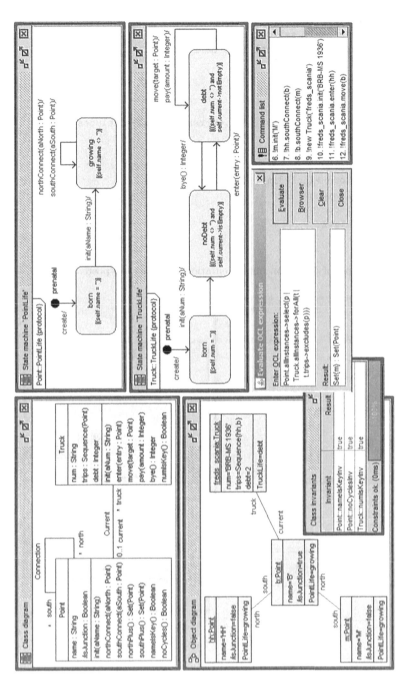

Fig. 1. Example model toll collect.

```
Truck::move(target:Point)
  begin self.trips:=self.trips->including(target);
        self.debt:=self.debt+1;
        delete (self,self.current) from Current;
        insert (self,target) into Current;
  end
pre currentExists:
  self.current->notEmpty
pre targetReachable:
  self.current.north->union(self.current.south)->includes(target)
post debtIncreased:
  self.debt@pre+1=self.debt
post tripsUpdated:
  self.trips@pre->including(target)=self.trips
post currentAssigned:
  target=self.current
post allTruckInvs:
  numIsKey()
```

**Fig. 2.** Example of operation implementation and pre- and postconditions.

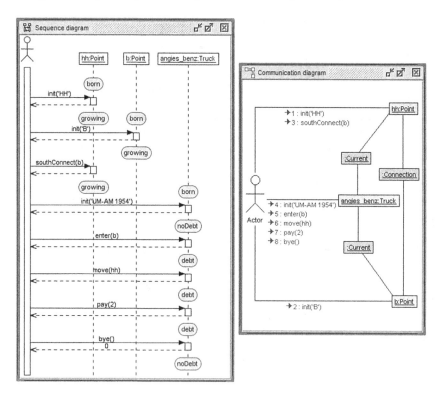

**Fig. 3.** Sequence diagram with statechart states on lifelines (some details suppressed) and equivalent communication diagram.

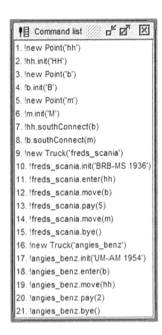

**Fig. 4.** Command list for used interaction diagrams.

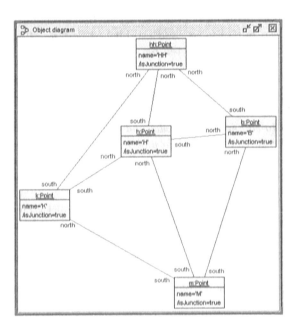

**Fig. 5.** Example for motorway connections.

operations are implemented in a Simple OCL-like Imperative programming Language (SOIL). An example for an operation contract and an operation implementation in SOIL [2] is shown in Fig. 2. Figure 3 displays a shortened variation of the scenario that the paper will discuss in detail in form of a sequence diagram and an equivalent communication diagram.

In Fig. 4, we show a longer command list where the single commands either generate objects with a specified object identity or call operations on generated objects. This command list and the commands determined by the respective operation implementation in SOIL are used in the following as the basis for the discussed interaction diagrams. This command list represents one test case, and this test case shows the *consistency* of the operation contracts in the sense that at least one scenario is possible where all operations are called (and thus *all pre- and postconditions* are valid) and *all invariants* are valid at times when no operation is active. The considered motorway connections are a toy example with the largest German towns Hamburg (hh), Berlin (b), and Munich (m). A slightly larger motorway example allowing to travel between western and eastern points as well is shown in Fig. 5. The complete USE model is given in the Appendix.

# 3 General Behavioral Modeling Issues: Abstraction, Best Practices, Tool Support

Before we go into the details of our approach we want to discuss crucial questions between our work and general issues in behavioral modeling: To what extent does our approach support behavioral modeling *abstraction* mechanisms? What is the relationship between our proposal and established *best practices* in behavioral modeling? How is our work supported by *tools*?

**Abstraction:** The motivation for modeling and the relationship to abstraction has been formulated to the point in [21] (and other works by the same author): *Why do engineers build models? (a) To understand problems and solutions, (b) to communicate model and design intent, (c) to predict interesting characteristics of the system under study, and (d) to specify the implementation of the system under study. Building models is realized by selecting statements through abstraction, i.e., reduction of information preserving properties relative to a given set of concerns.*

In our view structural and behavioral modeling must go hand in hand. As our background is database and information system modeling, we typically start with structural modeling and later involve behavioral aspects. Other IT disciplines as, for example, embedded systems may prefer to start with behavioral issues and continue with structural ones. In our view, behavioral aspects are inherently more complex than structural issues because in information systems the behavioral descriptions must be aware of and respect the structural requirements. Thus finding good abstraction techniques that *reduce information* are even more relevant for behavioral modeling.

As said already before, we use UML interactions for the analysis of a system which has been described structurally with a class diagram including class invariants and behaviorally with operation pre- and postconditions, operation implementations, and statecharts. One focus here is on UML interaction diagrams in form of communication diagrams. Communication diagram are able to present all details of a behavioral scenario and bear the danger to overwhelm the modeler with too many messages which are the basic cornerstones of a scenario. Thus in particular for communication diagrams proper and adequate abstraction mechanisms are strongly needed. This demand leads in our approach to a proposal for allowing views on interaction diagrams that take into account message number intervals, message depth, and message kind abstraction mechanisms in order to show that part of a scenario that the modeler regards as important.

**Best practices:** UML sequence and communication diagrams are employed for showing interactions, i.e., message exchanges between objects (or object roles) in order to perform a task. *Both sequence and communication diagrams show interactions, but they emphasize different aspects. A sequence diagram shows time sequence as a geometric dimension, but the relationship among [object] roles are implicit. A communication diagram shows the relationships among [object] roles geometrically and relates messages to the connectors, but time sequences are less clear because they are implied by the sequence numbers. Each diagram should be used when its main aspect is the focus of attention* (quoted from [20]). If one wants to capture the difference along the slogan *Time vs Space*, one would classify the sequence diagram into the *Time* dimension and the communication diagram into the *Space* dimension.

However, there is only little methodological help on the question when to use which diagram. Our observation is that sequence diagrams are more frequently used than communication diagrams. It seems that sequence diagrams can be used intuitively easier due to explicitly displayed message order. The message order must be mentally retrieved in communication diagrams. However, as said before, communication diagrams show the relationship between objects which is neglected in sequence diagrams.

**Tool support:** Both sequence and communication diagrams are supported by UML tools. However, a general common view mechanism on the underlying interactions is not explicitly stated in UML. This leads to different features for interactions diagrams in different tools.

Our proposal here is to offer the same view mechanisms in both interaction diagrams. The motivation for an (as far as possible) uniform treatment of sequence diagrams and communication diagrams comes from the fact that both diagram forms treat the same model elements: interactions, i.e., objects and messages between them. For example, if one starts from a complex interaction in form of a sequence diagram and one selects a subset of the involved objects for viewing, then it should be possible to do the same selection in the corresponding communication diagram. The same holds if the selection is made for messages. A conversion between both diagram forms is in principle possible because of identical underlying elements (objects and messages) and because of the fact that the geometrical ordering in the sequence diagram has its equivalent in the numerical ordering in the communication diagram. However the relationships between objects present in the communication diagram do not have an equivalent in the sequence diagram and thus cannot be represented. With respect to the underlying static structure (the class diagram) both interaction diagrams use the same elements arising from the class diagram, basically commands for the creation and deletion of objects and links, for the manipulation of attributes and for operation calls.

Interaction diagrams can be looked at from different angles. One can view interactions in both sequence and communication diagrams along the object or along the message dimension. Furthermore, apart from interactively selecting relevant parts in a scenario, we discuss how to employ OCL for systematically accessing objects and messages.

The discussed features are implemented in our tool USE. Sequence diagrams have been present in USE from the very beginning, and only later communication diagrams were added. Integrated views on both kinds of interaction diagrams with common features are currently under development. The aim of the newly added view features is to better support new abstraction mechanisms for behavioral modeling, in particular in connection with communication diagrams that are only poorly supported in present UML tools as far as voluminous scenarios are concerned.

## 4   Validation and Verification with USE

OCL can be employed in USE for various tasks: in class diagrams for (a) class invariants, (b) operation contracts, (c) attribute and association derivation rules, and (d) attribute initializations; in protocol state machines for (e) state invariants and (f) transition pre- and postconditions; furthermore for (g) ad-hoc OCL queries in object diagrams, and for (h) expressions within SOIL. In USE, class diagrams and protocol machines enriched by invariants, operation contracts, statechart constraints and SOIL operation implementations determine system structure and behavior. Sequence and communication diagrams are employed in USE for visualizing and analyzing specified test cases in form of scenarios. Interaction diagrams are not used for restricting system behavior, but to document, analyze, and understand the interactions. These diagrams are built after a complete model including the SOIL operation implementation has been constructed.

The overall aim of USE is to support development by reasoning about the model through (a) validation, i.e., checking informal expectations against formally given properties, for example, by stating OCL queries against a reached system state (object diagram) and (b) verification, i.e., checking formal properties of the model, for example by considering model consistency or the independence of invariants as in [7]. That contribution also shows how USE supports making deductions from the stated model on the basis of a finite search space of possible system states (object diagrams). Such checks are realized in form of positive and negative scenarios which can be thought of as being test cases for the system under consideration. Thus USE supports the development of tests.

In OCL operation contracts as well as pre- and postconditions can be general OCL formulas. In postconditions, one can refer with @pre to attribute and association end values at precondition time. Postconditions can state general requirements and are not restricted to the specification of changes to attribute and association end values. Thus the actual changes made by the operation are described in SOIL and are checked against the contract. Concerning the protocol state machines, concurrency is currently not supported, and operation call sequences which do not fit to the protocol are rejected. The definition of protocol state machines is optional.

Various validation and verification use cases for the USE tool are discussed in [9]. A comparison between the USE verification method for behavioral aspects and another approach is discussed in [11]. The so-called 'filmstripping' technique within USE for mapping behavioral descriptions into structural problems is proposed in [8].

## 5   UML Metamodel for Interactions

The interactions part of the UML metamodel[2] [18, p. 473ff.] was developed to visualize concrete traces of event occurrences and in addition to allow the definition of all possible traces of an interaction. The former can be used in early design stages to be able to communicate with designers and to some extent with stakeholders. A concrete trace does not show alternatives or loop constructs, because it describes a single message trace (or command trace) in the system. Elements like alternatives or loops can be used in later design phases to express all possible traces (cf. [18, p. 473]). Interactions can be visualized by different diagrams. Two of the more common ones are sequence diagrams and communication diagrams. Both diagrams focus on slightly different aspects of interactions. While sequence diagrams highlight the time line of an interaction, communication diagrams focus on the different elements participating in an interaction and their relationship.

Figure 6 shows an excerpt of the UML metamodel required to briefly discuss the representation of event occurrences inside interaction diagrams. A more detailed presentation can, for example, be found in [15]. On the right side of this figure, meta classes from the structural modeling part of the UML are shown. These are needed to completely model message occurrences. On the left side, the relevant parts of the interaction meta classes are shown. Consider the occurrence of the message enter(hh) shown in the following sequence diagram in Fig. 3 and in the (following) communication diagram in Fig. 8. This part of both diagrams can be expressed as an object diagram of the metamodel, as it is done in Fig. 7. Again, on the right side the structural part is shown, e. g., the two classes which participate in the message occurrence: Truck as the class of the receiving

---

[2] UML metamodel novices might skip this section on first reading and continue with the next section. UML metamodel followers are invited to dive deep.

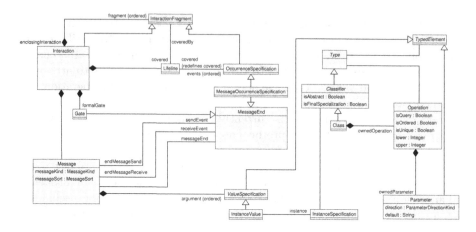

**Fig. 6.** Relevant parts of the UML interactions metamodel.

instance[3] and `Point` which is used as the type of the parameter of the operation
`enter`. Further, both instances used in the interaction diagrams (`freds_scania`
and `hh`) are placed there, too. On the left side, the example scenario is given as
an instance of `Interaction`. Since we consider the single message occurrence
`enter(hh)`, the object diagram contains few interaction related instances. First,
the `Gate gSend` acts as the source of the message occurrence. It is linked to the
interaction as a formal gate to signal that the source of the event is outside of
this interaction. The receiving end of the message is represented by the instance
`recEnter` of type `MessageOccurenceSpecification`. This instance is linked to
the `Lifeline` named `freds_scania:Truck`. The payload of the message `mEnter`
is given by the `InstanceValue` argument linked to the instance `hh` of the class
`Point`.

## 6   Sequence Diagrams

As USE allows the developer to employ UML protocol machines to restrict the
model behavior and to document test scenarios with sequence diagrams, it is
desirable to show the protocol machine state of objects on sequence diagram
lifelines, when the developer thinks this may be useful. Thus we have implemented this option for lifelines.

In Fig. 3, a fraction of the test scenario from Fig. 4 is displayed. We have
manually selected the lifeline of only two `Point` objects and one `Truck` object and
have activated the display of states from protocol state machines. For example,

---

[3] In the current version of the UML metamodel, a lifeline can only represent con-
nectable elements like properties or parameters. Since our tool allows a lifeline to
represent a concrete instance, this fact cannot be expressed using the current UML
metamodel. This is an open issue reported to the OMG [5].

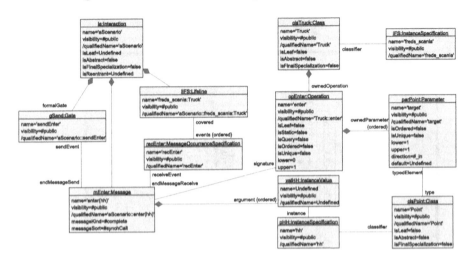

**Fig. 7.** Send message event as an instance of the UML metamodel.

one can directly trace the development of the Truck object and the state changing through operation calls with init(..), enter(..), move(..), pay(..), bye(): from born to noDebt to debt and then again to noDebt. In the case that more money has been paid than is needed for paying the journey, the operation bye returns the overpayment.

UML sequence diagrams also allow the developer to use combined fragments, which define a combination of interaction fragments. A combined fragment consists of an interaction operator, an appropriate interaction operands and, if required, so-called guards (Boolean expressions).

Altogether, the UML supports 12 interaction operators. Some of these operators could be introduced in USE by representing SOIL operations as sequence diagrams. The *alternatives* and *option* operators, for example, could be realized via SOIL's conditional execution support (*if-then-else*). And the *loop* operator could be implemented via the SOIL iteration statement (*for-in-do-end*).

Sequence diagrams also support *interaction use* elements, which allow developers to call other interactions to simplify or reuse shared interactions. This could be represented in SOIL with corresponding operation calls, thus covering the *reference* interaction operator.

## 7   Communication Diagrams

Figure 8 shows the communication diagram representing the messages from the test scenario in Fig. 4 and additionally all messages that are executed within the operation calls by the SOIL implementation. As usual in communication diagrams, the ordering of messages is determined by message numbers, and sub-messages (i.e., messages that are triggered by one message) are displayed by a structured message number with a dot as separator. For example, message 18 has

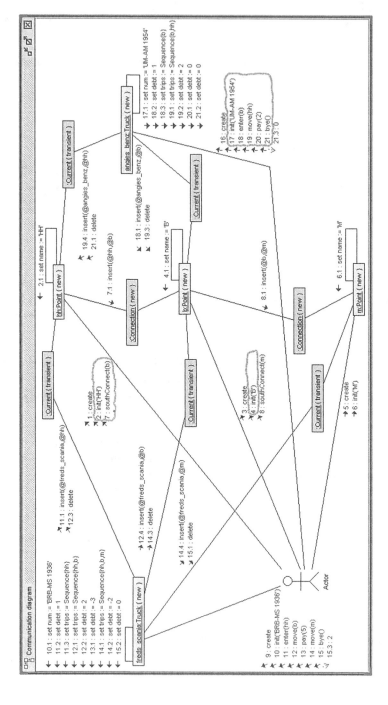

**Fig. 8.** Communication diagram with details shown (framed messages also in Fig. 3).

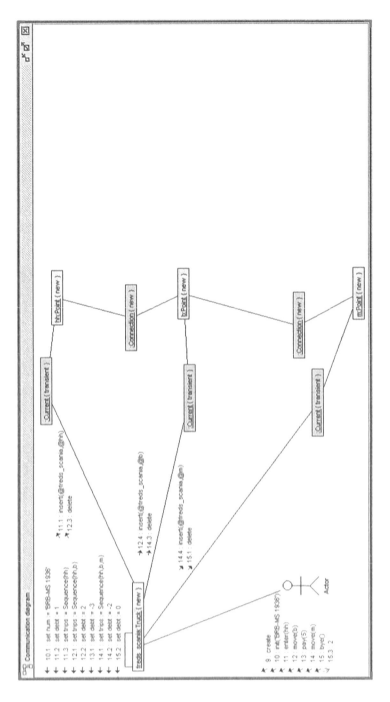

Fig. 9. Communication diagram displaying only messages 9–15.

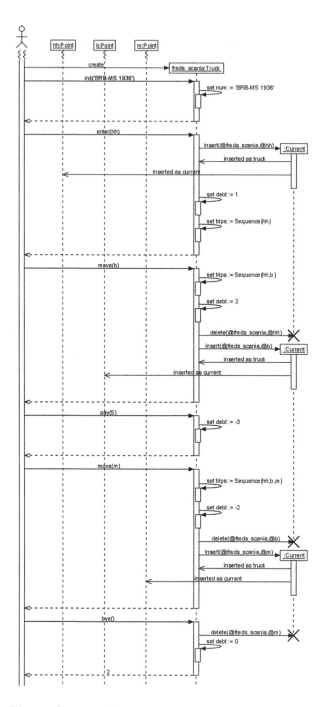

**Fig. 10.** Sequence diagram displaying only messages 9–15.

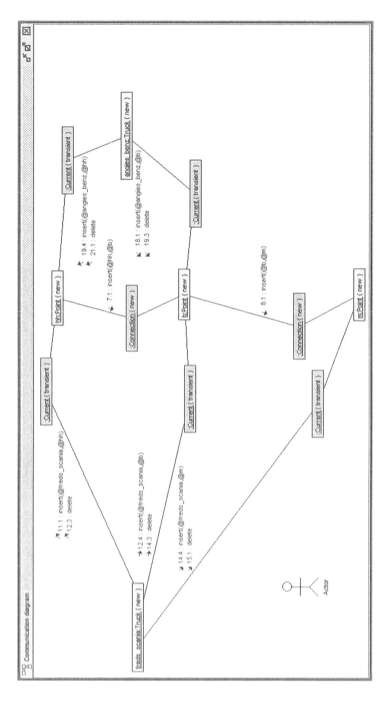

Fig. 11. Communication diagram displaying only link insertion and deletion.

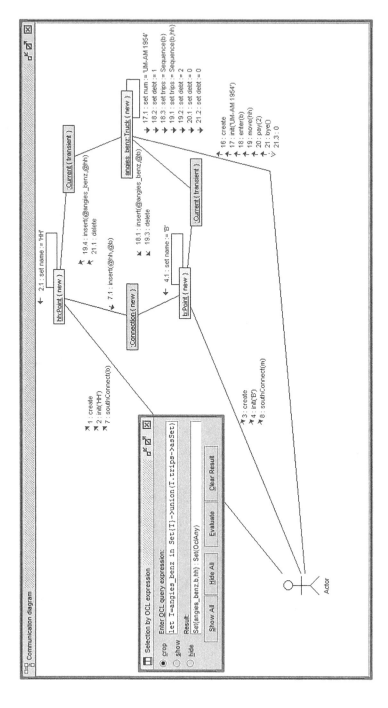

**Fig. 12.** Communication diagram with OCL selection for truck object by identity.

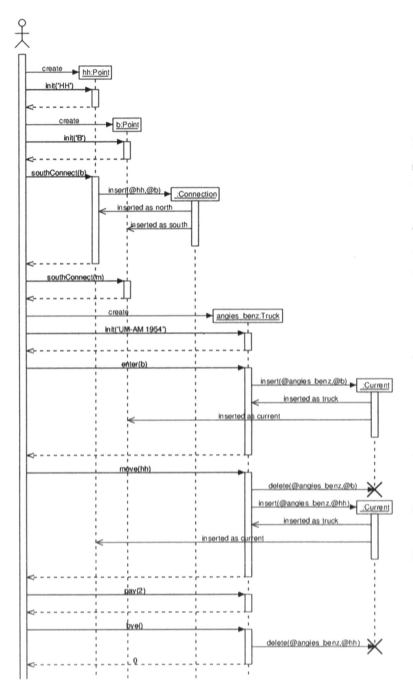

Fig. 13. Sequence diagram corresponding to communication diagram in Fig. 12.

the sub-messages 18.1, 18.2, and 18.3, i.e., the enter(b) call on the Truck object angies_benz is implemented by a link insertion (18.1) in association Current, an assignment (18.2) for attribute debt and an assignment (18.3) for attribute trips. As usual in communication diagrams, the specifications new, transient, resp. destroyed refer to objects that are newly introduced, newly introduced and deleted, resp. deleted during the interaction.

The relationship to the sequence diagram in Fig. 3 has been indicated manually by messages that are lying inside free drawn frames. These eight framed messages correspond to the eight messages in the sequence diagram.

For a smart representation of a communication diagram in an interactive GUI, the main objective is to provide a good overview and comprehensibility of the diagram. Bigger communication diagrams with multiple operation calls and messages become quickly difficult to follow (see Fig. 8). To improve this situation, some straightforward ideas have proven to be helpful:

1. Limiting the view of the diagram to a range of messages (see Fig. 9).
2. Cropping of different message types to only display those messages that are relevant to understand the shown process (see Fig. 11).
3. Cropping of objects and links to only display those relevant in the shown process (see Fig. 12).
4. Combinations of the above.

The communication diagram in Fig. 8 shows the complete sequence of messages (1–21), which can be roughly split into the *initialization of a road network* and two *navigations of trucks*. Figure 9 focuses on the navigation of the first truck only (messages 9–15) and thereby this sequence is easier to understand.

A similar effect occurs when focusing on a subset of message types. Figure 11 only shows link insertion and deletion messages in the communication diagram and thereby increases the focus on the development of the links. A similar feature is available for sequence diagrams, allowing to show or hide the message types create, destroy, insert, delete and set.

Lastly, single objects and links that are not relevant to understand the current process can be removed from the view of the diagram in favor of a better accessibility, e.g., in Fig. 12 only one truck, the two points that it visits and the links in between these objects are displayed. The other parts of the route as well as the second truck are hidden.

Thus, to help with the selection of large quantities of objects communication diagrams, the *selection by OCL expression* feature of the USE tool has been taken over from the object diagram (see Fig. 12). With this feature, certain objects can be shown, hidden or cropped.

## 8    Selection Mechanisms in Communication and Sequence Diagrams

To further illustrate and compare the selection mechanisms in sequence and communication diagrams, the following three examples demonstrate selecting views on the complete interaction from Fig. 8 where one particular aspect is emphasized in each example. Where appropriate, the corresponding sequence diagram is also displayed with the same filters applied.

1. **Interval selection:** Figure 9 restricts the messages according to a message number interval: only the messages 9 to 15 including their sub-messages are stated. This part of the interaction handles the first `Truck` object and shows its initialization and movements. Figure 10 shows the corresponding sequence diagram with the same selection applied.
2. **Message kind selection:** Figure 11 presents a view on the complete interaction along a different dimension than message numbers. Only messages concerning a particular message kind are displayed, in this diagram the insertion and deletion of links. As in UML different message kinds are available, such a restriction can be useful. In USE we currently support the following message kinds: object creation, object destruction, link creation, link destruction, attribute assignment, and operation call.
3. **OCL selection:** Figure 12 makes a selection in the communication diagram with the help of an OCL expression. In this case the OCL expression picks a `Truck` object together with the `Point` objects that are visited. The result is typed as `Set(OclAny)` because objects of different classes show up. All messages between the selected objects are shown. This object and message selection cannot be achieved with a message number interval or a message kind specification. Figure 13 shows the corresponding sequence diagram with the same selection applied, however `set` statements are hidden.

The selection mechanisms shown in the communication diagrams in Figs. 8 and 12, are currently implemented (modulo some required improvements in the user interface). USE also supports the selection mechanisms shown in Figs. 9 and 11.

## 9   Systematic Selection Mechanisms for Views in UML Interactions and Further Use of OCL

Currently, the selection mechanisms for UML sequence and communication diagrams in our tool USE are different. This is due to the fact that the design and implementation has been done at different times with different people involved. Our plan is to unify the selection mechanisms and offer a unified view mechanism for both interaction diagrams. We currently identify the following options. An overview in form of a generic interaction together with the object and message dimensions and the resulting presentation options is presented in Fig. 14.

**Selection focusing on objects:** Objects could be selected through the following possibilities:

1. Interactive show, hide or crop for objects individually or by class.
2. Interactive multiple selection by shift key and mouse click.

*Model behavior determined by*
- *Class diagram with class invariants and operation pre- and postconditions*
- *Statecharts with state invariants and transition pre- and postconditions*

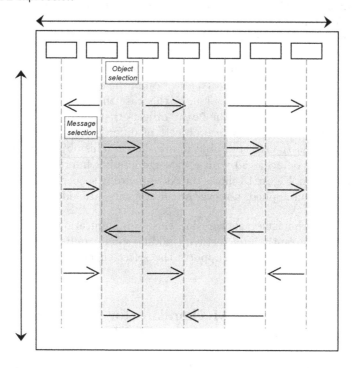

Object selection through
- Manual selection or selection by enumeration
- Class selection (objects of particular classes)
- Operation selection (objects sending/receiving calls of particular operations)
- OCL expression

Message selection through
- Manual selection or selection by enumeration
- Class selection (messages in particular classes)
- Operation selection (messages of particular operations)
- Message interval
- Message kind
- Message depth

**Fig. 14.** Overview on interactions with object and message dimension.

3. Objects satisfying resp. violating an OCL invariant during interaction.
4. Objects satisfying resp. violating an ad-hoc OCL formula during interaction.

**Selection focusing on messages:** Messages could be selected through the following possibilities:

1. Interactive show, hide or crop for messages.
2. Selection through an OCL object query identifying the sending object.
3. Selection through a satisfied resp. violated OCL pre- or postcondition.
4. Selection through a satisfied resp. violated ad-hoc OCL formula at pre- or postcondition time during an operation call.
5. Selection by message kind: object creation, object destruction, link insertion, link deletion, attribute assignment, operation call.
6. Selection by message number depth.
7. Determination of a message interval defined by
    (a) interactively fixed start message and end message.
    (b) start OCL formula and end OCL formula.
    (c) a statechart start state and a statechart end state for a fixed object.

The OCL expressions that we employ in communication diagrams are currently working on the last system state. However, the communication diagram contains information that is not selectable using plain OCL in this way, i.e., removed objects and links in general. For example the OCL expression `allInstances()` to select all instances of a class will currently not select transient or destroyed objects, yet they are still displayed in the communication diagram.

Consequently, to get full access to the elements in the communication diagram, the syntax and accordingly the evaluation of OCL has to be extended. First, it is desired to access the system's pre- and post states of each message to get access to all time steps of the communication diagram. In addition, access to the elements of a range of messages or the global sequence of messages is helpful for the selection. Temporal extensions for OCL often include functionality to formulate expression about the past (see e.g., [24]) and can be considered to be integrated.

The temporal extension of OCL would not only improve the selection of elements in the GUI. The access to the new properties increases the possibilities of validation tasks formulated on the communication diagram.

## 10   Related Work

Behavior modeling with UML interactions has relationships to other important approaches. A definition of the UML interaction semantics in terms of the System Model can be found in [3]. In [12], a comparison between software model verification approaches using OCL and UML interaction diagrams among others is performed. The work in [16] focuses on the interaction problem in the context of aspect-oriented programming. It explains how Aspect-UML can be translated into Alloy and shows how to verify aspect interactions with Alloy's model analyzer. In [17], the synthesis of test cases from UML interaction diagrams by a systematic interpretation of flow of controls is discussed. Improvements to the UML interaction metamodel concerning message arguments and loops are proposed and demonstrated in [23]. The approach in [14] is strongly related to the USE approach because of the emphasis on protocol modeling. That work is however closer to programming through the use of Java, whereas we are closer to modeling because of using OCL. The proposals in [4,13] discuss test case generation from interaction diagrams. Our approach is the only one that employs OCL for selecting relevant parts in the interactions under consideration. The current work differs from our previous contributions (like [7,10]) in that we did not consider sequence diagrams with statechart states on lifelines or communication diagrams at all.

## 11   Conclusion

This contribution has discussed how to handle UML interaction diagrams in a model validation tool and has pointed to the link between protocol machine and interaction diagrams. We have set up desirable selection mechanisms for both kinds of UML interaction diagrams, namely sequence and communication diagrams.

Future work has to complete our current implementation with the missing features in both interaction diagrams. In particular, message kind selection and message interval selection seem to offer useful analysis options. We have discussed how to extend the options for interaction analysis with temporal OCL query features. Larger examples and case studies need to validate the already existing and planned features for better support of interaction diagrams that advance behavioral modeling.

## Appendix: Complete USE Model for Toll Collect

```
-------------------------------------------------- model TollCollect
model TollCollect
-------------------------------------------------- class Truck
class Truck
attributes
  num:String             init: ''
  trips:Sequence(Point)  init: Sequence{}
  debt:Integer           init: 0
operations
  init(aNum:String)
    begin self.num:=aNum end
  enter(entry:Point)
    begin insert (self,entry) into Current; self.debt:=1;
    self.trips:=self.trips->including(self.current) end
  move(target:Point)
```

```
    begin self.trips:=self.trips->including(target);
    self.debt:=self.debt+1; delete (self,self.current) from Current;
    insert (self,target) into Current end
  pay(amount:Integer)
    begin self.debt:=self.debt-amount end
  bye():Integer
    begin delete (self,self.current) from Current;
    result:=self.debt.abs(); self.debt:=0 end
  ----------------------------------------------------------------
  numIsKey():Boolean=
    Truck.allInstances->forAll(self,self2|
      self<>self2 implies self.num<>self2.num)
  ----------------------------------------------------------------

statemachines
  psm TruckLife
  states
    prenatal:initial
    born    [num='']
    noDebt [num<>'' and current->isEmpty]
    debt    [num<>'' and current->notEmpty]


  transitions
    prenatal -> born    { create }
    born        -> noDebt { init() }
    noDebt    -> debt    { enter() }
    debt        -> debt    { move() }
    debt        -> debt    { pay() }
    debt        -> noDebt { bye() }
  end
end


------------------------------------------------------- class Point
class Point
attributes
  name:String init: ''
  isJunction:Boolean derived: north->union(south)->size()>=2
operations
  init(aName:String)
    begin self.name:=aName end
  northConnect(aNorth:Point)
    begin insert (aNorth,self) into Connection end
  southConnect(aSouth:Point)
    begin insert (self,aSouth) into Connection end
  ------------------------------------------------------------------
  northPlus():Set(Point)=north->closure(p|p.north)
  southPlus():Set(Point)=south->closure(p|p.south)
  ------------------------------------------------------------------
```

```
  nameIsKey():Boolean=
    Point.allInstances->forAll(self,self2|
      self<>self2 implies self.name<>self2.name)
  noCycles():Boolean=
    Point.allInstances->forAll(self|
      not(self.northPlus()->includes(self)))
    -----------------------------------------------------------------

statemachines
  psm PointLife
  states
    prenatal:initial
    born    [name='']
    growing [name<>'']
  transitions
    prenatal -> born    { create }
    born     -> growing { init() }
    growing  -> growing { northConnect() }
    growing  -> growing { southConnect() }
  end
end

----------------------------------------------- association Current
association Current between
  Truck[0..*] role truck
  Point[0..1] role current
end
---------------------------------------------- association Connection
association Connection between
  Point[0..*] role north
  Point[0..*] role south
end

-------------------------------------------------------- constraints
constraints
-------------------------------------------------------- invariants
context Truck inv numIsKeyInv:
  numIsKey()
context Point inv nameIsKeyInv:
  nameIsKey()
context Point inv noCyclesInv:
  noCycles()

-------------------------------------------------------- Point::init
context Point::init(aName:String)
pre freshPoint:
  self.name='' and self.north->isEmpty and self.south->isEmpty
pre aNameOk:
  aName<>'' and aName<>null
post nameAssigned:
```

```
  aName=self.name
post allPointInvs:
  nameIsKey() and noCycles()
```

```
------------------------------------------------- Point::northConnect
context Point::northConnect(aNorth:Point)
pre aNorthDefined:
  aNorth.isDefined
pre freshConnection:
  self.north->excludes(aNorth) and self.south->excludes(aNorth)
pre notSelfLink:
  self<>aNorth
pre noCycleIntroduced:
  aNorth.northPlus()->excludes(self)
post connectionAssigned:
  self.north->includes(aNorth)
post allPointInvs:
  nameIsKey() and noCycles()
```

```
------------------------------------------------------- Truck::init
context Point::southConnect(aSouth:Point)
pre aSouthDefined:
  aSouth.isDefined
pre freshConnection:
  self.south->excludes(aSouth) and self.south->excludes(aSouth)
pre notSelfLink:
  self<>aSouth
pre noCycleIntroduced:
  aSouth.southPlus()->excludes(self)
post connectionAssigned:
  self.south->includes(aSouth)
post allPointInvs:
  nameIsKey() and noCycles()
```

```
------------------------------------------------------- Truck::init
context Truck::init(aNum:String)
pre freshTruck:
  self.num='' and self.trips=Sequence{} and self.debt=0 and
  self.current->isEmpty
pre aNumOk:
  aNum<>'' and aNum<>null
post numAssigned:
  aNum=self.num
post allTruckInvs:
  numIsKey()
```

```
------------------------------------------------------ Truck::enter
context Truck::enter(entry:Point)
pre noDebt:
  0=self.debt
```

```
pre currentEmpty:
  self.current->isEmpty
pre entryOk:
  entry<>null
post debtAssigned:
  1=self.debt
post currentAssigned:
  entry=self.current
post allTruckInvs:
  numIsKey()
--------------------------------------------------------- Truck::move
context Truck::move(target:Point)
pre currentExists:
  self.current->notEmpty
pre targetReachable:
  self.current.north->union(self.current.south)->includes(target)
post debtIncreased:
  self.debt@pre+1=self.debt
post tripsUpdated:
  self.trips@pre->including(target)=self.trips
post currentAssigned:
  target=self.current
post allTruckInvs:
  numIsKey()
--------------------------------------------------------- Truck::pay
context Truck::pay(amount:Integer)
pre amountPositive:
  amount>0
pre currentExists:
  self.current->notEmpty
post debtReduced:
  (self.debt@pre-amount)=(self.debt)
post allTruckInvs:
  numIsKey()

--------------------------------------------------------- Truck::bye
context Truck::bye():Integer
pre currentExists:
  self.current->notEmpty
pre noDebt:
  self.debt<=0
post resultEqualsOverPayment:
  self.debt@pre.abs()=result
post zeroDebt:
  self.debt=0
post currentEmpty:
  self.current->isEmpty
post allTruckInvs:
  numIsKey()
-----------------------------------------------------------------
```

# References

1. Büttner, F., Bartels, U., Hamann, L., Hofrichter, O., Kuhlmann, M., Gogolla, M., Rabe, L., Steimke, F., Rabenstein, Y., Stosiek, A.: Model-driven standardization of public authority data interchange. Sci. Comput. Program. **89**, 162–175 (2014)
2. Büttner, F., Gogolla, M.: Modular embedding of the object constraint language into a programming language. In: Simao, A., Morgan, C. (eds.) SBMF 2011. LNCS, vol. 7021, pp. 124–139. Springer, Heidelberg (2011)
3. Calegari, D., Cengarle, M.V., Szasz, N.: UML 2.0 Interactions with OCL/RT Constraints. In: FDL, pp. 167–172. IEEE (2008)
4. Chen, H.Y., Li, C., Tse, T.H.: Transformation of UML Interaction Diagrams into Contract Specifications for Object-oriented Testing. In: IEEE [12], pp. 1298–1303 (2007)
5. Chonoles, M.M.J.: Issue 15123: Sequence Diagram and Communication Diagrams should Support Instances as Lifelines (uml2-rtf), March 2010. http://www.omg.org/issues/uml2-rtf.html#Issue15123
6. Georg, G., France, R.: An Activity Theory Language: USE Implementation. Colorado State University, Computer Science, Technical report CS-13-101 (2013)
7. Gogolla, M., Büttner, F., Richters, M.: USE: a UML-based specification environment for validating UML and OCL. Sci. Comput. Program. **69**, 27–34 (2007)
8. Gogolla, M., Hamann, L., Hilken, F., Kuhlmann, M., France, R.B.: From Application Models to Filmstrip Models: An Approach to Automatic Validation of Model Dynamics. In: Fill, H., Karagiannis, D., Reimer, U. (eds.) Proceedings Modellierung (MODELLIERUNG'2014), pp. 273–288. GI, LNI 225 (2014)
9. Gogolla, M., Kuhlmann, M., Hamann, L.: Consistency, Independence and Consequences in UML and OCL models. In: Dubois, C. (ed.) TAP 2009. LNCS, vol. 5668, pp. 90–104. Springer, Heidelberg (2009)
10. Hamann, L., Hofrichter, O., Gogolla, M.: On integrating structure and behavior modeling with OCL. In: France, R.B., Kazmeier, J., Breu, R., Atkinson, C. (eds.) MODELS 2012. LNCS, vol. 7590, pp. 235–251. Springer, Heidelberg (2012)
11. Hilken, F., Niemann, P., Gogolla, M., Wille, R.: Filmstripping and unrolling: a comparison of verification approaches for UML and OCL behavioral models. In: Seidl, M., Tillmann, N. (eds.) TAP 2014. LNCS, vol. 8570, pp. 99–116. Springer, Heidelberg (2014)
12. Knapp, A., Wuttke, J.: Model checking of UML 2.0 interactions. In: Kühne, T. (ed.) MoDELS 2006. LNCS, vol. 4364, pp. 42–51. Springer, Heidelberg (2007)
13. Machado, P.D.L., de Figueiredo, J.C.A., Lima, E.F.A., Barbosa, A.E.V., Lima, H.S.: Component-based Integration Testing from UML Interaction Diagrams. In: IEEE [12], pp. 2679–2686 (2007)
14. McNeile, A.T., Simons, N.: Protocol modelling: a modelling approach that supports reusable behavioural abstractions. Softw. Syst. Model. **5**(1), 91–107 (2006)
15. Micskei, Z., Waeselynck, H.: The many meanings of UML2 sequence diagrams: a survey. Softw. Syst. Model. **10**(4), 489–514 (2011)
16. Mostefaoui, F., Vachon, J.: Design-level detection of interactions in aspect-UML models using Alloy. J. Object Technol. **6**(7), 137–165 (2007)
17. Nayak, A., Samanta, D.: Model-based test cases synthesis using UML interaction diagrams. ACM SIGSOFT Softw. Eng. Notes **34**(2), 1–10 (2009)
18. OMG, (ed.) UML Superstructure 2.4.1. Object Management Group (OMG), August 2011

19. OMG, (ed.) Object Constraint Language, Version 2.3.1. OMG (2012). http://www.omg.org. OMG Document
20. Rumbaugh, J., Jacobson, I., Booch, G.: The Unified Modeling Language 2.0 Reference Manual. Addison-Wesley, Massachusetts (2003)
21. Selic, B.: The Theory and Practice of Modeling Language Design. Tutorial at MODELS 2012 (2012). http://models2012.info/
22. Warmer, J., Kleppe, A.: The Object Constraint Language: Precise Modeling with UML, 2nd edn. Addison-Wesley (2003)
23. Wendland, M.-F., Schneider, M., Haugen, Ø.: Evolution of the UML interactions metamodel. In: Moreira, A., Schätz, B., Gray, J., Vallecillo, A., Clarke, P. (eds.) MODELS 2013. LNCS, vol. 8107, pp. 405–421. Springer, Heidelberg (2013)
24. Ziemann, P., Gogolla, M.: OCL extended with temporal logic. In: Broy, M., Zamulin, A.V. (eds.) PSI 2003. LNCS, vol. 2890, pp. 351–357. Springer, Heidelberg (2004)

# A Set of Metrics of Non-locality Complexity in UML State Machines

Gefei Zhang[1]($\boxtimes$) and Matthias M. Hölzl[2]

[1] Celonis GmbH, München, Germany
gefei.zhang@pst.ifi.lmu.de
[2] Ludwig-Maximilians-Universität München, München, Germany
matthias.hoelzl@pst.ifi.lmu.de

**Abstract.** One of the barriers to widespread adoption of behavior modeling languages lies in the complexity of the models. We show in the context of UML state machines how non-locality, i.e., the information for the current behavior of a model being spread over several model elements instead of being locally available, may make seemingly intuitive and simple models rather complex and error-prone. We present a set of metrics to measure the complexity of UML state machines arising from different kinds of non-locality. Our metrics give a better understanding of the complexity of UML state machines, and may alert the modeler to pay more attention to pitfalls in *apparently simple* UML state machines.

## 1 Introduction

In Software Engineering research, Model-Driven Engineering (MDE) has been recognized as "a promising approach to address the inability of third-generation languages to alleviate the complexity of platforms and express domain concepts effectively" [6]. However, in practice, MDE has not yet experienced broad acceptance. The reasons are manifold [7]. In our opinion, one important reason that has not yet been widely discussed in the literature is that behavioral models are, despite the best intention of the modeler, sometimes counter-intuitive and hard to comprehend.

UML state machines are widely used to model software system behaviors and have been described as "the most popular language for modeling reactive systems" [2]. In literature about software or behavior modeling, UML state machines are generally considered to be simple and intuitive. However, these intuitions can easily be misleading when UML state machines are used to model non-trivial behaviors [13].

In general, a state machine is only simple and intuitive as long as the effect of transitions is kept local: if a transition only deactivates the state it originates from, and only activates the state it leads to, the modeler can visually follow the control flow, and the model is easy to understand.

In many realistic state machines, however, states are parallel and contain orthogonal regions. In such state machines it is quite common for a transition to activate not only its target, and to deactivate not only its source, but also

© Springer International Publishing Switzerland 2015
E. Roubtsova et al. (Eds.): BM-FA 2009-2014, LNCS 6368, pp. 59–81, 2015.
DOI: 10.1007/978-3-319-21912-7_3

states that are visually not directly connected to it. Conversely, a state can be activated or deactivated not only by a transition directly connected to it, but also by visually "remote" transitions. Moreover, transitions and states in different regions may depend on each other in complex ways. In these situations the modeler has to carefully study all information carried by remote model elements to avoid introducing errors into the state machine.

It is therefore important to study this kind of complexity, which we call non-locality complexity. In this paper, we discuss in detail "hidden" activations and deactivations as well as cross-region dependencies, and we define a set of metrics to measure the non-locality complexity caused by states or transitions, that is, how many states—visually connected or not—are actually activated or deactivated by a certain transition, how many transitions—visually connected or not—may actually activate or deactivate a certain state, how many transitions—in different regions—are fired in one execution step, and how many states—in different regions—may prevent each other from getting active. These metrics quantify various non-local effects of a state machine's behavior and may alert developers to potential pitfalls.

The remainder of the paper is structured as follows: in the following Sect. 2, we give a brief overview of the concrete syntax and informal semantics of UML state machines, and show how non-locality complexity may arise. In Sect. 3 we discuss the non-local effects in more detail, define our metrics, and give some application samples of how the metrics may indicate possible flaws in a state machine. Related work is discussed in Sect. 4, before we conclude and outline some future work in Sect. 5.

## 2 UML State Machines

A UML state machine provides a model for the behavior of an object or component. Figure 1 shows a state machine modeling (in a highly simplified manner) the behavior of a player during a part of a game.[1] The behavior of the player—a magician—is modeled in the state Play, which contains two concurrent regions and models two different *concerns* of the magician's conduct. The upper region describes the possible movements of the player: she starts in an entrance hall (Hall), from there she can move to a room in which magic crystals are stored (CrystalRoom), and move on to a room containing a Ladder. From this room the player can move back to the hall.

The lower region specifies the magician's possible activities. She may be Idle, gathering power for the next fight, Spelling a hex, or Fighting. She may escape from the fight and try to spell another hex, or, if she wins the fight, finish the game.

### 2.1 Concrete Syntax and Informal Semantics

According to the UML specification [5], a UML state machine consists of *regions* which contain *vertices* and *transitions* between vertices. A vertex is either a *state*,

---

[1] This example is inspired by [14].

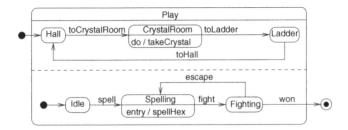

**Fig. 1.** Example: UML state machine

which may show hierarchically contained regions; or a *pseudo state* regulating how transitions are compounded in execution. Transitions are triggered by *events* and describe, by leaving and entering states, the possible state changes of the state machine. The events are drawn from an *event pool* associated with the state machine, which receives events from its own or from other state machines.

A state is *simple*, if it contains no regions (such as Hall in Fig. 1); a state is *composite*, if it contains at least one region; a composite state is said to be *orthogonal* if it contains more than one region, visually separated by dashed lines (such as Play). A region may also contain states and other vertices. A state, if not on the top-level itself, must be contained in exactly one region. To simplify the notation in later sections we assume in this paper that the top-level state is enclosed in a region top, so that each state is contained in exactly one region. A composite state and all the states directly or recursively contained in it thus build a tree. A state may have an *entry*, a *do*, and an *exit* action, which are executed before, whilst, and after the state is active, respectively.

Transitions are triggered by events (toCrystalRoom, fight). Completion transitions (not shown in this paper) are triggered by an implicit *completion event* emitted when a state completes all its internal activities. Events may be *deferred* (not shown), that is, put back into the event pool if they are not to be handled currently. A transition may have an *effect*, which is an action to be executed when the transition if fired. Very briefly speaking, the result of firing a transition is that the source state of the transition (and potentially other states, see Sect. 3.3) is left, its target state (and potentially other states, see Sect. 3.2) entered, and the entry and exit actions are executed; for more details, see below. Transitions may also be declared to be *internal* (not shown), thus skipping the activation-deactivation scheme. An *initial* pseudo state, depicted as a filled circle, represents the starting point of the execution of a region. A *junction* pseudo state, depicted as a dot, chains transitions together. A *final* state, depicted as a circle with a filled circle inside, represents the completion of its containing region; if all top-level regions of a state machine are completed then the state machine terminates. For simplicity, we omit the other pseudo state kinds: entry and exit points, fork and join, shallow and deep history, choice, and terminate. These vertices, except for joins, can be simulated using states and transitions only, see [10]; joins require a slight extension of the methods presented in this paper.

At run time, states get activated and deactivated as a consequence of transitions being fired. The active states at a stable step in the execution of the state machine form the active *state configuration*. Active state configurations are hierarchical: when a composite state is active, then exactly one state in each of its regions is also active; when a substate of a composite state is active, so is the containing state, too. The execution of the state machine can be viewed as different active state configurations getting active or inactive upon the state machine receiving events.

When an event in the event pool is processed, first the maximum set of enabled conflict-free transitions is calculated. We refer to transitions where the source state is active, the trigger is the current event, and the guard is evaluated to `true` as *enabled* transitions. At runtime, if there are several enabled transitions where the source states are in different regions, then all the transitions are in general contained in the set, and should be fired in one execution step.[2] A special case, however, is when the source of one of the enabled transitions is contained in the source of another enabled transition. In this case, only the transition with the *innermost* source state is contained in the maximum set of conflict-free enabled transitions. If there are several enabled transitions whose sources are in the same region, then they all have the same source state, since in one region there is at most one active state (here: exactly one). In this case, we say the enabled transitions (from the same source) are *conflicting*, and only one of them, chosen non-deterministically, is contained in the maximum set of conflict-free enabled transitions.

The transitions in the maximum set of conflict-free enabled transitions are then fired in one execution step. More specifically, first the source states, and other states to be deactivated (see Sect. 3.3), are deactivated, then their exit actions are executed, then the effects of the transitions are executed, then the entry actions of the target states, and other states to be activated (see Sect. 3.2), are executed, and finally these states are activated. For the entry and exit actions, the UML Specification [5] imposes a partial order of execution: for two states $s$ and $S$, if $s$ is directly or recursively contained in $S$, then the entry action of $S$ is executed before that of $s$ when the states are activated, and the exit action of $s$ is executed before that of $S$ when the states are deactivated. In the other cases, where $s$ and $S$ are in different regions and are not contained in each other, no special order of execution is specified. In the metrics we are going to define in this paper, we do not make use of this partial order. In the future, more precise metrics can be defined if this partial order is also taken into account.

Since the maximum set of enabled transitions is determined *before* the execution of the entry actions, the transitions' effects, and the exit actions, these actions have no effect on the choice of transitions to be fired.

In our example of Fig. 1, an execution trace, given in terms of active state configurations the state machine, might be (`Play`, `Hall`, `Idle`), (`Play`, `Hall`,

---

[2] Strictly using the terms defined in the UML Specification, this is a special case of the *run-to-completion* step. For simplicity, we do not use the concept run-to-completion in this paper. Since we ignore most of the pseudo states, see Sect. 3.1, a run-to-completion event is actually very similar to our execution step.

Spelling), (Play, Hall, Fighting), followed by the final state, which terminates
the execution trace.

## 2.2   Non-locality Complexity

While the simplest UML state machines may be intuitively comprehensible,
the complexity increases rapidly when the behavior under modeling gets more
involved [13]. There are several reasons for this increase in complexity. One is
that the language is low-level, providing only *if-then-else* and *goto* like constructs
(see [10]). In this sense, modeling with state machines is similar to programming
in assembly language, where the programmer has to implement every program
structure without the benefit of abstractions built into the language.

The metrics we propose in this paper are, however, mostly concerned with
another cause for complexity in state machines: the control flow in a region is
often determined not only by information that is available "locally", i.e., stored in
currently active states or transitions just before or after being fired. Instead, relevant information is "hidden" in model elements that are not directly connected
with active states and transitions. Recall, for instance, that when a transition $t$ is
fired, not only is its target $s$ activated, but, if $s$ is a substate in a composite state
$S$ not containing the source of $t$, so is the state $S$ (if a substate is active, then
so is its containing state, too). Therefore, in each region of $S$ exactly one of the
contained states, although not connected directly with $s$ or $t$, is also activated.
Similarly, when a transition $t$ is fired, not only is its source $s$ deactivated, so are
all states $S$ containing $s$ but not the target of $t$, and hence all states that are
directly or recursively contained in $S$, although they are not connected directly
with $s$ or $t$.

As an example, consider Fig. 1. The transition leaving the initial pseudo state
activates not only Hall in the upper region, but also Idle in the lower region;
the transition leaving Fighting deactivates not only this state, but also the
state in the upper region which is currently active. Considering that this kind of
"remote" activation and deactivation may be recursive, it may cause significant
potential for misinterpretation of the state machine's actual behavior by the
modeler.

Moreover, different, parallel regions of a state are not executed independently
of each other. Instead, there often exist cross-region dependencies within a state.
For instance, enabled transitions with the same trigger and source states in
different regions are normally fired in the same execution step—unless something
(like a guard in a nested region) prevents some of these transitions from firing.
To understand what a state machine is supposed to do, the reader of the machine
has thus to keep track of a lot of non-local information—a guard that prevents a
transition from firing does not have to be guarding the transition it inhabits or,
for that matter, be anywhere close to this transition in the visual representation
of the state machine.

We will present more examples of this kind of complexity, which we call
*non-locality complexity*, later on. In the following, we define metrics to measure
non-locality complexity.

# 3   Metrics

We first review the metamodel of UML state machines, define auxiliary functions, and then define metrics to capture the non-locality complexity.

## 3.1   Notation

The abstract syntax of UML state machines we consider in this paper is shown in Fig. 2. UML allows many syntactic variations that complicate static analysis of state machines. Therefore, we require some minor restrictions in addition to the UML Specification [5]:

1. A composite state may contain at most one region $r$ without an initial vertex; $r$ must contain directly or recursively a state which is the target of a transition $t$, and $t$'s source is not contained in $r$.[3]
2. The state machine must not contain junctions. All junctions, except the ones following an initial vertex, should be removed by the (semantics-preserving) transformation shown in Fig. 3, which essentially merges each pair of junction-connected transitions into one transition, with the conjuncture of the two original guards as new guard. For simplicity, we do not consider state machines with junctions following an initial vertex in this paper.

The first constraint applies only to states with multiple regions and serves to clarify their semantics: in the case of multiple regions the behavior of a state machine that does not satisfy this restriction is not clear. The second constraint actually slightly restricts the range of possible state machines; it would be possible to lift this restriction by a straightforward extension of our metrics.

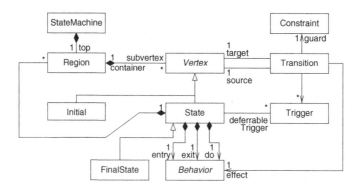

**Fig. 2.** Metamodel: UML state machines (simplified)

Given states $s_1$ and $s_2$, we write $\mathsf{LCR}(s_1, s_2)$ for the least region containing both $s_1$ and $s_2$, and $\mathsf{LCA}(s_1, s_2)$ for the least state containing both $s_1$ and

---

[3] In other words, $t$ is a *target-unstructured* transition, see below, Definition 3.

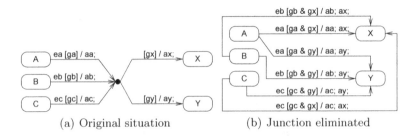

**Fig. 3.** Removing junctions

$s_2$. We suppose that on the top-level, a state machine consists in a region (called top), which contains the top-level vertices of the state machine, see Sect. 2.1. Therefore, for any $s_1$ and $s_2$, $\mathsf{LCR}(s_1, s_2)$ is well-defined. If there is no state containing both $s_1$ and $s_2$ (i.e., $\mathsf{LCR}(s_1, s_2) = \mathsf{top}$), we write $\mathsf{LCA}(s_1, s_2) = \perp$. In Fig. 1, $\mathsf{LCR}(\mathsf{Spelling}, \mathsf{Fighting})$ is the lower region of Play and $\mathsf{LCA}(\mathsf{Spelling}, \mathsf{Fighting}) = \mathsf{Play}$.

Given region $r$, we write $\mathsf{substate}^+(r)$ to represent all states (directly or recursively) contained in $r$. For a state $s$, we write $\mathsf{substate}^+(s)$ to represent $\bigcup_{r \in \mathsf{region}(s)} \mathsf{substate}^+(r)$ and write $\mathsf{substate}^*(s)$ to represent $\mathsf{substate}^+(s) \cup \{s\}$. We write $S \in \mathsf{superstate}^*(s)$ if $s \in \mathsf{substate}^*(S)$. We write $\mathsf{simple}(s)$ if state $s$ is simple. Given states $S$ and $s \in \mathsf{substate}^+(S)$, we write $s \in S$, otherwise we write $s \notin S$.

We refer to property $p$ of object $o$ as $p(o)$. If the name of a property is not given explicitly, we follow the common UML convention and use, independently of the multiplicity, the lower-cased name of its type as the property name. For example, we write $\mathsf{state}(r)$ for the state associated with a region $r$ according to UML metamodel given in Fig. 2.

In the following, we define some more auxiliary notations.

**Definition 1 (Initial Transition).** *If a region $r$ contains an initial vertex, we call the transition leaving this initial vertex the* initial transition *of $r$, and refer to it as $\mathsf{intr}(r)$.*

For example, in Fig. 1 the initial transition of the lower region is the one leading into the Idle state; the upper region does not have an initial transition.

**Definition 2 (Source Structured Transitions).** *A transition $t$ is called source structured, referred to as $\mathsf{struc}_{\mathsf{source}}(t)$, if its source is a direct subvertex of the LCR of its source and its target. More formally, $\mathsf{struc}_{\mathsf{source}}(t)$ is* **true** *if $\mathsf{source}(t) \in \mathsf{subvertex}(\mathsf{LCR}(\mathsf{source}(t), \mathsf{target}(t)))$.*

**Definition 3 (Target Structured Transitions).** *A transition $t$ is called target structured, referred to as $\mathsf{struc}_{\mathsf{target}}(t)$, if its target is a direct subvertex of the LCR of its source and its target. More formally, $\mathsf{struc}_{\mathsf{target}}(t)$ is* **true** *if $\mathsf{target}(t) \in \mathsf{subvertex}(\mathsf{LCR}(\mathsf{source}(t), \mathsf{target}(t)))$.*

Intuitively, a transition "goes through" the border of a composite state if it is source or target unstructured. Obviously, a transition may be both source and target structured, and does not need to be either. In Fig. 1, all transitions are target structured except for the one leading into state Hall from outside the Play state.

**Definition 4 (Container State in Region).** *Given a state s and a region r, the* container state *of s in region r is the state x which contains (directly or recursively) s and is a direct substate of r. More formally,* $\mathsf{Csr}(r, s) = \mathsf{subvertex}(r) \cap \{x \mid s \in \mathsf{substate}^+(x)\}$. *Obviously, if* $s \in \mathsf{substate}^+(r)$, *there is exactly one element in* $\mathsf{Csr}(r, s)$, *otherwise* $\mathsf{Csr}(r, s)$ *is empty. We therefore refer to this single element as* $\mathsf{Csr}(r, s)$.

In Fig. 1 no state has a container state in either the upper or lower region. The state Play is container state for Hall, CrystalRoom, Ladder, Idle, Spelling and Fighting in the region enclosing the whole state machine.

### 3.2 Metrics Regarding State Activation

The activation and deactivation of states in UML state machines is relatively complex, because concurrent and nested regions may be involved. We therefore introduce in Fig. 4 a slightly more complicated variant of the game in Fig. 1. The game now consists of two areas, a laboratory (Lab) in which the wizard may rest (in state Idle) or brew potions (in state BrewPotion) and the multi-room dungeon (Dungeon) in which fights take place. The wizard enters the level from the hall of the dungeon, and can use the ladder of the dungeon to escape to her lab and later return to the dungeon. In addition, she can take a potion before fighting (takeBrew) which will increase the power of her next spell tenfold (PowerSpelling and PowerFighting). In Sect. 3.5 we will use the metrics defined in this paper to show that this model has several possible modeling mistakes; for now we are only interested in the activation and deactivation of states by transitions.

According to the UML Specification [5], a state s can be activated in one of the following ways:

1. a transition t with target(t) = s is fired (transition spell to state Spelling) in Fig. 1,
2. a substate x of s is activated by a transition t where source(t) ∉ substate*(s) (Play when the "initial transition" from the outer region to Dungeon is fired; Dungeon, when the transition toLadder from state Idle in Lab is fired),
3. s is the target of an "initial transition" in a region, contained in composite state S, and transition t with target(t) = S is fired (Hall and Idle inside Dungeon in Fig. 4 when the "initial transition" to Dungeon is fired),
4. s is the target of an "initial transition" in a region, contained in composite state S, when a state x in one of the neighbor regions of s gets activated by a target-unstructured transition t with target(t) = x (state Idle in the lower region of Dungeon in Fig. 4 when toLadder from the state Idle in Lab is fired).

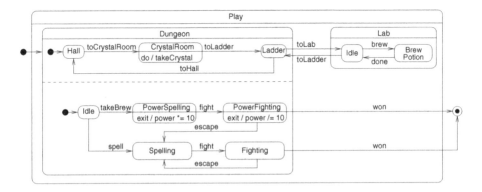

**Fig. 4.** Two-room game example

To capture this notion precisely we first define a function orth that returns the set of all states contained in regions orthogonal to the one containing $s$, i.e., all states either directly in a region orthogonal to the region containing $s$ or recursively contained in a state in such a region:

$$\text{superstate}(s) = \text{state}(\text{container}(s))$$
$$\text{orth}(s) = \{s' \in \text{substate}^+(\text{superstate}(s)) \mid \text{LCA}(s, s') \in \text{LCR}(s, s')\}$$

We can now define the set of transitions that may make state $s$ active, $A^{tr}(s)$ more precisely. $A^{tr}(s)$ is the least fixed point of the equations

$$A^{tr}(s) = T^{in}(s) \cup BT(s) \cup PT(s)$$

where

$$T^{in}(s) = \{t \mid \text{target}(t) = s$$
$$\vee (\text{source}(t) \not\subseteq \text{substate}^*(s) \wedge \text{target}(t) \in \text{substate}^+(s))\}$$

$$BT(s) = \begin{cases} \emptyset & \text{if } s \text{ is not target of an initial transition} \\ \bigcup_{s' \in IC(s) \setminus \{s\}} A^{tr}(s') & \text{otherwise} \end{cases}$$

$$IC(s) = \begin{cases} \{s\} & \text{if } s \text{ is not target}(\text{intr}(\text{container}(s))) \\ \{s\} \cup IC(\text{superstate}(s)) & \text{otherwise} \end{cases}$$

$$PT(s) = \begin{cases} \emptyset & \text{if } s \text{ is not target of an initial transition} \\ \{t \in \bigcup_{s' \in \text{orth}(s)} A^{tr}(s') \mid \text{source}(t) \not\subseteq \text{orth}(s)\} & \text{otherwise} \end{cases}$$

$T^{in}(s)$ covers the first two cases, whereas $BT(s)$ deals with the third and $PT(s)$ captures the fourth one. $A^{tr}$ is defined as fixed point to cover cases like the ones depicted in Fig. 5: Since both $B$ and $D$ are initial states in their respective regions, $A^{tr}(B)$ has to take into account $A^{tr}(D)$ when determining $PT(B)$, but $A^{tr}(D)$ in turn relies on $A^{tr}(B)$. In Fig. 5, the transition from A to B and the transition from C to D both activate states B and D.

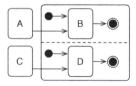

**Fig. 5.** State machine that illustrates the need for fixed points in $A^{tr}$

With these premises, we define the metric of *Number of Activating Transitions* of a state as the cardinality of the set of transitions that may activate it:

**Definition 5 (Number of Activating Transitions).** *Given a state $s$, its* Number of Activating Transitions *is*

$$NATr(s) = \#A^{tr}(s)$$

In Fig. 1 all states contained in `Play` are simple, therefore the number of activating transitions for each state is not surprising, e.g., for `Hall` it is 2, for `CrystalRoom` it is 1. In the lower region, the number of activating transitions for `Idle` is 1, the one for `Spelling` is 2 and the one for `Fighting` is 1.

Given a transition $t$, the set $Act(t)$ of states which may be activated by $t$ is as follows:

1. If $t$ is target structured and its target is a simple state, then it only activates its target.
2. If $t$ is target structured and its target is composite, then it activates all initial states directly contained in one of the regions of its target, and this activation continues recursively until simple states are reached.
3. If $t$ is not target structured, the chain of activations starts with the container state $S$ of its target in the region that contains both its source and target. This is the topmost state that can become active, since any state containing both source and target of $t$ has to be already active before $t$ can fire, and is not activated by $t$. If $S$ is itself the target of $t$, then, as in the previous case, all initial states recursively contained in $S$ are activated. If, however, $S$ is not target of $t$, then $S$ must contain the target state $s = \mathsf{target}(t)$. In this case, $t$ activates all regions of $S$ that are not in the "path" to $s$ in the usual way, whereas in regions that are on the way to $s$ it activates these states through which it passes, independently of whether they are targets of initial transitions or not.

$$Act(t) = \begin{cases} \{target(t)\} \\ \quad \text{if } struc_{target}(t) \wedge simple(target(t)) \\ \{target(t)\} \cup \bigcup_{r \in region(target(t))} Act(intr(r)) \\ \quad \text{if } struc_{target}(t) \wedge \neg simple(target(t)) \\ Act_s(t, Csr(LCR(source(t), target(t)), target(t))) \\ \quad \text{if } \neg struc_{target}(t) \end{cases}$$

where

$$Act_s(t, S) = \begin{cases} \{S\} \cup \bigcup_{r \in region(S)} Act(intr(r)) \text{if } target(t) = S \\ \bigcup_{r \in region(S), r \neq r'} Act(intr(r)) \cup Act_s(t, Csr(r', target(t))) \\ \quad \text{where } r' \in region(S) \wedge target(t) \in substate^+(r') \\ \quad \text{if } target(t) \neq S \end{cases}$$

With these premises, we define the metric *Number of Activated States* of a transition as the cardinality of the set of the states that may be activated by the transition:

**Definition 6 (Number of Activated States).** *Given a transition t, its* Number of Activated States *is*

$$NAS(t) = \#Act(t)$$

Applying this metric to the example given in Fig. 1, we get some interesting results. For example, let $t$ be the transition from the initial to Hall, then we have $NAS(t) = 3$, reflecting the fact that not only the obvious Hall is activated when $t$ is fired, but also Idle and Play. In this sense, $t$ is obviously more complex than the transition from Hall to CrystalRoom, which only has a $NAS$ of 1.

## 3.3 Metrics Regarding State Deactivation

According to the UML Specification [5], a state $s$ can be deactivated in one of the following ways:

1. a transition $t$ is activated, $source(t) = s$,
2. a transition $t$ is activated, $source(t) = S$, where $S$ is a state containing $s$,
3. a transition $t$ is activated, $source(t) = s'$, where $s'$ is in one of the neighbor regions of $s$ and $target(t)$ is in a region containing $s$.

An example for the first kind of deactivation is the transition from Fighting to Spelling in Fig. 4. A transition from Dungeon to Lab would be an example for the second case. The third kind of deactivation happens, e.g., for state Fighting when the transition from Ladder to Idle is taken.

More formally, let $D^{tr}(s)$ be the set of transitions that may deactivate state $s$, we have

$$D^{tr}(s) = \bigcup_{S \in \mathsf{superstate}^*(s)} T^{out}(S) \cup AT(s)$$

where

$$AT(s) = \bigcup \{t \mid \mathsf{target}(t) \notin \mathsf{LCA}(\mathsf{source}(t), s)\}$$

With these premises, we define the metric of *Number of Deactivating Transitions* of a state as the cardinality of the set of transitions that may deactivate the state:

**Definition 7 (Number of Deactiviting Transitions).** *Given a state $s$, its* Number of Deactivating Transitions *is*

$$NATr(s) = \#D^{tr}(s)$$

Deactivation is simpler than activation since no "cascading deactivations" may happen: A transition will deactivate all states in regions contained in its source and all states in regions "between" its source and target, but it may not trigger additional deactivations in regions inside its target state as is the case for activations. In Fig. 4, state `Fighting` has 3 deactivating transitions: from `Fighting` to `Spelling`, from `Fighting` to the final state, and from `Ladder` (in the upper region) to `Idle`.

Given a transition $t$, the set $Dct(t)$ of states which may be deactivated by $t$ is as follows:

1. A source-structured transition from a simple state deactivates only its source state.
2. A source-structured transition $t$ from a composite state $S$ deactivates $S$ and, potentially, all of its substates. More precisely, $t$ deactivates exactly one state in each of the active regions recursively contained in $S$. Since any of these states may be deactivated by $S$ we count the number of substates in $S$.
3. For a source-unstructured transition, the same considerations apply for states in regions not on the "path" of the transition; on the way from the source to the target of $t$ only these states through which $t$ passes may be deactivated.

$$Dct(t) = \begin{cases} \{\mathsf{source}(t)\} \\ \quad \text{if } \mathsf{struc}_{\mathsf{source}}(t) \wedge \mathsf{simple}(\mathsf{source}(t)) \\ \{\mathsf{source}(t)\} \cup \bigcup_{r \in R}\{x \mid x \in \mathsf{substate}^+(r)\} \\ \quad \text{if } \mathsf{struc}_{\mathsf{source}}(t) \wedge \neg\mathsf{simple}(\mathsf{target}(t)) \\ Dct_s(t, S) \\ \quad \text{if } \neg\mathsf{struc}_{\mathsf{source}}(t) \end{cases}$$

where

$$
Dct_s(t, S) =
\begin{cases}
\{S\} \cup \mathsf{substate}^*(S) \\
\quad \text{if } \mathsf{source}(t) = S \\
\bigcup_{r \in R, r \neq r'} \mathsf{substate}^*(r) \cup Dct_s(t, \mathsf{Csr}(r', \mathsf{source}(t))) \\
\quad \text{where } r' \in \mathsf{region}(s) \wedge \mathsf{source}(t) \in \mathsf{substate}^+(r') \\
\quad \text{if } \mathsf{source}(t) \neq S
\end{cases}
$$

With these premises, we define the metric *Number of Deactivated States* of a transition as the cardinality of the set of states that may be deactivated by the transition:

**Definition 8 (Number of Deactivated States).** *Given a transition t, its* Number of Deactivated States *is*

$$
NDS(t) = \#Dct(t)
$$

Let $t$ be the transition from `Fighting` to the final state, it has a high *NDS* of 5, because not only `Fighting`, but also `Hall`, `CrystalRoom`, `Ladder` and `Play` will get inactive once $t$ is fired.

## 3.4 Metrics Regarding Cross-Region Dependency

Cross-region dependencies may have two forms: some "actions" (transitions being fired, states being activated or deactivated) in different regions are carried out simultaneously, while others may prevent each other from being carried out. These dependencies crosscut model elements across several regions, their comprehension requires careful study of the state machine.

In the following, we use another extension of our computer game to illustrate cross-region dependencies, see Fig. 6. In this variant of the game, the navigation region contains another state `CrystalPedestal` that can be reached from the `CrystalRoom` upon the event `investigate` whenever the player is near a pedestal. The `Idle` state in the region responsible for the player's activities has been refined by a state machine that describes the various activities the player can perform while she is idle: she can `Wander` around the room; while wandering the player may `trip` and enter into a `Curious` state in which she has the possibility to `investigate` the reason for tripping, or to `ignore` the incident and continue wandering. If the player does investigate while she is in the `Curious` state two courses of action may unfold: Either there was no particular reason for tripping, in which case the investigation deducts some health points (not shown in the state machine) and the player continues to wander, or the player tripped over a hidden trap door (guard TD) in which case she discovers a trap door leading to fame and fortune, and thus immediately wins the level without having to fight. Whenever the player is in the `Idle` state she can `investigate` her surroundings and thereby gather new information about the room or objects nearby.

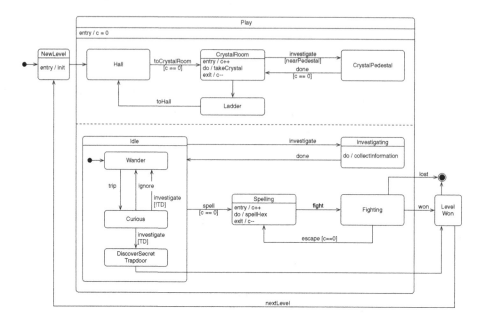

**Fig. 6.** Game with cross-region dependencies

In this version of the game we have used the `investigate` event on three different transitions: to change from the `CrystalRoom` to the `CrystalPedestal` with the guard `nearPedestal`, to change from `Idle` to `Investigating` unconditionally, and from `Wander` to `Curious` (both substates of `Idle`) when the guard TD holds. Whenever the transition inside the `Idle` state is enabled, the transition from `Idle` to `Investigating` cannot fire. This shows that submachines are not compositional, i.e., the addition of a submachine to a state may invalidate invariants of the containing machine. It is often convenient to model in this way. For example, if the `investigate` event is mapped to a physical event generated by controller hardware, the state machine in Fig. 6 represents the different results of pressing this button in various game situations in a very concise manner. However, the "stealing" of events by interior transitions is also a source of possible mistakes, in particular when working with modeling tools that allow modelers to hide nested states. Therefore we consider it useful to investigate metrics that can draw attention to these kinds of potential problems. In the following we will therefore propose some measures for the influence exerted by states or transitions on the execution of other regions of the state machine.

**Simultaneous Initial Transitions.** One simple case of transitions being fired in one execution step is that when a composite state $S$ is activated, either via a transition $t$, $\mathsf{target}(t) = S$, or via a transition $t'$, $\mathsf{target}(t') \in \mathsf{substate}^+(S)$, then the initial transitions of the regions of $S$ are also fired. Details were described in Sect. 3.2.

Given an initial transition $t$, for each state in the set $Act(t) \setminus \{target(t)\}$, there is another transition which is fired in the same execution step as $t$. The complexity measure for this situation is therefore given by the cardinality $NAS(t) - 1$, see page 11.

**Bonded Transitions.** Another case of transitions being fired in one execution step is that when transition $t_1$ is fired, another transition $t_2$ from a parallel region is also fired in the same execution step if all the four following conditions are satisfied:

1. the source states are both active,
2. $guard(t_1)$ and $guard(t_2)$ both hold,
3. both transitions have the same trigger,
4. the source states are in different, parallel regions.

To capture situations where these conditions may hold we define the set of transitions that are bonded to a given transition.

**Definition 9 (Bonded Transitions).** *Given a transition $t$, the set of transitions that are* bonded *to $t$ is $\overline{B}(t) = \{t' \mid \mathsf{Can}(t, t')\}$, where the predicate* $\mathsf{Can}$ *is defined as* $\mathsf{Can}(t, t') ::= \mathsf{trigger}(t) = \mathsf{trigger}(t') \wedge \mathsf{LCA}(\mathsf{source}(t), \mathsf{source}(t')) \in \mathsf{substate}^+(\mathsf{LCR}(\mathsf{source}(t), \mathsf{source}(t')))$.

The definition states that two transitions $t$ and $t'$ are *bonded*, written as $\mathsf{Can}(t, t')$, when the last two of the four conditions above are satisfied. The first part of the predicate $\mathsf{Can}$ reflects condition 3, and the second part reflects condition 4. However, the converse is not true: The information to determine if the other two conditions hold is only available at runtime. Since this paper is concerned with static analysis, we ignore these two conditions, and *over-estimate* the run-time value instead.

The set $\overline{B}(t)$ may also contain transitions that are not fired when $t$ is fired: suppose $t', t'' \in \overline{B}(t), \mathsf{source}(t'') \in \mathsf{substate}^+(\mathsf{source}(t'))$, and at some time during the state machine's execution, $\mathsf{source}(t'')$ (and therefore $\mathsf{source}(t')$) is active. If the current event is $\mathsf{trigger}(t) = \mathsf{trigger}(t') = \mathsf{trigger}(t'')$, then, according to the UML Specification [5], $t''$ is fired while $t'$ is not, since the source of $t''$ is a substate of $t'$. For example, when `Curious` (and thus `Idle`) is active, since one of the conditions `[TD]` and `[!TD]` is always `true`, the transition from `Idle` to `Investigating` in Fig. 6 will not be fired, even if the current event is `investigate`.

In the next definition, we restrict the set to contain only transitions that we know will definitely be fired when $t$ is fired. The flip side of the definition is that it may ignore those transitions $t'$ such that $\mathsf{Can}(t, t')$ holds but there is some $t''$, $\mathsf{source}(t'') \in \mathsf{substate}^+(\mathsf{source}(t')) \wedge \mathsf{Can}(t, t'')$.

**Definition 10 (Strictly Bonded Transitions).** *Given a transition $t$, the set of transitions that are* strictly bonded *to $t$ is $\mathcal{B}(t) = \{t' \mid \mathsf{Can}(t, t') \wedge \not\exists t'' \cdot [\mathsf{Can}(t, t'') \wedge \mathsf{source}(t'') \in \mathsf{substate}^+(\mathsf{source}(t'))]\}$*

These two relations are the most precise values we can compute by static analysis, since in general only by actually executing the state machine is it possible to find out whether source$(t'')$ will be active whenever source$(t')$ is active.

The relations are not symmetric, i.e., if $t' \in \overline{\mathcal{B}}(t)$, generally it does not hold that $t \in \overline{\mathcal{B}}(t')$ and if $t' \in \mathcal{B}(t)$, generally it does not hold that $t \in \mathcal{B}(t')$. Moreover, the relations are independent of the transitions' effects: since the transitions to fire are selected before their effects, if any, are executed, potential effects are transparent for (both strict and non-strict) bondedness of transitions.

Now we are in the position to define metrics for (strictly and non-strictly) bonded relationships.

**Definition 11 (Number of Bonded Transitions).** *Given a transition $t$, the number of transitions* bonded *to $t$ is*

$$\overline{NB}(t) = \#\overline{\mathcal{B}}(t)$$

**Definition 12 (Number of Strictly Bonded Transitions).** *Given a transition $t$, the number of transitions* strictly bonded *to $t$ is*

$$NB(t) = \#\mathcal{B}(t)$$

These two metrics reflect the complexity of transitions that may be fired simultaneously, i.e., within one execution step.

In Fig. 6 the transition $t_{CC}$ from CrystalRoom to CrystalPedestal is strictly bonded (and hence bonded) to each of the transitions triggered by the investigate event in the lower region: the transition $t_{CW}$ from Curious to Wander, the transition $t_{CD}$ from Curious to DiscoverSecretTrapdoor and the transition $t_{II}$ from Idle to Investigating. Therefore $\overline{NB}(t_{CW}) = NB(t_{CW}) = 1$, $\overline{NB}(t_{CD}) = NB(t_{CD}) = 1$ and $\overline{NB}(t_{II}) = NB(t_{II}) = 1$. These numbers show that each of these transitions may be accompanied by a simultaneous transition in an orthogonal region, but that if a concurrent execution step takes place in the orthogonal region, it always progresses by triggering the same transition for each of $t_{CW}, t_{CD}$ and $t_{II}$. (The metric is not precise enough to indicate that all three transitions are bonded to the same transition $t_{CC}$)

On the other hand, the transitions $t_{CW}$ and $t_{CD}$ are both strictly bonded to $t_{CC}$ since no transition starting from a substate of Curious exists. However the transition $t_{II}$ is bonded to $t_{CC}$ but not strictly bonded, since $t_{CW}$ and $t_{CD}$ are bonded to $t_{CC}$ and their initial states are substates of Idle. Therefore, we have $\overline{NB}(t_{CC}) = 3$, $NB(t_{CC}) = 2$. These metrics show that the behavior in the region orthogonal to $t_{CC}$ is much more complicated: There are at least two different transitions in the innermost relevant region that may each fire concurrently with $t_{CC}$, (because $NB(t_{CC}) = 2$), and there is one transition that may be inhibited by locally invisible transitions inside its source state (because $NB(t_{CC}) = \overline{NB}(t_{CC}) + 1$). When looking at bonded transitions, the measures $NB$ and $\overline{NB}$ for the transitions bonded to a transition $t$ are more revealing than the measures for $t$ itself: By seeing the numbers $NB(t_{CC})$ and $\overline{NB}(t_{CC})$ when looking at $t_{II}$ we are immediately alerted that there are other transitions that may prevent $t_{II}$ from firing, even when the submachine inside Idle is hidden.

**Competing States.** There are also states which are, at least under certain conditions, not supposed to be active simultaneously. This is often implemented in state machines by adding `entry`, `do`, or `exit` actions to a state that change the value of some variable $x$, while there are states in other regions with incoming transitions where $x$ is consulted; [11] discusses implementation of mutual exclusion using this technique in greater detail.

We have to take care of two facts:

1. the target of the transition may be a composite state, or a substate of some composite state, and therefore firing this transition may actually cause many other states to be active and their entry actions to be executed;
2. the source of the transition may be a composite state, or a substate of some composite state, and therefore firing this transition may actually cause many other states to be inactive and their exit actions to be executed.

While in case 1 we can precisely calculate the states to be activated and thus their entry actions, in case 2 it is in general not possible to calculate statically the precise "path" of state deactivation and thus the exit actions. We therefore make some approximation for this case.

We first define auxiliary functions for the entry and exit actions that are executed when composite state or their substates get active or inactive.

**Definition 13 (Compound Entry Action).** *Given a transition $t$, we define its* Compound Entry Action *as* $\text{Entry}_C(t) = \{\text{entry}(s) \mid s \in Act(t)\}$.

**Definition 14 (Compound Exit Action).** *Given a transition $t$, we define its* Compound Exit Action *as* $\overline{\text{Exit}_C}(t) = \{\text{exit}(s) \mid s \in Dct(t)\}$.

Note that $\overline{\text{Exit}_C}(t)$ also contains actions that are not executed, since $Dct(t)$ contains states that are not active when $t$ is fired. Again, finding out which states are actually active when $t$ is fired requires actually executing the state machine; static analysis does not suffice.

**Definition 15 (Strict Compound Exit Action).** *Given a transition $t$, we define its* Strict Compound Exit Action *as*

$$\text{Exit}_C(t) = \{\text{exit}(S) \mid S \in \text{substate}^*(\text{Csr}(\text{LCR}(\text{source}(t), \text{target}(s)))) \\ \wedge \text{target}(t) \in \text{substate}^*(S)\}).$$

$\text{Exit}_C(t)$ *underestimates* the exit actions, since it only contains the exit actions of those states that are *definitely* deactivated when $t$ is fired, i.e., all composite states containing $\text{source}(t)$, contained in the region $\text{LCR}(\text{source}(t), \text{target}(s))$.

**Definition 16 (Modified Variables).** *Given a transition $t$, the set of variables it modifies,* $\overline{\mathcal{W}}(t)$ *is the set of all variables written by* $\overline{\text{Exit}_C}(t) \cup \{\text{effect}(t)\} \cup \text{Entry}_C(t)$.

**Definition 17 (Strictly Modified Variables).** *Given a transition $t$, the set of variables it strictly modifies,* $\mathcal{W}(t)$ *is the set of all variables written by* $\text{Exit}_C(t) \cup \{\text{effect}(t)\} \cup \text{Entry}_C(t)$.

**Definition 18 (Do-Modified Variables).** *Given a state $s$, the set of variables it do-modifies is the set $\mathcal{W}(s)$ of all variables written in $do(s)$.*

As stated in Sect. 2.1, in order to calculate our metrics, we ignore possible orders of execution of these actions, and instead simply assume a non-deterministic execution order.

**Definition 19 (Read Variable).** *Given a transition $t$, the set of variables it reads is $\mathcal{R}(t) = \{v \in \mathcal{V} \mid v \text{ is read by } \mathsf{guard}(t)\}$.*

Now we can define relations describing cross-region dependencies:

**Definition 20 (Controlling).** *Given a transition $t_1$ and a state $s_2$, we say $s_2$ is (weakly) controlled by $t_1$, and write $\overline{\mathsf{control}}(t_1, s_2)$, if there exists a transition $t_2$ with target $s_2$ such that $t_1$ modifies a variable read by $t_2$, i.e., if*

$$\exists t_2 \cdot \exists v \in \mathcal{V} \cdot [\mathsf{target}(t_2) = s_2 \wedge v \in \overline{\mathcal{W}}(t_1) \wedge v \in \mathcal{R}(t_2)].$$

*Given two states $s_1$ and $s_2$, we say $s_2$ is (weakly) controlled by $s_1$ if there exists a transition $t_1$ with target $s_1$ that controls $s_2$ or if the do activity of $s_1$ modifies a variable that is read by a transition leading into $s_2$, i.e., if*

$$\exists t_1, t_2 \cdot \exists v \in \mathcal{V} \cdot [\mathsf{target}(t_1) = s_1 \wedge \mathsf{target}(t_2) = s_2$$
$$\wedge (v \in \overline{\mathcal{W}}(t_1) \vee v \in \mathcal{W}(s_1)) \wedge v \in \mathcal{R}(t_2)]$$

*We write this as $\overline{\mathsf{control}}(s_1, s_2)$. If $v \in \mathcal{W}(t_1) \vee v \in \mathcal{W}(s_1)$ holds in the above formula instead of $v \in \overline{\mathcal{W}}(t_1) \vee v \in \mathcal{W}(s_1)$, then we say $s_1$ strictly controls $s_2$ and write it as $\mathsf{control}(s_1, s_2)$.*

A state $s_1$ therefore controls a state $s_2$ if there exists a variable $v$ such that a guard in at least one transition $t$ leading into $s_2$ depends on $v$ and either (1) a transition leading into $s_1$ modifies $v$ in its compound entry action, its effects or its compound exit actions, or (2) the do activity of $s_1$ modifies $v$. This can also be expressed as

$$\left( \bigcup_{\mathsf{target}(t_i)=s_1} \overline{\mathcal{W}}(t_i) \cup \mathcal{W}(s_1) \right) \cap \mathcal{R}(t) \neq \emptyset$$

If $s_1$ controls $s_2$ it may only influence some paths leading into $s_2$, or it may control all transitions leading into $s_2$. The latter case is important if we want to ensure, e.g., mutual exclusion between states. We therefore define the notions of partial and total control:

**Definition 21 (Partial Control).** *Given two states $s_1$ and $s_2$, we say $s_2$ is partially controlled by $s_1$, and write $\mathsf{control}^p(s_1, s_2)$, if $s_2$ is controlled by $s_1$ but there exists a transition $t$ with target $s_2$ that is not controlled by $s_1$, i.e., if the predicates*

$$\exists t \cdot \left[ \mathsf{target}(t) = s_2 \wedge \left( \bigcup_{\mathsf{target}(t_i)=s_1} \overline{\mathcal{W}}(t_i) \cup \mathcal{W}(s_1) \right) \cap \mathcal{R}(t) \neq \emptyset \right]$$

$$\exists t \cdot \left[ \mathsf{target}(t) = s_2 \wedge \left( \bigcup_{\mathsf{target}(t_i)=s_1} \overline{\mathcal{W}}(t_i) \cup \mathcal{W}(s_1) \right) \cap \mathcal{R}(t) = \emptyset \right]$$

*both hold. If additionally* control$(s_1, s_2)$ *holds, then we say* $s_1$ *partially strictly controls* $s_2$ *and notate it by* control$^p(s_1, s_2)$.

**Definition 22 (Total Control).** *Given two states* $s_1$ *and* $s_2$, *we say* $s_2$ *is totally controlled by* $s_1$, *and write it as* $\overline{\text{control}^t}(s_1, s_2)$, *if* $s_1$ *controls all transitions leading into* $s_2$, *more precisely, if* $\overline{\text{control}}(s_1, s_2)$ *and*

$$\forall t_1, t_2 \cdot [\text{target}(t_1) = s_1 \wedge \text{target}(t_2) = s_2 \implies (\overline{\mathcal{W}}(t_1) \cup \mathcal{W}(s_1)) \cap \mathcal{R}(t_2) \neq \emptyset].$$

*If* $(\mathcal{W}(t_1) \cup \mathcal{W}(s_1)) \cap \mathcal{R}(t_2) \neq \emptyset$ *holds in this equation instead of* $(\overline{\mathcal{W}}(t_1) \cup \mathcal{W}(s_1)) \cap \mathcal{R}(t_2) \neq \emptyset$, *then we say* $s_1$ *totally strictly controls* $s_2$ *and write it as* control$^t(s_1, s_2)$.

If $s_1$ totally controls $s_2$ we therefore have

$$\forall t \cdot \left[\text{target}(t) = s_2 \implies \left(\bigcup_{\text{target}(t_i)=s_1} \overline{\mathcal{W}}(t_i) \cup \mathcal{W}(s_1)\right) \cap \mathcal{R}(t) \neq \emptyset\right]$$

and if there are any transitions leading into $s_2$ this is a necessary and sufficient condition for total control.

Based on the controlling relationship, we now define the following metrics:

**Definition 23 (Number of Partially Controlled States).** *Given a state* $s$, *its Number of Partially Controlled States is*

$$NPC(s) = \#\{s' \mid \overline{\text{control}^p}(s, s')\}$$

*and its Number of Partially Strictly Controlled States is*

$$NPSC(s) = \#\{s' \mid \text{control}^p(s, s')\}$$

**Definition 24 (Number of Totally Controlled States).** *Given a state* $s$, *its Number of Totally Controlled States is*

$$NTC(s) = \#\{s' \mid \overline{\text{control}^t}(s, s')\}$$

*and its Number of Partially Strictly Controlled States is*

$$NTSC(s) = \#\{s' \mid \text{control}^t(s, s')\}$$

As indicated above, these metrics may be used to determine possible sources of concurrency errors: if $NTC(s) < NPC(s)$ the state machine contains a state $s'$ whose reachability on some paths depends on $s$ but some other transitions into $s'$ do not depend on $s$. If $s'$ is meant to be mutually exclusive to $s$ this may indicate synchronization bugs. (Note that an analysis based solely on these metrics is not sufficiently precise to determine whether $s$ and $s'$ are synchronized or not since, e.g., predecessor states of $s'$ may be synchronized with $s$ and therefore prevent the unguarded transitions from being reached).

## 3.5    Applications

While the metrics presented in this paper represent only a rough estimate of the complexity caused by behavior depending on non-local properties, we believe that they could serve a useful purpose in alerting modelers to unexpected features of their state machines. In the following, we demonstrate the usefulness of our metrics by means of two simple extensions of the game, which contain several potential modeling mistakes that can be identified using our metrics, see Figs. 4 and 6.

**Hidden Deactivation.** Figure 4 contains several potential mistakes. The first one is that the wizard can escape to her laboratory whenever she is in the ladder room, even during a fight. This is not immediately obvious from the lower region of the state machine which describes the behavior of the wizard, and a developer focusing on this region might suppose that casting a spell always leads to a fight, and that fights are always terminated by either winning or escaping. However, the number of deactivating transitions for every state in the lower region is higher than the number of directly visible transitions, which clearly indicates that there are other ways to exit the states in this region than the locally visible ones. For example, in state Fighting there are two locally visible transitions (to Spelling and to the final state), but the number of deactivating transitions is 3. By looking at the metrics the developer is therefore immediately alerted to the existence of deactivating transitions operating in a "more global" manner.

**Post-Domination.** While a simple comparison of locally visible activations and deactivations with the metrics proposed in this paper is strong enough to point to some problems, this analysis is relatively indiscriminate and may capture non-local effects intended by the system's designers. By combining the metrics with flow-analysis techniques it becomes possible to identify more precisely situations which are likely to be incorrect.

For example, a slightly more sophisticated analysis of Fig. 4 shows that it is possible for the wizard to obtain arbitrarily large power ups: Taking into account only local transitions, state PowerFighting *post-dominates* [1] state PowerSpelling, i.e., each path from PowerSpelling to a final state goes through PowerFighting. This is an important property because states that release acquired resources or undo changes to variables have to post-dominate all resource acquisitions or variable changes for the state machine to be correct. In the example, the player obtains a boost of its power in state PowerSpelling which is undone in state PowerFighting.

Looking only at the lower state machine one might thus be led to assume that the exit action of PowerFighting will always be executed after state PowerSpelling has been entered. However, the measure $D^{tr}$ of deactivating transitions for PowerSpelling has the value 3; since there are only two locally visible outgoing transitions it is clear that it is, indeed, possible to exit this state by a non-local transition: If the player enter state PowerSpelling while in the Ladder room, she can take the transition toLadder to exit from PowerSpelling without decreasing the value of the power variable.

By combining the metrics presented in this paper with static analysis it would therefore be possible for tools to identify possible sources of errors resulting from non-local activations or deactivations.

**"Stolen" Events.** One of the pitfalls of the semantics of UML state machines is that if several transitions with the same trigger are enabled, and for two of them, say $t_1$ and $t_2$, it holds that source($t_1$) is directly or recursively contained in source($t_2$), then only $t_1$ is fired. This is a bit dangerous since when modeling on a higher level of abstraction (with states on a higher level in the hierarchy), the modeler may intend to have several transitions bonded, i.e., they should be fired at the same time, and this bondedness may easily get lost when one of the higher level states is later refined and a substate reacts to the same event. For example, in Fig. 6, since state Curious also reacts to event investigate (and one of the conditions [TD] and [!TD] is always true), the transition from Idle (which contains Curious) to Investigating will not be fired when Curious is active. Using our metrics, this mistake can be easily detected: Let $t$ be the transition from CrystalRoom to CrystalPedestal, then $\overline{NB}(t) \neq NB(t)$, and the modeler can be alerted to double check this transition and those bonded to it.

**Mutual Exclusion.** Another important application of our metrics is the detection or validation of mutual exclusions of states. In general, mutual exclusion is in UML state machines often hard to model and to comprehend, since the exclusion logic is "hidden" in several model elements, scattered in several regions [11]. A mechanism to make mutual exclusions in a state machine "visible" is therefore desirable.

Our metrics provide a simple means to make hidden mutual exclusions visible. For two states $s_1$ and $s_2$, we say $s_1$ *excludes* $s_2$ if $s_1$ strictly controls $s_2$, and there do not exist transitions $t_1, t_2$, target($t_1$) $= s_1$, target($t_2$) $= s_2$, such that after $t_1$ has been fired (and all exit actions, $t_1$'s effect, and all entry actions have been executed), the guard of $t_2$ is satisfiable. If $s_1$ excludes $s_2$ and $s_2$ excludes $s_1$, then $s_1$ and $s_2$ mutually exclude each other from being active. For example, in Fig. 6, the states CrystalRoom and Spelling mutually exclude each other, since the condition for CrystalRoom to be active (via any transition) is c==0, and its entry action then increases the value of umlc, setting it to 1, thus making it impossible for the guard of any of the transitions leading to Spell satisfiable; and in the same manner, entering Spell also prevents CrystalRoom from getting active. This way, mistakes of the modeler failing to constrain any of transitions leading to these states are easy to detect by the measures for partial and total control as described on p. 20.

## 4   Related Work

Complexity metrics of state machines have been recognized as useful indicators [9]. Hierarchical states are considered in [3,4]. Strictly speaking, these approaches do not consider UML state machines, but rather State Transition Systems (STSs). The syntax of STSs is considerably simpler than that of UML state machines, and their semantics do not contain cross-region effects, such as bonded transitions, stolen transitions, or a transition originating from one region deactivating states in another. In comparison, our approach provides a set of metrics for UML state machines, where it is much more involved to determine the model elements that may activate or deactivate certain states. Moreover, it is also clearer which elements are actually responsible for the complexity.

Cyclomatic complexity [8] is a very widely-used metric for state-based systems. Like the approaches cited above, cyclomatic complexity is also only applicable to flat state transition systems, and is therefore, in the domain of UML, not as direct as our approach.

Our previous paper [12] was the first one to study remote activation and deactivation of states. The current paper extends [12] by the metrics regarding cross-region dependencies.

The determination of the transitions activating or deactivating a certain state is also an essential technique for weaving aspect-oriented state machines [14].

## 5   Conclusions and Future Work

We have discussed in detail the activation and deactivation of (hierarchical) composite states in UML state machines, and, based on this discussion, defined metrics to reflect the complexity of transitions leading to or leaving composite states, as well as the complexity caused by cross-region dependencies. Our metrics give a better understanding of the complexity of UML state machines than traditional metrics. They also show where the modeler or reader of UML state machines must pay attention, and may alert them to potential modeling mistakes.

Based on this work, we plan to define more precise metrics which also take into account, e.g., the partial order of the execution of entry and exit actions when composite states are activated or deactivated. Metrics on their own can only provide relatively coarse indications of problems in state machines, and tools based solely on metrics will probably often report possible errors when structural properties of the state machine are used by designers to ensure invariants of the model. Therefore we also intend to pursue the integration of the measures presented in this paper with stronger structural analysis techniques for state machines. Finally, we plan to validate our metrics in more realistic models, as well as to implement support for the metrics in modeling tools.

**Acknowledgment.** This work has been partially sponsored by the EU project ASCENS, 257414.

# References

1. Cytron, R., Ferrante, J., Rosen, B.K., Wegman, M.N., Kenneth Zadeck, F.: An efficient method of computing static single assignment form. In: Conference Record of the 16$^{th}$ Annual ACM Symposium Principles of Programming Languages (POPL 1989), pp. 25–35. ACM Press (1989)
2. Drusinsky, D.: Modeling and Verification Using UML Statecharts. Elsevier, Amsterdam (2006)
3. Guo, L., Sangiovanni-Vincentelli, A.L., Pinto, A.: A complexity metric for concurrent finite state machine based embedded software. In: 8$^{th}$ IEEE International Symposium on Industrial Embedded Systems (SIES 2013), pp. 189–195. IEEE (2013)
4. Hall, M.: Complexity metrics for hierarchical state machines. In: Cohen, M.B., Ó Cinnéide, M. (eds.) SSBSE 2011. LNCS, vol. 6956, pp. 76–81. Springer, Heidelberg (2011)
5. Object Management Group. OMG Unified Modeling Language (OMG UML), Superstructure, Version 2.4.1. Specification, OMG (2011). http://www.omg.org/spec/UML/2.4.1/Superstructure
6. Schmidt, C.D.: Model-Driven Engineering. IEEE Comput. **39**(2), 25–31 (2006)
7. Vallecillo, A., Koch, N., Cachero, C., Comai, S., Fraternali, P., Garrigó, I., Gómes, J., Kappel, G., Knapp, A., Matera, M., Meliá, S., Moreno, N., Pröll, B., Reiter, T., Retschitzegger, W., Rivera, J.E., Schauerhuber, A., Schwinger, W., Wimmer, M., Zhang, G.: MDWEnet: A practical approach to achieving interoperability of model-driven web engineering methods. In: Koch, N., Vallecillo, A., Houben, G.-J. (eds.) Proceedings of the 3$^{rd}$ International Workshop on Model-Driven Web Engineering (MDWE 2007), vol. 261 of CEUR-WS (2007)
8. http://en.wikipedia.org/wiki/Cyclomatic_complexity. Accessed on 2014–04-30
9. http://code.google.com/p/umple/wiki/MasuringStateMachineComplexity. Accessed on 2014–04-30
10. Zhang, G.: Aspect-Oriented State Machines. Ph.D thesis, Ludwig-Maximilians-Universität München (2010)
11. Zhang, G.: Aspect-oriented modeling of mutual exclusion in UML state machines. In: Vallecillo, A., Tolvanen, J.-P., Kindler, E., Störrle, H., Kolovos, D. (eds.) ECMFA 2012. LNCS, vol. 7349, pp. 162–177. Springer, Heidelberg (2012)
12. Zhang, G., Hölzl, M.: A set of metrics for states and transitions in UML state machines. In: Proceedings of the 6$^{th}$ International Workshop on Behaviour Modeling-Foundations and Applications (BM-FA 2014). ACM, New York (2014)
13. Zhang, G., Hölzl, M.: HiLA: high-level aspects for UML state machines. In: Ghosh, S. (ed.) MODELS 2009. LNCS, vol. 6002, pp. 104–118. Springer, Heidelberg (2010)
14. Zhang, G., Hölzl, M.M.: Weaving semantic aspects in HiLA. In: Hirschfeld, R., Tanter, É., Sullivan, K.J., Gabriel, R.P. (eds.) Proceedings of the 11th International Conference on Aspect-Oriented Software Development, (AOSD 2012), pp. 263–274. ACM Press (2012)

# A Customizable Execution Engine
# for Models of Embedded Systems

Karolina Zurowska$^{(\boxtimes)}$ and Jürgen Dingel

School of Computing, Queen's University, Kingston, ON, Canada
{zurowska,dingel}@cs.queensu.ca

**Abstract.** In the Model Driven Development (MDD) paradigm analysis of models is important. We propose an approach to the analysis which uses a customizable execution engine. Such customization can improve scalability and provide more support for variations of semantics. We exemplify these benefits with several customizations of semantics that are abstractions. They are applied to models of embedded systems implemented in the UML-RT language. The goal of abstractions is to replace original semantics with semantics that generates smaller state spaces. Different execution semantics of UML-RT models are provided terms of operational semantics style execution rules. We describe the design of the toolset called Toolset for UML-RT Execution, illustrate execution rules with examples, and present the results of preliminary evaluation.

## 1  Introduction

In Model Driven Development (MDD) analysis techniques are important, since they provide better understanding of models. Moreover, they enable debugging and verification. In this paper we propose an approach to the analysis of MDD models based on a customizable execution semantics engine. The engine can execute models with the standard semantics, but we can adjust it, so that the execution state space becomes smaller or simpler or it explores only portions of models important w.r.t. the desired analysis. The goal of making execution engines customizable is also to facilitate model analysis through, e.g., better scalability and support for variations in semantics and for flexible displays of executions.

The standard notion of abstraction in MDD and behavioral modeling deals with representing elements of modeled systems in a way that is simple but yet contains sufficient details [17]. We propose to extend this notion and apply it to the analysis and verification of models. In this context the abstraction is used to overcome one of the most important challenges, that is, the scalability of analysis. We realize abstractions by providing non-standard execution semantics of models. These semantics are implemented in our execution engine dedicated to one of the industrial MDD languages, namely, the UML-RT modeling language. Therefore we also address another challenge of modern MDD, which is a lack of tools dedicated to the industrial languages.

© Springer International Publishing Switzerland 2015
E. Roubtsova et al. (Eds.): BM-FA 2009-2014, LNCS 6368, pp. 82–110, 2015.
DOI: 10.1007/978-3-319-21912-7_4

The customization of executions realized as abstractions can serve the analysis of MDD models in two ways. Firstly, it can support verification, that is, exhaustive checking whether certain desired properties are satisfied in a model. In this case abstractions can reduce the state space and make the exhaustive exploration possible. The reduction of the sizes of the state space comes with a price, which in case of some our abstractions is the overapproximation and the possibility of false positive (or negative) results. We can deal with such results either by checking the paths against the model or by being more specific which parts of the state space we abstract away (we proposed a model checking technique based on this idea [21]). The second way abstractions are useful is to help visualize the executions. Thanks to the substantial reduction in complexity of models we can show the execution of a model, and such an execution can be inspected.

In this paper we illustrate our ideas by presenting a Toolset for UML-RT Execution (TUMLE) that enables execution of UML-RT models with various semantics. TUMLE includes a rule-based engine in which a set of rules defines the semantics. These rules are tailored to UML-RT models and we describe the set of rules necessary to simulate the semantics of the standard UML-RT language. Variations of this semantics enable us to perform abstract executions. We distinguish three abstractions: symbolic execution, structural abstraction and state aggregation. Symbolic execution is used to deal with the values of variables in a model, structural abstraction is used to simplify the structure of models and state aggregation is used to simplify state machines. The changes in rules required by these abstractions can be aggregated, so that we can provide more powerful and directed abstractions.

The use of interpreters for models has been advocated among others by Bran Selic in [18]. However, most of the MDD tools, including the tool for UML-RT (i.e. IBM RSA RTE), support only the basic execution of models and they typically require code generation. The majority of general analysis methods uses translations of UML-like models to an input language of an existing tool [9,10,15,16]. Although these tools allow for the comprehensive verification, their support for execution and abstractions is limited. On the other hand abstractions have long been used in model checking to reduce the sizes of state spaces [5,6]. These works, however, are not directly applicable to MDD models. Finally, the variations in semantics of models have been recognized in for instance in [4,13], but the goal of these works is to capture different variants of state machines.

In Sect. 2 we indicate benefits of customizations and we show the design of our tool. In Sect. 3 we summarize the UML-RT language. In Sect. 4 we describe the design of the engine. In Sect. 5 we report on experiments and in Sect. 7 we discuss related work.

## 2    Analysis Support with Customizable Execution Engine

In this work we use the UML-RT modeling language described in more detail in Sect. 3. UML-RT models are executable, so we associate *executions* with them.

In the simplest case the execution of a UML-RT model is a sequence of execution states and transitions that represent a change in a state. The execution is the result of *exploration* of states of a model and sometime we will use these two terms interchangeably.

The standard execution semantics of UML-RT models is defined in the IBM RSA RTE tool., Making the execution engine customizable can bring advantages such as:

1. *Reducing complexity of executions.* To simplify executions, we can use abstractions. Additionally, we can focus on certain aspects or views of executions, and abstract out portions that are irrelevant w.r.t. required analysis.
2. *Support for variations of semantics.* Variations in semantics may be due to several reasons. Firstly, there might be variation points in the design of the modeling language (such as in UML 2). Secondly, the modeling languages change with time, e.g., with updates of tools.
3. *Support for flexible display of executions.* There are many aspects in which we may want to customize the visualization of executions. For instance, we may want to display only some elements of execution states.
4. *Support for partial models.* By providing semantics for elements that are tentative, missing or not well-formed we can support the execution of models that are still under development.

In order to achieve the above advantages we propose a toolset whose structure is presented in Fig. 1. We can distinguish three major areas of the tool: formalization, execution and verification. The formalization step is necessary to simplify UML-RT models to enable the analysis. This step is divided into two parts: ATL transformation of structural elements of UML-RT models and symbolic execution of action code associated with transitions and states. The symbolic execution is performed using our custom built symbolic execution engine. The output from this step is a model in our formal representation of UML-RT models called Communicating Functional Finite State Machines (see Sect. 3). The execution part of our toolset is given by an execution engine that uses rules for execution. This engine and the rules are described in more details in the following sections. Finally, the toolset includes a model checker for UML-RT models [21].

## 3   Overview of the UML-RT Language

In our work we use the UML-RT modeling language and in this section we introduce its basic features using the example of a model of traffic lights. A specification of a UML-RT model consists of a *structure diagram* and a *state machine* for each *capsule*, i.e., a component.

Figure 2 presents the structure diagram of a capsule `TrafficController`. The capsule has 2 internal parts: `cars` and `walk`. A *part* in a capsule is an instance of some other capsule, in this case of `CarLights` and `WalkLights`, respectively. Besides parts, the capsule also contains *ports*: `carsManager` and `walkManager` to

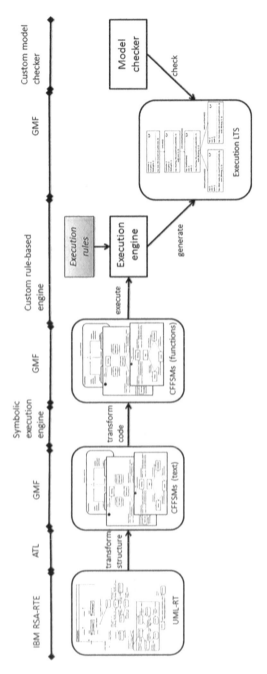

**Fig. 1.** The design of toolset for analysis of UML–RT models.

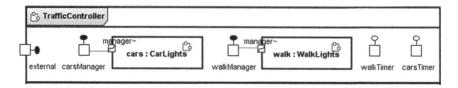

**Fig. 2.** Structure diagram of `TrafficController` capsule. Inspired by [19].

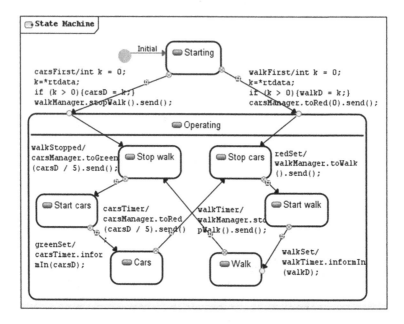

**Fig. 3.** A structure and behavior of capsule `TrafficController`. Labels of transitions are of the forms: `port.signal` or `port.signal/action_code`. From [19].

communicate with the parts, `external` to receive signals from the environment and `carsTimer` and `walkTimer` to receive timer signals. Ports can be *base* or *conjugated* and we only connect ports of different types. Ports have a type, called a *protocol*. For instance, a protocol for `carsManager` is called *CarsProtocol*. Protocols gather *events* that can be received or sent through this port; events can be used as triggers on transitions. Events may contain variables that carry values when they are sent. A capsule in a model may include also typed *attributes* (not shown in the structure diagram). The values of attributes receive default values, which can be updated during execution.

The behavior of each capsule is specified with a UML-RT State Machine, which is a variant of UML 2 State Machines [2]. The state machines for capsules in our model are shown in Figs. 3 and 4. They have *states* and *guarded transitions*, which can contain *actions*. For instance, in Fig. 3 a transition between the states `Starting` and `Stop cars` checks for the value of input received with the trigger

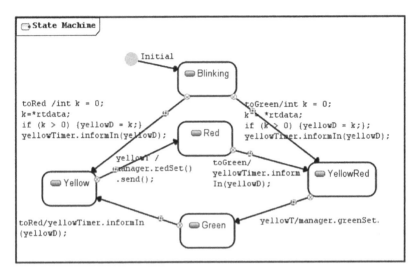

(a) CarLights

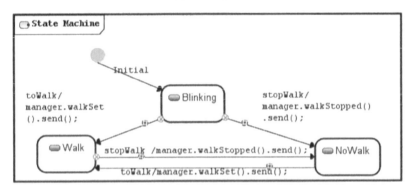

(b) WalkLights

**Fig. 4.** A structure and behavior of capsules CarLights and WalkLights. Labels of transitions are the same as in Fig. 3. From [19]

(through a pointer *rtdata) and if the value is greater than 0, it is assigned to the attribute walkD of this capsule. Next, with the help of the send operation, the signal toRed is sent using the port carsManager. Another example of an action is shown between states Stop walk and Walk. This action is used to start the timer walkTimer, which after the prescribed time generates a timeout event. Figure 4(a) and (b) present state machines for CarLights and WalkLights capsules. The state machine of CarLights in Fig. 4(a) initializes the part and cycles through different lights using timers to control Yellow and YellowRed transitions. The behavior of the capsule WalkLights is shown in Fig. 4(b) and it alternates between the states walk and no Walk.

**Table 1.** Informal description of the mapping of the structural elements from UML-RT models to CFFSMs. Parameters of elements are given in parentheses.

| UML-RT element | CFFSMs element |
|---|---|
| capsule | module |
| part (type) | part (type) |
| (base port, protocol, out event(variable)) | out signal(out variable) |
| (conjugated port, protocol, in event(variable)) | |
| (base port, protocol, in event(variable)) | in signal(in variable) |
| (conjugated port, protocol, out event(variable)) | |
| (connector(base port, conjugated port, owner), protocol, out event) | connector(owner, out signal (base port, protocol, out event), owning part(base port), in signal (conjugated port, protocol, out event), owning part (conjugated port), variables) |
| (connector(base port, conjugated port, owner), protocol, in event) | connector(owner, out signal (conjugated port, protocol, in event), owning part(conjugated port), in signal (base port, protocol, in event), owning part (base port), variables) |

We formalize syntax and semantics of a subset of UML-RT models using Communicating Functional Finite State Machines (CFFSMs)[19]. The structure of CFFSMs is very similar to that of UML-RT and we present the mapping of structural elements in Table 1 and of state machine elements in Table 2. In the structure of CFFSMs we simplify the communication and we use only *signals* and *connectors*, which represent the combination of ports and protocols. Additionally, *connectors* combine events, ports and protocols.

State machines in CFFSMs are flat and we use *functions* to summarize action code attached to transitions and states. These functions are obtained using symbolic execution of the action code. Each function is a set of *cases*, and each case is a pair consisting of a condition and effects such as the update of attributes. The work presented in this paper has been defined for CFFSMs, so any modeling language that can be translated to CFFSMs can be used.

**Table 2.** Mapping of the state machine elements from UML-RT to CFFSM.

| UML-RT | CFFSMs |
|---|---|
| non-composite state | state |
| (transition chain (start state, target state), trigger) | transition (start state, target state, trigger) |
| (transition chain (code), entry and exit code from states) | transition (functions ) |
| transition chain (guard code) | transition (guard) |

## 4    Elements of the Execution Engine

The execution engine which is a part of our toolset (see Sect. 2) uses execution rules. A set of applied rules determine the execution semantics we wish to use. We start this section with the description of the basic elements of rules used and then we show how different sets of rules can be used to obtain different execution semantics.

### 4.1    Elements of Execution Rules

Figure 5 presents the elements of rules used in our execution engine. A rule contains `variables`, `conditions` and `effects`. A *rule variable* represents a type of an element of a model (such as execution part or a state machine location). The operation `getValues` returns the currently possible values of the rule variable and these values are stored. A *rule variable value* is a pair consisting of a rule variable and a value, that is, an element of a current execution state (e.g., a current execution part, a current value of an attributes) or of the original model (e.g., a location, a transition in a state machine). Rule variable values are gathered in a `mapping`. A *rule condition* represents a condition that must be satisfied in order to fire a rule. For instance, a rule condition can be a check whether a trigger is external. Rule conditions are evaluated with the `match` method, which uses a mapping to refer to the respective elements of an execution state, i.e., values of rule variables. A *rule effect* describes changes to an execution state and the `fire` methods realizes these changes. For instance, such an effect can be changing a state machine location or updating values of attributes based on the update effect. Similar to rule conditions, they refer to the necessary elements of an execution using rule variables and the values stored in the assignments.

*Example 1.* Let us assume that in a very simplistic engine we have only one execution rule, which is called `SimpleRule` defined by its elements: three variables `LocationVariable` (refers to a location in a state machine), `TransitionVariable` (refers to a transition in state machine), `CaseVariable` (refers to a set of cases assigned to a transition). The variables refer to the elements of a state machine mentioned in their names. This very simple rule has:

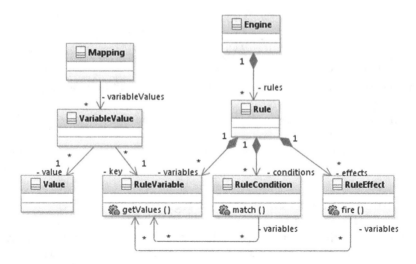

**Fig. 5.** A class diagram used for execution rules.

- one condition `IsExternal`, which uses `TransitionVariable` and which in its
  `match` method checks if a transition is external,
- one effect `TargetLocation`, which uses `TransitionVariable` and which in its
  `fire` method updates a location in a target execution to be a target location
  of a transition

The above specification of an engine can refer to any model. We refer to a specific
model after declaring mappings of variables, that is, after providing their specific
values.

Given the set of execution rules we perform an exhaustive exploration of a
model, that is we make sure that if a rule is applicable it will be fired including all
its effects. The exploration is done for a given execution state with Algorithm 1
used to explore such a state. The algorithm iterates through all rules (line 2).
For each rule we generate all possible mappings for its rule variables (line 3).
For each possible mapping we check whether it fulfills the necessary conditions
(line 5) and if so we generate a new execution state. The necessary changes (rule
effects) are applied to this new execution state in line 7. The updated state is
then included in the set of returned results.

Generating mappings uses the `getValues` method for each variable and it is
outlined in Algorithm 2. First, we create some initial empty mapping. Next, in
line 2 we iterate through all variables and using `getValues`, we generate values
for them according to the current execution state and to the current mapping
(line 5). Because a set of possible values might have more than one element, for
each such value we need to copy the current mapping (line 7) and add this value
to the new mapping (line 8). The new mapping `mappingNew` with a variable and
value pair is added to the set of all mappings (line 9).

---

**Algorithm 1.** An outline of `explore(executionState)`.

---

**Require:** a set of rules rules
**Require:** a current execution state executionState
    results ← ∅
    for all rule ∈ rules  do
3:      mappings ← generateMappings(rule.variables, executionState)
      for all mapping ∈ mappings do
        if match(rule.conditions,mapping) then
6:          executionStateNew ← copy(executionState)
          fire(rule.effects,mapping,executionStateNew)
          results ← results ∪ {executionStateNew}
9: return  results

---

**Algorithm 2.** An outline of `generateMappings(variables, executionState)`.

---

**Require:** a set of rules variables variables
**Require:** a current execution state executionState
    mappings ← {emptyMapping}
    for all variable ∈ variables  do
3:     for all mapping ∈ mappings do
       mappings ← mappings \ {mapping}
       values ← variable.getValues(executionState, mapping)
6:     for all value ∈ values do
       mappingNew ← copy(mapping)
       mappingNew ← mappingNew ∪ {variable ↦ value}
9:       mappings ← mappings ∪ {mappingNew}
   return  mappings

---

*Example 2.* We continue with the previous example and the rule SimpleRule. The rule has three variables and we have to generate mappings for them. For the sake of brevity let us assume that we have a model with just one state machine, its UML-RT version is presented in Fig. 3. In the current execution state we have the current location to be Starting. We start the procedure by creating an empty mapping and place it in the mappings set. We consider the first variable, i.e., LocationVariable. In the current execution state the getValues method of this rule variable returns only one location Starting. We iterate through all mappings, which at this point means using only an empty mapping. We copy this mapping and we add to it the pair {LocationVariable ↦ Starting}. The resulting mapping is included in the set mappings.

Next, we consider TransitionVariable. We start with the single mapping we created for the previous variable. The getValue method of this variable returns outgoing transitions from a location mapped by LocationVariable. According to Fig. 3 we have two of them carsFirst and walkFirst (we assume their names are the names of their triggering signals). We copy the original mapping and we add to it the pair TransitionVariable ↦ carsFirst to it, which results in a mapping {LocationVariable ↦ Start, TransitionVariable ↦ carsFirst}. For the next value of TransitionVariable we start with the original mapping and we add the variable value pair with the value walkFirst. This gives us mappings: {{LocationVariable ↦ Start, TransitionVariable ↦ carsFirst}, {LocationVariable ↦ Start, TransitionVariable ↦ walkFirst}}.

We now move to the last variable CaseVariable. Its getValue method returns the cases of the transition mapped by TransitionVariable. As required by the algorithm we iterate through two existing mappings. The first one is {LocationVariable ↦ Starting, TransitionVariable ↦ carsFirst}. For this mapping we get values for CaseVariable, that is, cases assigned to the carsFirst transition, which are {(carsFirstVar > 0), (carsFirstVar <= 0)} (names are after the conditions of the cases and carsFirstVar is an input variable). We add (CaseVariable ↦ (carsFirstVar > 0)) to the copy of the current mapping. We do the same for the second value, i.e., (carsFirstVar <= 0). We move to the the second mapping, i.e., {LocationVariable ↦ Starting, TransitionVariable ↦ walkFirst}. For this mapping values for CaseVariable are cases assigned to the walkFirst transition, which are {(walkFirstVar > 0), (walkFirstVar <= 0)}. We add both of these values to a current mapping and it gives us the following set of mappings mappings = {

{LocationVariable ↦ Starting, TransitionVariable ↦ carsFirst,
CaseVariable ↦ (carsFirstVar > 0)},

{LocationVariable ↦ Starting, TransitionVariable ↦ carsFirst,
CaseVariable ↦ (carsFirstVar <= 0)},

{LocationVariable ↦ Starting, TransitionVariable ↦ walkFirst,
CaseVariable ↦ (walkFirstVar > 0)}

{LocationVariable ↦ Starting, TransitionVariable ↦ walkFirst,
CaseVariable ↦ (walkFirstVar <= 0)}}

Our execution engine detects the *similarity* of execution states. If the state that is a result of application of all effects is the same as some other existing state we stop exploration. The similarity is defined recursively for all execution parts in the model and may slightly differ for different execution semantics.

## 4.2    Execution Rules for Standard and Abstract Semantics

In this section we introduce the execution rules for different execution semantics. We start with the rules for the standard execution that mimics the UML-RT behavior. Next, we show the adjustments to those basic rules that need to be applied to provide abstractions. For each rule we provide a set of rule variables it uses as well as conditions and effects. For conditions and effects we provide the necessary rule variables in parentheses.

Table 3 summarizes rules in the *standard execution semantics*. We have five rules:

- the **Default Rule** needs just an execution part which is in its initial state. Initializing such a part will fire initial transitions and evaluate cases assigned to them,
- the **Match Rule** also needs the execution part, but additionally it requires the current location of its the state machine, a transition outgoing from this location along with guards assigned to it, case conditions, case effects and the execution signal from the queue. We have several rule conditions including one that checks whether a trigger on the transition and an execution signal are the same. Additionally, case and guard conditions have to be satisfied.

If this is true, the current location is changed to the target location of the transition, the execution signal is removed from the queue and a set of effects assigned to the case are executed.

– the `External Rule` is very similar to the match rule, and it differs only in that there is no queue involved and the valuation of input variables is generated (as opposed to being taken from the queue). Also in this rule the case condition and guard must be satisfied and the rule effects change the location and evaluate the considered case.

– the `Timeout Rule` differs from the external rule only in that a timeout signal is used as trigger and the corresponding timer must be present in the execution state of the execution part we apply the rule to. In the rule effects we remove the timer from the set of set timers, so the timer that goes off disappears.

– the `Drop Rule` simply removes the current execution signals from the queue, if it cannot be used as trigger on any transitions.

In the standard execution semantics we say that states are similar if they are identical. States are identical if the contents of all queues is the same and if the execution states for each execution part are the same with respect to their locations, values of attributes and the set of active timers. If we find some state to be similar with one of already explored states we do not explore it.

*Example 3.* We use the UML-RT model shown in Sect. 3. Figure 6 shows an example of a concrete execution. Each execution state consists of two parts. The first one includes the contents of queues in a model, in the example, each capsule has its own queue. The second part includes details of the execution state of each part in the model. The details contain a current location, values of attributes declared in a capsule and the set of currently active (i.e., set) timers. In the first execution state the queues are empty, the states of all parts are initial and the attributes have default values. Because at least one part is in the initial state, the `Default rule` is fired and the location of the top part and all its children is updated. Next, we can apply the `External Rule` and the top level part receives one of the external signals `carsFirst` or `walkFirst`. In Fig. 6 we show only two out of all possible values received with an incoming signal. In both cases values received with input signals are greater than zero, so we will update values of respective attributes. In the labels of transitions we have the type of the transition, which is the same as the type of the rule. Next, we show the full name of the part involved in the transition as a sequence of part names that the part is in contained in $<$ and $>$. Finally, we have the input signal received and all output signals generated during the transition.

## 4.3   Execution Rules for Abstract Execution Semantics

In this section we show the execution rules for abstractions with the concrete execution rules as the basis. We present the necessary changes to obtain rules for symbolic execution, structural abstraction and state aggregation.

**Table 3.** Rules in the standard execution.

| Default Rule | |
|---|---|
| Variables: | Part, Transition, CaseEffects, AttributesVal |
| Conditions: | IsInitial (Part) |
| Effects: | Initialize(PartVar) |
| | EvalauteInitialEffects(CaseEffects,AttributesVal) |

| Match Rule | |
|---|---|
| Variables: | Part, Location, AttributesVal, Transition, Trigger, Guard, |
| | CaseConditon, CaseEffects, Queue, ExecutionSignal, |
| | InputVariablesVal |
| Conditions: | NotIsInitial (Part) |
| | TriggerInQueue (Trigger,ExecutionSignal) |
| | CaseSatisfied (CaseCondition,InputVariablesVal, |
| | AttributesVal) |
| | GuardSatisfied (Guard,InputVariablesVal, |
| | AttributesVal) |
| Effects: | TargetLocation(Part,Transition) |
| | Dequeue(Part,ExecutionSignal,Queue) |
| | EvaluateEffects(Part, CaseEffects, InputVarVal,AttributesVal) |

| External Rule | |
|---|---|
| Variables: | Part, Location, AttributesVal, Transition, Trigger, Guard, |
| | CaseConditon, CaseEffects, InputVarValGenerated |
| Conditions: | NotIsInitial (Part) |
| | TriggerIsExternal (Trigger) |
| | CaseSatisfied (CaseCondition,InputVarValGenerated,AttributesVal) |
| | GuardSatisfied (Guard,InputVarValGenerated,AttributesVal) |
| Effects: | TargetLocation(Part,Transition) |
| | EvaluateEffects(Part, CaseEffects, InputVarValGenerated, |
| | AttributesVal) |

| Timeout Rule | |
|---|---|
| Variables: | Part, Location, AttributesVal, Transition, Trigger, Guard, CaseConditon, |
| | CaseEffects |
| Conditions: | NotIsInitial (Part) |
| | TriggerIsTimer (Trigger) |
| | TimerIsSet (Part,Trigger) |
| | CaseSatisfied (CaseCondition,AttributesVal) |
| | GuardSatisfied (Guard,AttributesVal) |
| Effects: | TargetLocation(Part,Transition) |
| | EvaluateEffects(Part, CaseEffects, AttributesVal) |
| | RemoveTimer(Part,Trigger) |

| Drop Rule | |
|---|---|
| Variables: | Part, Location, Queue, ExecutionSignal |
| Conditions: | NotIsInitial (Part) |
| | ExecutionSignalNotTriggered (Location,ExecutionSignal) |
| Effects: | Dequeue(Queue) |

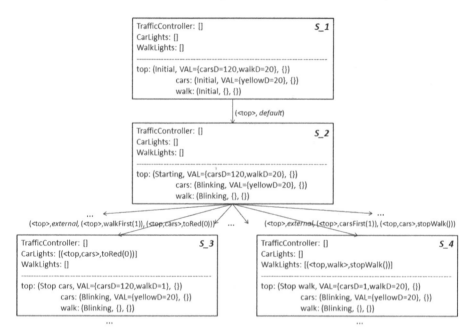

**Fig. 6.** First execution states of a UML-RT model in a standard execution semantics.

In *symbolic execution* (see Table 4) we use symbols instead of concrete values of input variables and we maintain conditions on these symbols to distinguish between execution paths. The rules used in this semantics are similar to the standard rules. The default and the drop rule are exactly the same. In all other rules we update the check of the guard and case conditions. Instead of checking if they are satisfied in the current state we check whether the conditions are satisfiable in the current state (i.e., no contradictions are introduced). Another adjustment is for the external rule, in which we use symbolic input variables instead of standard ones. We also check whether the combined path constraints are satisfiable. Effects in the symbolic execution engine are very similar to one in the standard execution semantics, with an additional one, which adds case conditions and guards to the current path constraints, that is constraints that need to be satisfied to follow certain branch of execution.

Symbolic execution is exact, so no spurious paths are introduced and no paths are removed from the execution [19]. This means that checking properties of UML-RT models yields the same results in the standard and symbolic execution. This is very useful and desired property of any execution engine. For instance, consider checking reachability of locations in our traffic lights model. If we are checking reachability of an execution state in which the top level part is in the Stop cars location (see Fig. 3), we get the same results using symbolic or standard execution, that is, the state is reachable, no matter if we use concrete or symbolic variables as an input in the signal carsFirst.

**Table 4.** Rules in symbolic execution.

| Default Rule - the same as in Table 3 |
|---|
| **Match Rule, Timeout Rule** |

| | |
|---|---|
| Variables: | the same as in Table 3 |
| Conditions: | the same as in Table 3 with: |
| | `CaseSatisfiable (CaseCondition,InputVariablesVal,AttributesVal)` |
| | `GuardSatisfiable (Guard,InputVariablesVal,AttributesVal)` |
| | `CombinedPCSatisfiable(CaseCondition, Guard)` |
| Effects: | the same as in Table 3 and |
| | `AddToPC(Guard, CaseCondition, AttributesVal, InputVarVal)` |

| **External Rule** | |
|---|---|
| Variables: | the same as in Table 3 with: |
| | `InputVarValSymbolic` instead of `InputVarValGenerated` |
| Conditions: | `NotIsInitial (Part)` |
| | `TriggerIsExternal (Trigger)` |
| | `CaseSatisfiable (CaseCondition,InputVarValSymbolic,AttributesVal)` |
| | `GuardSatisfiable (Guard,InputVarValSymbolic,AttributesVal)` |
| | `CombinedPCSatisfiable(CaseCondition, Guard)` |
| Effects: | the same as in Table 3 and |
| | `AddToPC(Guard, CaseCondition, AttributesVal, InputVarValSymbolic)` |

| `Drop Rule` the same as in Table 3 |
|---|

In the case of symbolic execution we define similarity as in the case of the standard execution with one adjustment. We say two states are similar if they are exactly the same (including path constraints) or if they are the same modulo symbolic input variables. This helps to detect similarity for execution states that differ only in the order of received input variables.

*Example 4.* We present symbolic execution using the UML-RT model from Sect. 3. The first execution states S_1,S_2 are shown in Fig. 7. Two of them are exactly the same as in the case of standard execution. However, the states explored after the application of the `External Rule` are different. We introduce a new variable `carsFirst_var1` (and `walkFirst_var1`) to represent the input value received with the input signal `carsFirst` (and `walkFirst`). These variables are used to update the value of attributes. They are also used to update the path constraints so that the condition from the action code attached to the transition is represented.

When using *structural abstraction*, the user first identifies the parts that are to be abstracted. Then, only the unabstracted parts are executed as before with the exception that whenever an unabstracted part p requires input from an abstracted part q (i.e., to be able to take a transition, p requires a trigger that is generated by q), then that input is simply assumed to exist and provided to p, without checking if q can actually produce this input to p in the current state. The rules necessary to realize the above semantics are gathered in Table 5. They are the same as those of the standard execution semantics, with an extra

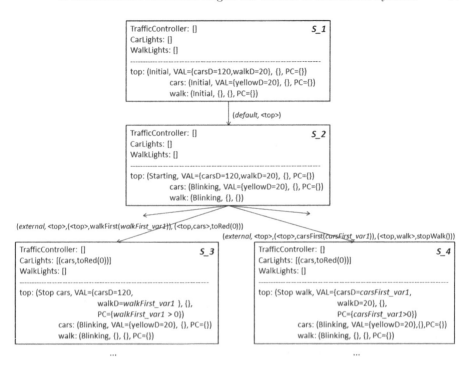

**Fig. 7.** An example of execution states in symbolic execution in the UML-RT model from Figs. 2, 3 and 4.

rule **Abstracted Signal Rule** to account for using triggers from abstracted parts. This rule has a condition that checks whether the sender of a trigger is one of the abstracted parts.

The presence of the extra **Abstract Signal Rule** results in triggering transitions that otherwise would not be triggered. This makes structural abstraction an overapproximation, because we may introduce additional execution paths not present in the original state space. So, as with analyses based on overapproximations in general, structural abstraction needs to be handled with a bit of care: if the analysis reveals some undesired behaviours, we need to check them against the unabstracted model; however, if the analysis does not find any undesired behaviours, then we can be assured that the original, unabstracted model does not contain any, either. For instance, if in the traffic lights model we abstract away the <top,walk> part and if we show unreachability of an execution state in which the <top,cars> part is in its Green location (see Fig. 4(a)) and the <top> part is in Walk (see Fig. 3), we are certain that such an execution state is also unreachable in unabstracted execution.

Moreover, for many combinations of properties and choices of parts to be abstracted out using structural abstraction, the fact that the abstraction cannot introduce any spurious analysis results can be deduced from the model quite easily. For instance, when checking the reachability of the location Red in the part

**Table 5.** Rules in structural abstraction.

| |
|---|
| `Default Rule, Match Rule, External Rule,` `Timeout Rule, DropRule-` the same as in Table 3 |

| `Abstracted Signal Rule` | |
|---|---|
| Variables: | `Part, Location, AttributesVal, Transition, Trigger, Guard,` `CaseConditon, CaseEffects, InputVarValGenerated` |
| Conditions: | `NotIsInitial (Part)` |
| | `TriggerSenderIsAbstracted (Trigger)` |
| | `CaseSatisfied (CaseCondition,InputVarValGenerated,` `AttributesVal)` |
| | `GuardSatisfied (Guard,InputVarValGenerated,` `AttributesVal)` |
| Effects: | `TargetLocation(Part,Transition)` |
| | `EvaluateEffects(Part, CaseEffects, InputVarValGenerated,` `AttributesVal)` |

<top, cars> in the traffic lights model (see Fig. 4(a)), a structural abstraction to abstract out the part <top, walk> will not introduce any spurious results, because to reach this location the part <top, cars> does not interact with the part <top, walk> at all. For another example, consider an analysis to determine the signals exchanged between the parts <top> and <top, walk>; here, the execution paths introduced by the interactions with <top, walk> are irrelevant, and <top, walk> can again be safely abstracted out.

The similarity detection of execution states in the case of the structural abstraction is the same in the case of standard abstractions assuming that states of abstracted parts are the same. Note that if an execution part is abstracted it remains such for the entire execution and its execution details will always be empty.

*Example 5.* We use the UML-RT model from Sect. 3. Figure 8 presents some of the execution states when the model is executed with structural abstraction applied to the execution part <top,walk>. The initial execution states from S_1 to S_4 of this model are similar as in Fig. 6. The only difference is that the part that is abstracted, that is <top,walk> is marked with an empty execution, that is, ∅. We label the last execution state as S_4'. Let us consider the execution part <top>. The current location of this part is `Stop walk`. The only outgoing transition from this location is triggered by the `walkStopped` signal (see Fig. 3), which is delivered by the <top,walk> part. Since this execution part is abstracted we can apply `Abstracted Signal Rule`. Application of this rule will result in state S_5'.

In *state aggregation* (see Table 6) we aggregate user-specified locations of state machines and we treat them as one location. We call this abstraction state aggregation initially to relate to states in original UML-RT state machines, but more accurate term is location aggregation. We specify disjoint aggregation

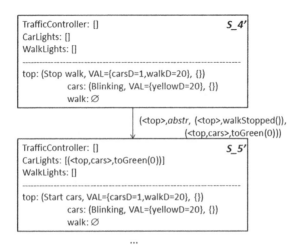

**Fig. 8.** Execution states in the structural abstraction of the UML-RT model in Figs. 2, 3 and 4.

groups, which group locations we wish to aggregate. Rules used in the semantics are almost the same as in the standard execution semantics, but instead of using a single location as a rule variable we now use a set of locations. Additionally, we add an extra effect which will make sure that when taking a transition the target locations include all locations in a given aggregation group.

As in the case of structural abstraction, state aggregation is an overapproximation, because we can trigger transitions outgoing from all locations in the current aggregation groups. In the standard execution we consider transitions outgoing from only one such location. However, as in case of the structural abstraction, we can accept such spurious paths if they are irrelevant to the analysis. For instance, if in the traffic lights example we have an aggregation group for all states in <top,cars> part and we wish to check reachability of the location Cars in the top level part (see Fig. 3) the result will be the same as if the analysis was performed without the aggregation. This is possible because the transitions between the locations we aggregate depend on the triggers provided by the top level part (or timers which are set after receiving such triggers), so the transitions in <top,cars> would be fired anyway.

The similarity detection for execution states explored using the state aggregation semantics is very much as in the standard execution semantics. Note that in this case we need to compare sets of locations and we use standard equality between sets.

*Example 6.* We continue the previous example of a UML-RT model. In Fig. 9 we present execution states of the model using state aggregation abstraction. We assume that we have one aggregation group {Start cars, Stop walk}. From the execution state S_1 we take a transition triggered by carsFirst. This transition takes us to the location Stop walk. Because this location is in the aggregation

**Table 6.** Rules in state aggregation engine.

| Default Rule, Match Rule, External Rule, Timeout Rule | |
|---|---|
| Variables: | the same as in Table 3 with Locations instead of Location |
| Conditions: | the same as in Table 3 |
| Effects: | the same as in Table 3 with: TargetAddLocations() |

| Drop Rule the same as in Table 3 |
|---|

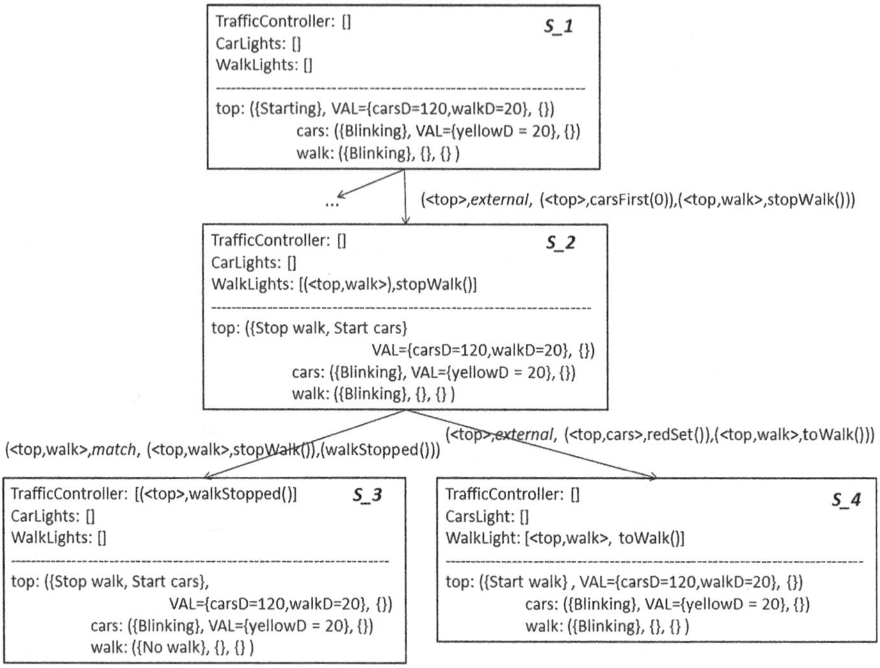

**Fig. 9.** Execution states of the UML-RT model (Figs. 2, 3 and 4) using state aggregation abstraction. We assume that **toRed** is external signal.

group we extend the target state to the entire aggregation group. Now, if we consider the execution state S_2 we need to check both locations in the aggregation group. We assume that **toRed** is external, therefore we can apply **External Rule**.

We can combine several abstractions to further increase the level of abstraction. For instance we can combine symbolic execution with either two other abstractions, to have some parts abstracted or some location aggregated and symbolic values used for input variables.

## 5    Results of Executing UML-RT Models

In this section we present the results of using the proposed tool. We show how the tool performs using several models. The performance is given using the number of states generated in each case. Unfortunately, we cannot compare ou tool with existing approaches, because the tools introduced in the literature are not publicly available.

We performed experiments with the execution engine using the version of the traffic lights model from Sect. 3. Figure 10 shows the structure of additional capsules we use in our experiments. IntersectionController represents an intersection and StreetController represent a street, that is, a sequence of several intersections. We increase the complexity of the models by increasing the number of intersections in the model up to 3. Additionally, we report on our experiments with a UML-RT model we obtained from our industrial partner, which is a model of a Private Branch Exchange (PBX) as used in the telecommunication industry. The experiments are performed on 4 subsystems of the main model which have up to 6 capsules and between 4 K an 6.5 K lines of code after code generation.

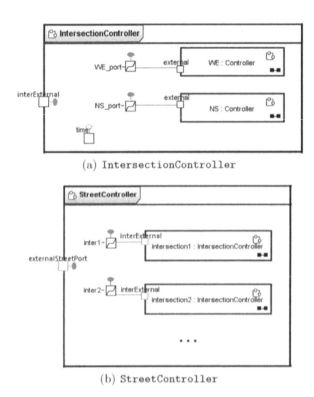

(a) IntersectionController

(b) StreetController

**Fig. 10.** Structure diagrams of capsules IntersectionController and Street Controller. From [19]

The results of our experiments are presented in terms of the number of execution states when using different execution rules. We used a standard PC with with processor Intel i7 (3.07 GHz) and with 4 GB of RAM memory. We omit the times necessary to execute the models, because they are proportional to the number of states and in case of the model with 1 intersection are seconds, with 2 or 3 intersections and PBX subsystems are less than 20 min and for 3 intersections and PBX subsystems in cases when OutOfMemoryException is thrown are more than 24 hours. For all experiments we detect similarity of states and we stop the exploration if the same states are detected.

## 5.1   Symbolic Execution

We start by presenting results of experiments with symbolic execution performed on several models. If possible we compare the sizes of the state space between symbolic and standard execution semantics. When using the standard execution we assume that the domain of all possible integer input values is limited to the intervals: (-1,1) and (-4,4). In the tables below we label the executions that use these intervals as 'Concrete (-1,1)' and 'Concrete (-4,4)' respectively.

**Table 7.** Number of states in the symbolic execution of StreetController model with different number of intersections. From [19].

| Module | Symbolic | Concrete(-1,1) | Concrete(-4,4) |
|---|---|---|---|
| StreetController with 1 intersection | 188 | 226 | 862 |
| StreetController with 2 intersections | 10 587 | 26 597 | 45 849 |
| StreetController with 3 intersections | >136 000 | >136 000 | >136 000 |

Table 7 presents the number of states in state spaces that are results of experiments with StreetController model with 1, 2 and 3 intersections. The models with 1 and 2 intersections were explored fully, but the exploration for the model with 3 intersection was interrupted by an OutOfMemoryException. The size of the state space increases with each additional intersection. Also state spaces resulting from standard (concrete) execution are larger than those arising from symbolic execution. For interval (-1,1) the state space is larger by 20 % and 150 % compared to symbolic execution, whereas for interval (-4,4) the increase is 5 and 10 times.

We also performed experiments with symbolic execution of subsystems of the PBX model. Table 8 gathers the results of these experiments. We show only results of symbolic execution, because the state space created during standard execution is too large. Even symbolic execution in most of the cases is partial. The largest discovered state space was in case of CallController and the smallest of OAMManager.

**Table 8.** Number of states in the symbolic execution of PBX subsystems. From [19].

| Model | CallController | DeviceManager | OAMSubsystem | ProxyManager |
|---|---|---|---|---|
| Size of state space | > 350 000 | > 250 000 | 65 582 | > 200 000 |

Symbolic execution is an abstraction that can reduce the size of execution state space of models if they rely on external inputs. However, the abstraction is the most efficient for smaller models such as StreetController with 1 or 2 intersections. For models larger than that we cannot explore the entire state space without further abstraction even if symbolic variables are used.

## 5.2   Structural Abstraction

In this section we present structural abstraction of StreetController model with 1, 2 and 3 intersections and to subsystems of the PBX model. In all cases we will combine structural abstraction with symbolic execution to get smaller and more manageable state spaces.

Table 9 presents results of applying several structural abstractions to the model with 1 intersection when combined with symbolic execution. In the table we present the results of increasingly more aggressive abstractions, when the larger number of execution parts are abstracted out. We start with abstracting walk parts in both NS and WE parts. Next, we perform abstraction in cars parts. The state space size decreases more if cars parts are abstracted, because this part has more interactions in the model. In the next row are results of abstracting parts with prefixes: <top,intersection1,NS> or <top,intersection1,NS>. This effectively means that we abstract all cars and walk parts. Next, we additionally abstract <top,intersection1,NS> and <top,intersection1,WE>, so we abstract parts with the prefix <top,intersection1>. This means that not abstracted parts are <top> and <top,intersection1>. The last row abstract all parts except for <top>. We can see that the number of states is reduced with more parts being abstracted.

**Table 9.** Number of states in symbolic execution state space of StreetController model with 1 intersection with different structural abstractions. i1 stands for intersection1 part and * indicates any parts with the prefix.

| Abstracted parts | Symbolic |
|---|---|
| none | 188 |
| $< top, intersection1, NS, walk >$, $< top, intersection1, WE, walk >$ | 157 |
| $< top, intersection1, NS, cars >$, $< top, intersection1, WE, cars >$ | 112 |
| $< top, intersection1, NS, * >$, $< top, intersection1, WE, * >$ | 86 |
| $< top, intersection1, * >$ | 15 |
| $< top, * >$ | 6 |

We perform similar abstractions of the model StreetController with 2 intersections. The results are given in Table 10. However, we distinguish a case when only parts from intersection1 are abstracted (first column in the table) and when we apply abstractions to both intersection1 and intersection2 (second

**Table 10.** Number of states in symbolic execution state spaces of `StreetController` model with 2 intersection parts with different structural abstractions. i is `intersection1` part or `intersection1` and `intersection2` parts and * indicates any parts with the indicated prefix.

| Abstracted parts | i = {intersection1} | i = {intersection1, intersection2} |
|---|---|---|
| none | 10 587 | 10 587 |
| < top, i, NS, walk >, < top, i, WE, walk > | 9 577 | 8 353 |
| < top, i, NS, cars >, < top, i, WE, cars > | 8 265 | 4 627 |
| << top, i, NS, * >, < top, i, WE, * > | 6 947 | 3 043 |
| < top, i, * > | 3 117 | 337 |
| < top, * > | 546 | 10 |

**Table 11.** Number of states in state spaces of `StreetController` model with 3 intersection parts with different structural abstractions. i stands for all `intersection` parts and * indicates any parts with the indicated prefix.

| Abstracted parts | i = all intersection parts |
|---|---|
| < top, i, NS, cars >, < top, i, WE, cars > | 69 022 |
| << top, i, NS, * >, < top, i, WE, * > | 51 757 |
| < top, i, * > | 4 791 |
| top,* | 546 |

column in the table). The difference between abstracting parts from one or both intersections is apparent in cases when more parts are abstracted. In the case of abstracting `walk` parts we have reduced the state space by 12 % if all `walk` parts from both intersections are considered. The difference becomes more substantial when more parts are abstracted. For instance, if abstracting `walk` and `cars` parts from both intersections we reduce the state space by 56 %.

Table 11 presents the results of experimenting with `StreetController` with 3 intersections if parts of all intersections are abstracted. Even though the initial model is too large for exhaustive exploration, by abstracting away execution parts we can substantially reduce the execution state space.

Structural abstraction also is useful for performing a unit analysis of individual capsules in isolation. We achieve that by abstracting away all parts that are not a part we are interested in. In this way we can inspect the execution of a state machine associated with a capsule.

Table 12 presents the sizes of state spaces in symbolic and concrete execution (with values between -4 and 4). The behavior of a capsule `WalkLights` is the same in case of symbolic and concrete execution, because it does not depend on external signals with variables. The sizes of the resulting state spaces are very small and can be easily verified.

**Table 12.** Number of states in state space of `TrafficLights` model with different structural abstractions used to extract a single module.

| Module | Symbolic | Concrete(-4,4) |
|---|---|---|
| WalkLights | 7 | 7 |
| CarLights | 15 | 121 |
| Controller | 33 | 95 |
| IntersectionController | 20 | 284 |
| StreetController for 1 intersection | 6 | 22 |
| StreetController for 2 intersections | 10 | 26 |
| StreetController for 3 intersections | 22 | 38 |

**Table 13.** Number of states in execution of PBX subsystems model with different structural abstractions used to extract a behavior of a single module.

| Module | Symbolic | Concrete(-4,4) |
|---|---|---|
| CallController | | |
| Call | 16 | 40 |
| OrigSession | 9 | 353 |
| TermSession | 13 | 13 |
| OAMSubsystem | | |
| GMSC | 20 | 52 |
| SystemAdminProxy | 39 | 103 |
| HLR | 182 | 43 650 |
| DeviceManager | | |
| Phone | 41 | 89 |
| ProxyManager | | |
| CellPhoneEventFilter | 3 563 | 3 571 |

We also performed this kind of unit analysis on several modules of PBX subsystems. Table 13 presents the results. Most of the capsules have rather limited state spaces. The largest one is for `CellPhoneEventFilter`, because it models the reception of pressing keys on the phone, and combination of those must be considered. We can also observe that most of the capsules depend on external inputs and the sizes of their symbolic execution state spaces are smaller.

This section shows the results of experiments with structural abstractions. We can see how powerful this abstraction can be. This is valid even for models, that cannot be exhaustively explored such as `StreetController` with 3 intersections and PBX subsystems. Depending on parts that are abstracted, structural abstraction may substantially reduce the execution of models. We also show how structural abstraction can be used to support unit analyses and inspect the behaviour of individual capsules in isolation. As mentioned earlier structural abstraction is an overapproximation and may produce spurious execution paths, so the analysis results should be treated with care.

## 5.3  State Aggregation

In this section we present results of experimenting with state aggregation abstraction. We apply this semantics to the StreetController model with 1 and 2 intersections using different aggregation groups.

Table 14 presents the results of applying state aggregation abstractions to the StreetController model with 1 intersection (in the first we repeat the number of states without any abstraction). In the first experiment we use an aggregation that groups all the operating locations in IntersectionController. This abstraction enables the reduction of the number of states by more than 70 %. In the following experiment we use an aggregation group that gathers initalization locations in the TrafficController. This abstraction does not change the number of states, because we aggregate states for which triggers need to be present in a respective queue and simply enabling extra transitions is not sufficient for a transition to actually be fired. Finally we use 2 aggregation groups with Yellow and YellowRed for both cars parts. In this case the larger number of enabled transitions result in extra states and the execution is larger.

**Table 14.** Number of states in execution of StreetController model with 1 intersection with different state aggregation abstractions.

| Aggregation | Symbolic | Concrete (-4,4) |
|---|---|---|
| none | 188 | 862 |
| Operating in intersection | 62 | 196 |
| Initialization in intersection | 188 | 862 |
| Yellow and YellowRed in both cars parts | 222 | 970 |

We gather results of applying state aggregation to the StreetController model with 2 intersections in Table 15. Aggregation groups are similar to the ones used in the previous experiment and we also present the full size of the

**Table 15.** Number of states in execution of StreetController model with 2 intersections with different state aggregation abstractions.

| Aggregation | Symbolic | Concrete (-4,4) |
|---|---|---|
| none | 10 867 | 45 849 |
| Operating in both intersections | 2 807 | 9 417 |
| Initialization in both intersections | 10 867 | 45 849 |
| Yellow and YellowRed in all cars | 16 423 | 65 325 |

state space in the first row of the table. Next we show the results of state aggregation for two aggregation groups, each of which includes locations responsible for operating an intersection. Similarly to the previous model, this abstraction reduces the number of execution states. Using the next aggregation group has no effect on the number of states. Finally, aggregation with 4 aggregation groups containing locations `Yellow` and `YellowRed` generates more execution states than standard or symbolic execution.

State aggregation abstraction enables grouping locations in state machines. The groupings can be arbitrary, but we can also follow the hierarchies of states in the original UML-RT State Machine. Unlike the previous abstraction, this abstraction may have none or even a negative effect, that is, we may not achieve the reduction in the number of states or we may increase that number. Therefore, it is crucial to carefully select locations to be grouped. Similarly to the structural abstraction, state aggregation is an overapproximation.

## 5.4  Summary

Figure 11 summarizes the results of using different execution semantics for 1, 2 and 3 intersections. The dashed lines indicate executions for which we could not produce any results because of `OutOfMemoryException`. We selected one of the structural abstractions (namely `<top,i,*`) and one of the aggregation groups in state aggregation (namely Operating). Structural abstraction is more aggressive and is the only execution type we could get results for `StreetController` with 3 intersections.

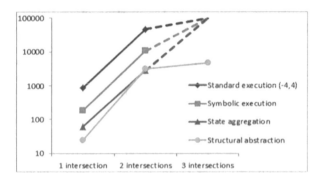

**Fig. 11.** Number of states in the execution of `StreetController` using different execution semantics (Y-axis is logarithmic with base 10).

# 6   Extending TUMLE to Support Additional Customizations

In the current version of the tool we support the basic abstractions and their combinations. In order to realize the full possibilities of customizable abstractions (from Sect. 2) we have to extend the existing tool in the following ways:

- easy support for user-defined semantics: the tool should support any semantics, by allowing the user to define new execution rules with easy interface (currently it can be done only in the source code). It should be possible to reuse execution rules as well as to introduce new rules.
- extended parametrization of abstractions: some of the proposed abstractions have parameters, such as parts to abstract or states to aggregate. We wish to extend possible parameters to other elements of models. For instance, we may have new abstractions that act on specific signals or functions.
- selective application of abstractions: in the current work we can combine existing abstractions. We would like to extend such combinations to any semantics with parameters indicating which semantics should be used for which parts of execution and/or of the models.

# 7   Related Work

UML-RT models are executable in the IBM RSA RTE [1] with code generation. However, IBM RSA RTE does not support abstractions or alternative semantics.

The prevailing works in the general analysis of UML like models is concerned with translation of models to the existing other tools. For instance, HUGO RT [9,16] is a toolset that offers translation of collections of UML State Machines SPIN, UPPAAL and other. In the context to of UML-RT translations to Promela/Spin [15], to AsmL language [10] and others were proposed. Although these tools allow verification of properties, they are usually limited in their abilities to exhaustively execute or the models. Also, the semantics used in the models are fixed, and the adjustments in executions can be made only through models.

In model checking abstractions are used to reduce the complexity of verification [11]. In [5] it is shown that for certain CTL properties (only universal path quantifiers) it is possible to check them on the abstracted model $\mathcal{M}_a$ as long as there is a simulation relation between $\mathcal{M}$ and $\mathcal{M}_a$. This approach is similar to abstract interpretation [6], in which the semantics of certain operations is replaced and simpler state spaces are generated. There were also other numerical abstraction methods proposed for model checking [7,8]. In our approach we use abstractions in a similar way, but we provide abstractions dedicated to the UML-RT models we are using.

One of the abstraction we use is symbolic execution, it is also supported in Symbolic JPF [14]. This tool performs symbolic execution for Java, but in [12] is extended to support single state machines. In [4] the problem of heterogeneity of state based models is addressed and implemented with a tool based on JPF. We also proposed the tool for symbolic execution of UML-RT models [20]. The tool presented here introduces also other abstractions.

There are also other tools that support specification of the semantics of domain specific languages. We can specify the entire language (such as XSemantics for XText [3]) or we can use state machines templates [13].

To the best of our knowledge, the proposed tool is the first interpreter for UML-RT model with varying semantics.

## 8  Conclusions

In this paper we present Toolset for UML Execution (TUMLE). The toolset enables execution of models with various semantics and to support abstractions that will reduce the size of the state space. We show the design of the tool, which is based on rules and we show the specification of rules necessary to perform different abstractions. Thanks to the rule-based design we can reuse internal elements, but we can also reuse the implementation of the graphical display. We performed experiments with the tool and we showed how abstractions can reduce the size of the state space of more complex models.

## References

1. IBM Rational Software Architect, RealTime Edition, Version 8.0.2. http://publib.boulder.ibm.com/infocenter/rsarthlp/v7r5m1/
2. Unified Modeling Language (UML 2.0) Superstructure. http://www.uml.org/
3. Xsemantics. http://xsemantics.sourceforge.net/
4. Balasubramanian, D., Păsăreanu, C.S., Karsai, G., Lowry, M.R.: Polyglot: systematic analysis for multiple statechart formalisms. In: Piterman, N., Smolka, S.A. (eds.) TACAS 2013 (ETAPS 2013). LNCS, vol. 7795, pp. 523–529. Springer, Heidelberg (2013)
5. Clarke, E.M., Grumberg, O., Long, D.E.: Model checking and abstraction. ACM Trans. Program. Lang. Syst. **16**(5), 1512–1542 (1994)
6. Cousot, P.: Abstract interpretation based formal methods and future challenges. In: Wilhelm, R. (ed.) Informatics: 10 Years Back, 10 Years Ahead. LNCS, vol. 2000, pp. 138–156. Springer, Heidelberg (2001)
7. Dwyer, M.B., Hatcliff, J., Joehanes, R., Laubach, S., Păsăreanu, C.S.: Tool-supported program abstraction for finite-state verification. In: ICSE (2001)
8. Loustinova, N., Sidorova, N.: Abstraction and flow analysis for model checking open asynchronous systems. In: Software Engineering Conference (2002)
9. Knapp, A., Merz, S., Rauh, C.: Model checking timed uml state machines and collaborations. In: Damm, W., Olderog, E.-R. (eds.) FTRTFT 2002. LNCS, vol. 2469, pp. 395–414. Springer, Heidelberg (2002)
10. Leue, S., Stefanescu, A., Wei, W.: An AsmL semantics for dynamic structures and run time schedulability in UML-RT. Technical report, University of Konstanz (2008)
11. Manna, Z., Colón, M.A., Finkbeiner, B., Sipma, H.B., Uribe, T.E.: Abstraction and modular verification of infinite-state reactive systems. In: Broy, M. (ed.) RTSE 1997. LNCS, vol. 1526, pp. 273–292. Springer, Heidelberg (1998)

12. Mehlitz, P.C.: Trust your model - verifying aerospace system models with Java pathfinder. In: IEEE Aerospace Conference (2008)
13. Niu, J., Atlee, J.M., Day, N.A.: Template semantics for model-based notations. IEEE Trans. Softw. Eng. **29**(10), 866–882 (2003)
14. Păsăreanu, C.S., Rungta, N.: Symbolic PathFinder: symbolic execution of Java bytecode. In: ASE (2010)
15. Saaltink, M., Meisels, I.: Using SPIN to analyse RoseRT models. Technical report, ORA Canada (1999)
16. Schäfer, T., Knapp, A., Merz, S.: Model checking UML state machines and collaborations. Electron. Notes Theoret. Comput. Sci. **55**(3), 357–369 (2001)
17. Selic, B.: A short catalogue of abstraction patterns for model-based software engineering. Int. J. Softw. Inform. **5**(1–2), 313–334 (2011)
18. Selic, B.: What will it take? A view on adoption of model-based methods in practice. Softw. Syst. Model. **11**(4), 513–526 (2012)
19. Zurowska, K.: Language specific analysis of statemachine models of reactive systems. Ph.D. thesis, Queen's University, June 2014
20. Zurowska, K., Dingel, J.: Symbolic execution of communicating and hierarchically composed UML-RT state machines. In: Goodloe, A.E., Person, S. (eds.) NFM 2012. LNCS, vol. 7226, pp. 39–53. Springer, Heidelberg (2012)
21. Zurowska, K., Dingel, J.: Model checking of UML-RT models using lazy composition. In: Moreira, A., Schätz, B., Gray, J., Vallecillo, A., Clarke, P. (eds.) MODELS 2013. LNCS, vol. 8107, pp. 304–319. Springer, Heidelberg (2013)

# New Ways of Behaviour Modelling:
# Events in Modelling

# Programming Animation Using Behavioral Programming

David Harel[✉] and Shani Nitzan

Department of Computer Science and Applied Mathematics,
Weizmann Institute of Science, 76100 Rehovot, Israel
dharel@weizmann.ac.il, Shani.Lesser@gmail.com

**Abstract.** We propose a simple, user-friendly way of creating computer programs for hybrid systems whose execution involves animation. This is done by adapting *behavioral programming*, a recently proposed approach to software development that is aligned with how people describe system behavior, for use in programming animation. Users can define discrete and continuous behavior, which are then run simultaneously, interacting with each other, and resulting in a smooth hybrid animation.

## 1 Introduction

We define a natural and intuitive method for programming animation through scenarios. Each scenario describes a certain part of the motion of an object, and can correspond to an individual requirement, specifying what can, must, or may not happen following a sequence of events. Ideally, such motion scenarios should enable incremental development, allowing the user to add new scenarios without interfering with existing ones.

*Behavioral programming* (BP) is a recently proposed scenario-based programming paradigm that centers on natural and incremental specification of behaviors; see [8]. The BP approach was preceded by the language of *live sequence charts* (LSC) [1], which extends message sequence charts (MSC), and is a scenario-based language for reactive systems. LSCs add modalities to MSCs, allowing the specification of liveness and safety properties, as well as forbidden behaviors [1,2]. Two support tools for LSCs have been built, first the *Play-Engine* [2] and then *PlayGo* [3]. Later, the ideas where extended and embedded also in conventional programming languages like Java (resulting in BPJ, for behavioral programming in Java) [4], C++ [5], as well as Erlang and Blockly [6,7], thus providing a more classical programming point of view to this concept. See [8] for more details. In this paper we use BPJ.

Heretofore, behavioral programming had been used predominantly for programming discrete systems. In this article we propose and demonstrate its use for programming hybrid systems, whose execution can involve also continuous animation.

Animation programs can be executed by calculating the location of an object according to the time elapsed between clock ticks, while considering the location of the other objects. Although this can be made to produce satisfactory visual

© Springer International Publishing Switzerland 2015
E. Roubtsova et al. (Eds.): BM-FA 2009-2014, LNCS 6368, pp. 113–132, 2015.
DOI: 10.1007/978-3-319-21912-7_5

results, it is not always a natural way to describe animation. Over the years, much research has been carried out to simplify this by having moving objects assume more life-like behavior. Scenarios have been used for animation [9], and an initial attempt at using LSCs to create animations appears in [10]. A decision network framework for specifying and activating human behaviors has been introduced to create the behavioral animation of virtual humans [11].

Complex behavioral animation can also be obtained by defining simple, local rules between the various objects [12], which can rely on the objects having *synthetic vision* [13, 14]. Synthetic vision has been used with other interaction components (an attention component, a gaze generation component and a memory component) to create a virtual human animation [15]. It has been integrated with cognitive science work on human locomotion to model interactive simulation of crowds of individual humans [16]. Non-linear dynamical system theory, kinetic data structures, and harmonic functions have also been used for agent steering and crowd simulation [17]. Motion within a large crowd has also been modelled by integrating global navigation and local collision avoidance [18].

A hybrid system is usually defined as one that exhibits both continuous and discrete (reactive) behaviors. Continuous behaviors are those that create the motion of an object; discrete behaviors are those that control sudden changes in that motion. Thus, between bounces, a bouncing ball exhibits a continuous behavior, its movement determined by angle, velocity, speed and gravity, but when it hits the ground it undergoes a sudden change in motion, due to the hit and the release of energy, which is considered a discrete behavior.

Hybrid behaviors can be modelled in many ways, a well known one being hybrid automata [19]. A hybrid automaton is a finite-state machine, where each state can be governed by a set of differential equations, enabling continuous behaviors between discrete state changes.

In this article we introduce a system that integrates defining local rules between various objects that have synthetic vision, with the *behavioral programming* principles. Our method simplifies the creation of animation in several ways, notably in that it enables the implementation of the local rules by using different threads for different rules. The method of synchronization of these threads is built into the BP execution mechanism, and in a way is transparent to the user. This is explained later.

A bouncing ball can thus be modeled using two scenarios: **Move** and **Change-Direction**. The scenario **Move** is responsible for moving the ball according to its initial velocity and the force of gravity, and represents a continuous behavior. When the ball hits the ground, **ChangeDirection** calculates the new velocity of the ball, and it represents a discrete behavior. These scenarios can be implemented incrementally, so that for each step the physical correctness can be verified and simulated.

The code for all the examples presented in this article can be downloaded from:

https://www.dropbox.com/sh/yjxgpuq1pjzb2xd/AAAozws8Ql7l8ssAqmp KhmdAa?dl=0

# 2   Behavioral Programming

## 2.1   Basic Idioms

A behavioral program [8] consists of separate behavioral components (called *b-threads*) that generate a flow of events via an enhanced publish/subscribe protocol, as follows (see Fig. 1). Unlike regular threads, each b-thread runs atomically until it reaches a synchronization point, at which point it yields. When synchronizing, a b-thread specifies the following three sets of events:

- *Requested events:* The b-thread asks that these events be triggered, and to be notified when any of them is.
- *Waited-for events:* The b-thread asks to be notified when any of these events is triggered. It does not ask to trigger them.
- *Blocked events:* The b-thread prevents these events from being triggered.

When all the b-threads enter a synchronized point, some event is sought, which is in the requested events set of at least one of the b-threads, and is not in the blocked events set of any of the b-threads. One such event (if it exists) is selected for triggering, and when it is triggered all b-threads that requested or waited for it are notified, and their execution is resumed. Each of the resumed b-threads then proceeds with its execution, all the way to its next synchronization point, where it again presents its sets of requested, waited-for and blocked events. When all b-threads are again at a synchronization point the event selection process repeats. When more than one event is found as a legal candidate for triggering, i.e., it is requested by some b-thread and not blocked by any, the actual event to be triggered is chosen depending on the implemented execution semantics, of which there are several, see [8].

Each b-thread has local variables and global variables; events are defined globally. Since b-threads run atomically until a synchronization point is reached there is no need for safety measures, such as locks, to be taken in order to ensure that the b-threads work as expected.

BP principles can be implemented as part of various languages and programming approaches, with possible variations on the actual programming idioms. In addition to Java with the BPJ package, the idioms have been implemented in Erlang [6, 20], Blockly [7] and C++ [5]. The BP idioms have also been applied to PicOS, a programming environment for wireless sensor networks, using C [21]. In addition to the Play-Engine and PlayGo, a visual approach called *Synthesizing Biological Theories* (SBT) [22], a tool for biological modelling, was implemented using the BP principles.

## 2.2   Behavioral Programming in Java

BPJ is implemented using the special **BPJ package**. In BPJ, every b-thread is an instance of the class BThread, and events are instances of the class Event or classes that extend it. The logic of each behavior is coded as a method supplied

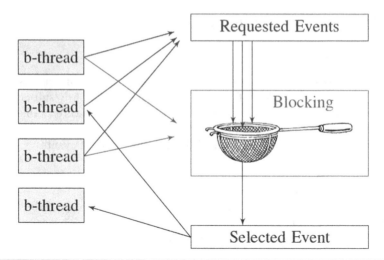

**Fig. 1.** An illustration of the BP execution cycle

by the programmer, which in turn invokes the method bSync to synchronize with other behaviors, and to specify its requested, waited-for and blocked events, as follows:

bSync(requestedEvents, waitedForEvents, blockedEvents);

When a b-thread calls bSync, it is suspended, and is resumed when a requested or waited-for event is triggered. To enforce predictable and repeatable execution the events selected at a synchronization point must be uniquely defined. This can be done in different ways. In BPJ every b-thread has a unique priority. When more than one event is requested and not blocked the event that will be triggered is the one requested by the b-thread with the lowest priority. If this b-thread requests more than one event the first event in the list of requested events that is not blocked is the one triggered (this is possible because in BPJ the requested events set is ordered).

*Example 1.* We illustrate the use of BPJ by a water flow control example taken from [4]. The goal is to have lukewarm water flow from a tap, by alternately letting a small amount of warm water and then a small amount of cold water flow. Hot and cold water are supplied by different sources, each of which supplies its type of water repeatedly. The alternation of the two is done by an external mechanism. The b-threads for the three relevant behaviors are as follows:

1. **AddHotThreeTimes:** This b-thread requests the event `addHot` three times. The event `addHot` represents opening the hot water-tap for a short time.
2. **AddColdThreeTimes:** This b-thread requests the event `addCold` three times. The event `addCold` represents opening the cold water-tap for a short time.
3. **Interleave:** This b-threads repeatedly waits for the event `addHot` and blocks the event `addCold`, and then waits for the event `addCold` and blocks the event `addHot`.

**AddHotThreeTimes** and **AddColdThreeTimes** can work independently of one another, resulting in the flow of only hot or cold water from the tap. To get lukewarm water, the b-thread **Interleave** is used to force the alternation of the events `addHot` and `addCold`, which results in lukewarm water (Fig. 2).

The BPJ package, the code of the water flow problem and other BPJ examples can be downloaded from:
http://www.wisdom.weizmann.ac.il/~bprogram/bpj/

## 2.3   Live Sequence Charts

The visual language *live sequence charts* (LSC) [1] is an extension of message sequence charts (MSC). Like MSC, LSC use vertical lifelines to represent objects and horizontal arrows to represent messages passed between them. Since time flow is from top to bottom, a partial order of occurrences of the events ensues.

However the partial order alone cannot express what scenarios are to be carried out and when. This is where the extension of LSCs comes into play. LSCs can express what must happen (hot), what may happen (cold), and what is not allowed to happen (forbidden). Scenarios that are to be executed proactively are also distinguished from those that are only to be observed and monitored.

An LSC is composed of two parts, a prechart, depicted as a dashed-line hexagon, and a main chart. The main chart contains instructions that should be executed, and to activate it the scenario in the prechart must have occurred. The chart in Fig. 3 is a part of an implementation of a cruise control. It represents the scenario of the brake being pressed, resulting in the cruise releasing control of the brakes and the accelerator and turning itself off.

**Play-in.** LSC allows a new way of coding, called play-in [2], which is similar to programming by example. With play-in the user specifies the scenario in a way that is close to how real interaction with the system occurs, and the programming itself is done via a GUI. In the example in Fig. 3, the user would click the brake (action of the prechart), which releases the control the cruise has on the brakes and accelerator (action of the main chart).

```
class AddHotThreeTimes extends BThread {
    public void runBThread() {
        for (int i = 1; i <= 3; i++) {
            bp.bSync( addHot, none, none );
        }
    }
}

class AddColdThreeTimes extends BThread {
    public void runBThread() {
        for (int i = 1; i <= 3; i++) {
            bp.bSync( addCold, none, none );
        }
    }
}

class Interleave extends BThread
    public void runBThread() {
        while (true) {
            bp.bSync( none, addHot, addCold );
            bp.bSync( none, addCold, addHot );
        }
    }
}
```

**Event log of
the coordinated run**

| addHot |
| --- |
| addCold |
| addHot |
| addCold |
| addHot |
| addCold |

**Fig. 2.** The water flow problem

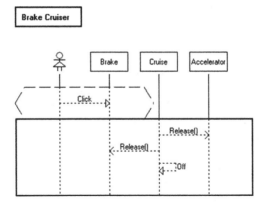

**Fig. 3.** LSC chart

**Play-out.** The play-out technique facilitates the execution of an LSC. Play-out does this by tracking the actions taken by the user and the system's environment. Events that may be selected next in all lifelines in all charts are tracked. When needed, play-out responds to an action accordingly, by selecting and triggering events. Play-out is also carried out via a GUI.

## 3    Animation in Behavioral Programming

Our method for creating animation with behavioral programming calls for each object to have b-threads that control its motion. Each of these b-threads represents a certain behavior of that object and they interact with one another through the BP synchronization mechanism. The b-threads are divided into those that represent discrete behaviors and those that represent continuous behaviors.

B-threads that represent discrete behaviors are called *control b-threads*. They influence *motion b-threads*, those that represent continuous behaviors, through synchronization. After a synchronization point, when a control b-thread senses that the motion of the object it is in charge of needs to be manipulated it will do so.

It should be noted that in this article continuous behaviors are implemented by discretization (the process of transforming a continuous model into discrete parts), since computers work in a discrete way. This can be analogous to a person walking. Even though the person is moving in a continuous way his/her motion can be divided into discrete steps.

Like in regular animation programs, small movements of an object are triggered by time ticks, which are controlled by the following b-thread:

`Sleep(Event endSleep, long timeOfSleep, double priorityOfBThread)`

When created, this b-thread sleeps for `timeOfSleep` milliseconds and then requests that the event `endSleep` be triggered. The b-thread gets priority `priorityOfBThread`. The b-thread `Sleep` is always created by a motion b-thread.

## 3.1   Motion B-Threads

Since motion b-threads represent an object's continuous behavior, and continuous behavior in animation is guided, among other things, by the velocity of an object, the most basic and simple pattern of a motion b-thread is an infinite loop that does the following: It first creates the b-thread `Sleep`, and then waits for the event `endSleep`. It then requests the event `takeStep`, and finally calculates the new position of the object.

| |
|---|
| **while** *true* **do** |
|    Create the b-thread **Sleep**. |
|    Wait for the event **endSleep**. |
|    Request the event **takeStep**. |
|    Calculate the new place of the object according to the velocity and the time passed. |
| **end while** |

**Algorithm 1.** Basic motion b-thread algorithm

To understand how a motion b-thread works, imagine a green ball rolling to the right. The ball has one continuous behavior, which is its movement. Its motion b-thread is as follows:

```
while (true) {
    createSleep(endSleep1, sleep, prio1);
    bp.bSync(none, endSleep1, none);
    bp.bSync(takeStep1, none, none);
    x1 += getTimePassed()*step; //updates coordinate
}
```

An example of this animation can be viewed here:
https://www.dropbox.com/s/jaoptmayfn1cm8c/Sec3Sub1.mp4.

Now suppose another ball is added; this time a blue ball rolling at half the speed of the green ball. Now there is a second continuous behavior, which is represented by another appropriate motion b-thread.

An example of this animation can be viewed here:
https://www.dropbox.com/s/56eoxjxwcybv3cb/Sec3Sub1_2.mp4.

With these two b-threads the two balls move simultaneously, each at its own pace. New moving objects can thus be added incrementally. Changing the direction or speed of one of the balls requires no change in the b-threads of the other balls.

## 3.2  Control B-Threads

Control b-threads can manipulate the motion of an object in different ways. In our example, one of the simplest is to block the event **takeStep**. The motion b-thread of the object being blocked terminates, which results in stopping the motion. Imagine the rolling green ball of the previous subsection, and that this ball is getting closer to a wall. When it reaches the wall we want it to stop rolling. The continuous behavior of the ball is the same, which means that the motion b-thread that represents it is the same as well, but now the following control b-thread can be added:

```
while(true){
    bp.bSync(none, endSleep1, none);
    if(collision()) { //checks if the ball has reached the wall
        bp.bSync(none, none, takeStep1);
    }
}
```

An example of this animation can be viewed here:
https://www.dropbox.com/s/oh5cxuex8ww8i2k/Sec3Sub2.mp4.

This b-thread adds a behavior without the user having to alter existing ones. More control b-threads can be added very easily. For example, all that needs to be done in order to add a new wall is to enhance the program with a new control b-thread that checks collision with the new wall and blocks **takeStep1** accordingly.

These basic algorithms for control and motion b-threads are the basis for implementing far more complex behaviors, as we show later.

## 3.3  Improving and Adding B-Threads

One problem that appears when integrating different b-threads for the balls, is that a ball does not stop exactly when it reaches the wall, but a little later. This is because the ball moves in steps and the wall will often be reached in between two steps. In some cases this kind of issue does not cause a problem. For example, if an object moves until it sees an obstacle 50 m away and it turns left, then it does not matter if the object turned left when it was 50 m away from the obstacle or 50 m and 1 cm away. However, in many cases, including the one above, this does matter. The ball should appear to stop at the wall, which means that it has to stop exactly when it gets to the wall.

To overcome this problem we make the control b-thread look ahead at the next step, and if a change of motion is in order, it is fixed. This is done by making small changes to both the motion and the control b-threads. The changes are demonstrated in the bouncing ball example. The motion b-thread calculates the new y-axis coordinate of the ball, and then requests the event takeStepY. After it is triggered, the new coordinate is updated. The motion b-thread is as follows:

```
while (true) {
    createSleep(endSleep, sleep, prio);
    nextY = calcNextY(); //calculates the next coordinate
    bp.bSync(takeStepY, none, none);
    y = nextY; //updates the new coordinate
}
```

After checkStep (the event that symbolizes looking ahead at the next step) is triggered, the control b-thread checks if the next coordinates will result in a collision between the ball and the ground. If so, the b-thread requests the event hitGround, and updates the next coordinate so that the ball is exactly on the ground. Since the ball should bounce and not just stop, then instead of blocking the event takeStepY the control b-thread calculates the new velocity, which is in the opposite direction of the previous velocity, and its speed is slower, due to friction. The control b-thread is as follows:

```
while (true) {
    bp.bSync(none, endSleep, none);
    bp.bSync(checkStep, none, none);
    if(ballHitGround()){ //checks if the ball collides with the ground
        bp.bSync(hitGround, none, none);
        nextY = calcNewNextY(); //calculates the new next coordinate
        calcNewInitVelocityY(); //calculates the new velocity
    }
}
```

By using only these two b-threads the ball continues to bounce on the floor forever, reaching increasingly lower latitudes. To stop the ball when its velocity is near zero, another control b-thread is added. This one waits for the event hitGround, then blocks the event endSleep if the velocity is near enough to zero. The b-thread is as follows:

```
while(true) {
    bp.bSync(none, hitGround, none);
    /*The velocity is near zero so motion should stop*/
    if(speedNearZero())
        bp.bSync(none, none, endSleep);
    }
```

An example of this animation can be viewed here:
https://www.dropbox.com/s/gg2m18rg5erjhjc/Sec3Sub3.mp4.

## 4   Using Behavioral Programming for Billiard

Our technique for creating animations using behavioral programming is fairly simple, yet it can handle many of the general problems that occur when trying to program animations. We now discuss billiard. The animation scenarios of a billiard game are described in Fig. 4. The game consists of 16 balls; here the balls are indexed 0–15, where 0 is the white ball. The event moveBall[i] is triggered when ball number $i$ starts moving (which happens when another ball hits it).

The b-thread that represents the continuous behavior of ball $i$ is **Move-Ball(i)**. Since the ball should only start moving when the event moveBall[i] is triggered, this b-thread repeatedly waits for it. After that, as long the velocity of the ball is not zero the ball should move while decreasing its velocity at each

1. **StartMove:** When a new move starts, the player can use the stick to hit the white ball.

2. **StickHitsWhiteBall:** When the stick hits the white ball, the white ball starts moving. Its velocity is calculated by the direction and impact of the hit.

3. **MoveBall:** As long as the velocity of the ball isn't zero, it moves and the velocity is decreased by friction. As long as the ball is moving a new move can't start.

4. **BallHitsBorder:** When a ball hits the border of the table, the ball's motion stops and it starts moving in the opposite direction.

5. **BallInHole:** When the ball enters one of the holes, it stops moving, disappears from the table, and other balls on the table should not consider it in their motion.

6. **WhiteBallInHole:** When a new move starts, if the white ball is inside a hole, it is put back in the middle of the table.

7. **BallHitsBall:** When balls collide, both balls stop moving and then start moving with a new velocity determined by the direction and impact of the hit.

**Fig. 4.** Description of the animation scenarios of a billiard game

time tick, due to friction. This is exactly what **MoveBall(i)** does, while block-ing the event startMove with every call to the function bSync. Therefore, a new move does not start while the ball is still moving. **MoveBall(i)** is as follows:

```
while(true){
    bp.bSync(none, billiard.moveBall[i], none);
    long t1 = System.currentTimeMillis(), t2 = t1; //initialized the time

    /*continues in a loop until the ball's velocity equals zero*/
    while(ballHasVelocity()){
        createSleep(endSleep[i], sleep, prio[i]);
        bp.bSync(none, endSleep[i], startMove);

        t2 = System.currentTimeMillis(); //updates the time
        calculateNextStep(t2-t1); //calculates the next coordinates of the
            ball

        bp.bSync(takeStep[i], none, startMove);

        takeNextStep(); //updates the coordinates of the ball
        t1 = t2;
    }
}
```

There are three discrete behaviors in the animation of a billiard game: a ball's collision with the borders of the billiard table (**BallHitBorder(i)**), a ball falling into one of the holes on the table (**BallInHole(i)**) and a ball colliding with another ball (**BallHitsBall(i,j)**). Every step these b-threads wait for the event endSleep[i] (which is only requested when ball $i$ has non-zero velocity).

Every time tick, **BallHitBorder(i)** checks if ball $i$ has collided with the borders of the table and updates the next coordinates of the ball and its velocity accordingly. **BallInHole(i)** does the same for the holes of the table, with one exception: when the ball falls into a hole it should stop moving altogether and other balls shouldn't check for collisions with it. To insure this as long as ball $i$ is inside the hole, the event ballOnTable[j] is blocked.

For every ordered pair of balls $i$ and $j$, the b-thread **BallHitsBall(i,j)** rep-resents ball $i$ colliding with ball $j$. When there is a collision, the coordinates and velocities of both balls should change accordingly, and if ball $j$ was motionless it should start moving. To enable this, every time a collision is detected, the event moveBall(j) is requested, which resumes the execution of the motion b-thread **MoveBall[j]**. After checking for a collision **BallHitsBall(i,j)** requests the event ballOnTable[j], which prevents this b-thread from continuing if ball $j$ is not on the table. **BallHitsBall(i,j)** is as follows:

```
while(true) {
    bp.bSync(none, endSleep[i], none);
    bp.bSync(checkCollision[i], none, none);

    //checks if there is a collision between balls i and j
    if(areBallsColliding(i ,j)){
        adjustPosition();
        adjustVelocities();

        bp.bSync(moveBall[j], none, none);
    }
    bp.bSync(ballOnTable[j], none, none);
}
```

All the control b-threads are independent of each other, while still affecting the motion b-thread when it is required. This is important, and makes it possible to add or remove discrete behaviors easily, without affecting other b-threads. The current example shows only one motion b-thread per object, which may not always be the case.

An example of this animation can be viewed here: https://www.dropbox.com/s/oukaccxcke2m26n/billiard.mp4.

The billiards animation was based on open source code that can be downloaded from here: http://ftparmy.com/193538-billard4k.html.

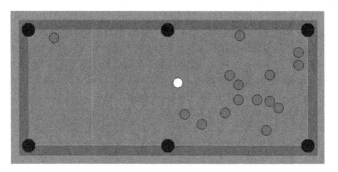

## 5    Adding Continuous Behaviors

Sometimes moving objects have more than one continuous behavior. When a ball is thrown it can be thought of having two continuous behaviors. The first is the motion in the direction the ball was thrown, and the second is the acceleration towards the ground, due to gravity. In our approach, like in many motion calculations, each of these behaviors can be represented by an independent motion b-thread, and integrating them is done using one or more control b-threads.

Separating an object's motion into multiple continuous behaviors simplifies the act of describing the motion. Describing a thrown ball with a single scenario is difficult, because the ball has a curve-like motion. When the motion is separated into the behaviors of movement with the initial velocity and movement towards the ground due to gravity, describing the motion becomes easy.

Like with discrete behaviors, adding continuous behaviors to an already working program should be done, as far as possible, without altering existing b-threads. The BP's incremental approach makes adding continuous behaviors of an object relatively easy. Moreover, implementing motion b-threads that represent such continuous behaviors creates additional benefits. For example, it makes the controlling of the motion simple. If there are several continuous behaviors that work at different times, scheduling them can be done by control b-threads.

## 5.1  How it is Done

To demonstrate the b-threads of a thrown ball having an initial velocity parallel to the x-axis, we use the example of a bouncing ball, which already has continuous behavior of the acceleration due to gravity. Thus, the motion in the direction that the ball was thrown is the only behavior that needs to be added.

The new b-thread has the same pattern as other motion b-threads. Each time the event endSleep is triggered this motion b-thread requests the event takeStepX, and then updates the new x-axis coordinate of the ball. The b-thread is as follows:

```
while (true) {
    bp.bSync(none, endSleep, none);
    bp.bSync(takeStepX, none, none);
    double x = calcNewX(); //updates new x-axis coordinates
}
```

Notice that the main difference between this motion b-thread and the earlier ones is the fact that this one does not trigger the b-thread **Sleep**. This is because the motion b-thread in charge of the motion towards the ground already does this. Since we assume that every object has a single clock and all its b-threads work in a way that is aligned with that clock, only one motion b-thread triggers **Sleep**. We call it the *main motion b-thread*. All other b-threads (control and motion) just wait for the event endSleep when a synchronization with the clock is called for.

This scenario presents a problem that can occur when programming animations using behavioral programming. Sometimes a control b-thread can affect more than one motion b-thread even when this is not desirable. The fact that both motion b-threads work with the same clock means that, automatically, when takeStepY is blocked due to the y-axis velocity being near zero the ball stops moving along the x-axis too. If this scenario is not desired, then creating the b-thread **Sleep** should not be done by the motion b-thread that represents the motion on the y-axis. Rather, it can be done by creating a new main motion b-thread.

In our example, every time the ball hits the ground the direction of the y-axis velocity is flipped and its speed decreases due to friction. Although the

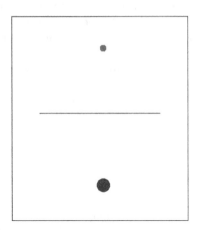

**Fig. 5.** Circle trying to pass an obstacle to get to its destination

x-axis velocity should not be flipped its speed should decrease. This can be done easily by adding a control b-thread that waits for the event `hitGround` and then decreases the speed of the x-axis velocity.

An example of this animation can be viewed here:
https://www.dropbox.com/s/ldy2wjv122s5lia/Sec5Sub1.mp4.

## 5.2    Blocking Unwanted Continuous Behaviors

When using more than one motion b-thread it is possible to block some of the events requested by some of those b-threads. Every time a specific motion is deemed unnecessary or harmful, an event requested by the motion b-thread representing it can be blocked by a control b-thread.

This is demonstrated by the following example, which involves a green circle that has to get to a destination point (depicted by a red circle), overcoming a mid-way obstacle (in the form of a line). The green circle has to first move to the closest edge of the obstacle and then move to the destination. There are three motion b-threads involved (Fig. 5):

1. **MoveY-** This b-thread adds one unit to the circle's y-axis coordinate every time tick, and is the main motion b-thread, since the circle's coordinates should be increased until it reaches its destination.
2. **MoveX1-** This b-thread adds one unit to the circle's x-axis coordinate every time tick.
3. **MoveX2-** This b-thread removes one unit from the circle's x-axis coordinate every time tick.

Since the circle is continuously moving forward on the y-axis, the b-thread **MoveY** should run until the circle reaches the destination. If the circle passes the obstacle from the right-hand side, **MoveX1** should run until the circle reaches the obstacle. The b-thread **MoveX2** should start running only when the circle reaches the obstacle, and should stop when it reaches the destination.

In this example there is one control b-thread. As long as the circle has not reached the obstacle it blocks the event moveX2. After that, as long as the circle has not reached the destination, this b-thread blocks the event moveX1. When the ball reaches the destination it should stop moving, which is why moveX1, moveX2 and moveY are blocked. The b-thread is as follows:

```
//continues until circle reaches the obstacle
while(!reachObstacle())
    bp.bSync(none, endSleep, moveX2);

//continues until circle reaches the destination
while(!reachDestination())
    bp.bSync(none, endSleep, moveX1);

//blocks all movement of circle
bp.bSync(none, none, new EventSet(moveY, moveX1, moveX2));
```

An example of this animation can be viewed here: https://www.dropbox.com/s/kad7uicwipwqfls/Sec5Sub2.mp4.

## 5.3   Random Continuous Behaviors

Imagine a winding corridor, and suppose that one should get an object from one end of the corridor to the other. There are many known ways to get the object to its destination. Here we show how animation using behavioral programming can be used for this (Fig. 6).

The solution to this problem using BP is very simple. There is a set of directions $D$ in which the object can move. These are defined ahead of time. For every direction $d \in D$ a motion b-thread (**Move**) and a control b-thread (**BlockMove**) are written.

The b-thread **Move** works in a different way from the motion b-threads presented so far. It waits for the event takeStep($d$), and then updates the coordinates of the object according to the time passed and the direction $d$. **Move** is as follows:

```
while (true) {
    bp.bSync(none, takeStep, none); //waits for takeStep(f)
    //updates coordinates according to the function f
    x += speedX;
    y += speedY;
}
```

Every time tick, **BlockMove** checks if moving the object in the direction $d$ will result in the object being too close to the walls of the corridor, and blocks the event takeStep($d$) if it does. Here is how this is programmed:

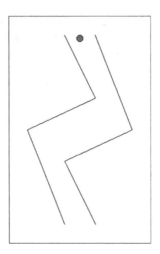

**Fig. 6.** An object that wants to get from one end of a winding corridor to the other

```
bp.bSync(none, endSleep, event);
while (true) {
    //checks if moving in the direction of function f results in
        intersection with the borders
    if(intersectWithBorders())
        bp.bSync(none, endSleep, takeStep); //blocks takeStep(f) until
            next time tick
    else
        bp.bSync(none, endSleep, none);
}
```

To trigger the event `takeStep`$(d)$, another b-thread is used, which is the main motion b-thread. It waits for a time tick and then arranges the events `takeStep`$(d)$ for every direction $d \in D$ in a random ordered list, and then requests the list. This results in the object taking a step in a random direction, but not in a direction that brings it too close to the walls of the corridor (because in this case the relevant event is blocked).

If the set of directions is chosen correctly (the average direction of the set is always in the general direction of the corridor) the object succeeds in getting from one side of the corridor to the other.

An example of this animation can be viewed here: https://www.dropbox.com/s/mqd239tu02xjbau/Sec5Sub3.mp4.

## 6   Flock Movements

Boids is an algorithm that simulates the flocking behavior of birds; see [23]. The basic algorithm consists of three rules that each bird follows:

1. Separation- maintain a small distance from other birds.
2. Alignment- try to match the velocity with the average velocity of the flock.
3. Cohesion- fly towards the center of mass of the flock.

Other behaviors can be added, such as flying away from the center of mass of the flock when there is a threat, maintaining a certain minimum and maximum speed, and keeping away from walls and other objects. In this example, the birds fly in a flock as long as there is no threat. When a threat occurs (simulated in our example by a mouse left-click) the birds fly away from the flock. When they stop flying in a united flock (the mouse is right-clicked) the birds continue flying, keeping away from each other and other objects, and they do not follow the alignment and cohesion rules.

Since this algorithm is based on the birds' individual behaviors, it can be easily implemented using behavioral programming. We set things up so that every bird in the flock has a motion b-thread for each rule. Control b-threads are used to block events requested by motion b-threads that represent rules that are not relevant to the state of the bird or flock.

Each bird has the following motion b-threads:

- **Boid-** Every time tick, this b-thread updates the coordinates according to the velocity and the time passed. This is the main motion b-thread.
- **MatchSpeed-** Every time tick, this b-thread requests the event `matchSpeed` and updates the velocity so that it is closer to the average velocity of the rest of the flock.
- **FlyTowardsCenterOfMass-** Every time tick, this b-thread requests the event `flyTowardsCenterOfMass`, and moves the bird towards the center of the flock.
- **FlyAwayFromCenterOfMass-** Every time tick, this b-thread requests the event `flyAwayFromCenterOfMass` and updates the velocity so that the bird flies away from the center of the flock.
- **KeepSpeed-** Every time tick, this b-thread updates the velocity of the bird to keep it between a given minimum and maximum.
- For every wall $K$ **SoftBounceFromKWall-** Every time tick, this b-thread requests the event `softBounceFromKWall` and updates the velocity of the bird to make it move away from the wall.
- For every wall $K$ **HardBounceFromKWall-** Every time tick, this b-thread requests the event `hardBounceFromKWall` and reverses the velocity of the bird to make it move away from the wall.
- For every other bird $i$ in the flock **KeepAway-** Every time tick, this b-thread requests the event `keepAway[i]` and moves the bird away from bird $i$.

We have the following control b-threads:

- **MouseReleased-** When the mouse is released from its left-click, the b-thread is created. It waits for the event `mousePressed` and blocks `flyAway-FromCenterOfMass`. This makes the birds fly as a flock with all the relevant behaviors.

- **Scared-** When the mouse is left-clicked, the b-thread is created. It waits for the event `mouseReleased` and blocks `matchSpeed` and `flyTwardsCenterOf-Mass`. This is so that the birds fly away from each other as fast as possible, to avoid the threat.
- **NotCooperative-** When the mouse is right-clicked, the b-thread is created. It waits for the event `mouseReleased` and blocks `matchSpeed`, `flyTwards-CenterOfMass` and `flyAwayFromCenterOfMass`. This way the birds continue to move, but not as a united flock.

Every bird in the flock has the following control b-threads:

- For every wall $K$ **CheckKWall-** Every time tick, this b-thread checks where the bird is with respect to the wall, and then blocks `hardBounceFromKWall` and `softBounceFromKWall` accordingly.
- For every pair of birds in the flock **CheckCollision-** Every time tick, this b-thread blocks the `keepAway` event of both birds if they are not close to each other. This is so they will not fly away from each other when there is no need to do so.

The b-threads above implement the Boid algorithm using BP. It is an example of how animation with BP integrates defining local rules between various objects that have synthetic vision with BP, to further simplify the creation of complex computerized animations.

Examples of this animation can be viewed here:
https://www.dropbox.com/s/g6zu5n34psxaoi3/flock.mp4, and here:
https://www.dropbox.com/s/yt7lhixhukuyu35/flock%205%20X2.avi

The boid animation was based on open source code that can be downloaded here: http://ultrastudio.org/en/Project:Boids.

## 7   Future Work

In the billiard and flock examples, each object had a number of behaviors. Since each of these was turned into a b-thread, there are many context switches between b-threads before the new coordinates of an object can be calculated. It takes a while to execute these context switches, because the system needs to check that the next event to be triggered is not blocked by any b-thread, so that it has to be compared to all the blocked events in the program.

In these two examples there is a relatively large number of objects. This can create a problem if the time between each clock tick is too short. When this occurs, an object with high priority can execute two or more moves, while an object with a lower priority does not move at all. This happens when the `endSleep` event of the higher priority object is requested before the `endSleep` event of the lower priority object is triggered, which results in the `endSleep` event of the higher priority object being triggered instead of the `endSleep` event of the lower priority object. When this happens, it can be seen on-screen; some of the objects move, while others do not. To solve this problem, the context switch between b-threads should be optimized.

In addition to optimizing the algorithm for the context switch between b-threads, further work should be done on behavioral programming with multiple time scales [20]. Our work on programming animation using BP enables using a different clock, and hence a different time scale, for each object. Although objects then move independently of each other, they still share common variables and events. More work can be done on rendering the behaviors of these objects truly independent, while still synchronizing their execution.

Our work simplifies programming animation, but is still far from becoming as simple as we would like. Research could be done on analyzing how animation is described informally in layman's terms, and then using the results to suggest formal programming language primitives to enhance the BP paradigm with means for specifying animation. Also, the physical calculations in this article are carried out in conventional code, and it would be beneficial for users to have a system that incorporates a feature that enables making these calculations directly from a mathematical formula. In addition, functionality should be added to BP, to give the user a better illusion that motion b-threads are actually continuous. This will make programming animation more user-friendly to non-programmers.

Additional work can also be done on more complex animation examples. What comes to mind are compound objects that have many moving parts, such as worm or a human. Another example is of an object with dynamic boundaries, such as a stress ball. Other complex animations would involve the merging and splitting of objects; cells, for example.

**Acknowledgements.** Part of this research was supported by the I- CORE program of the Israel Planning and Budgeting Committee and the Israel Science Foundation.

# References

1. Damm, W., Harel, D.: LSCs: breathing life into message sequence charts. Formal Methods Syst. Des. **19**(1), 45–80 (2001)
2. Harel, D., Marelly, R.: Come, Let's Play: Scenario-Based Programming Using LSCs and the Play-Engine. Springer, New York (2003)
3. Harel, D., Maoz, S., Szekely, S., Barkan, D.: PlayGo: towards a comprehensive tool for scenario based programming. In: Proceedings of the IEEE/ACM 25th International Conference on Automated Software Engineering (ASE 2010), Antwerp, Belgium, pp. 359–360 (2010)
4. Harel, D., Marron, A., Weiss, G.: Programming coordinated behavior in Java. In: D'Hondt, T. (ed.) ECOOP 2010. LNCS, vol. 6183, pp. 250–274. Springer, Heidelberg (2010)
5. Harel, D., Kantor, A., Katz, G.: Relaxing synchronization constraints in behavioral programs. In: McMillan, K., Middeldorp, A., Voronkov, A. (eds.) LPAR-19 2013. LNCS, vol. 8312, pp. 355–372. Springer, Heidelberg (2013)
6. Wiener, G., Weiss, G., Marron, A.: Coordinating and visualizing independent behaviors in erlang. In: Fritchie, S.L., Sagonas, K.F. (eds.) Erlang Workshop, pp. 13–22. ACM (2010)

7. Marron, A., Weiss, G., Wiener, G.: A decentralized approach for programming interactive applications with javascript and blockly. In: Proceedings of the 2nd Edition on Programming Systems, Languages and Applications Based on Actors, Agents, and Decentralized Control Abstractions, AGERE! 2012, pp. 59–70. ACM, New York (2012)

8. Harel, D., Marron, A., Weiss, G.: Behavioral programming. Commun. ACM **55**(7), 90–100 (2012)

9. Devillers, F., Donikian, S.: A scenario language to orchestrate virtual world evolution. In: SCA 2003: Proceedings of the 2003 ACM SIGGRAPH/Eurographics Symposium on Computer Animation, Aire-la-Ville, Switzerland, Switzerland, pp. 265–275. Eurographics Association (2003)

10. Atir, Y., Harel, D.: Using LSCs for scenario authoring in tactical simulators. In: Proceedings of Summer Computer Simulation Conference (SCSC 2007), pp. 437–442 (2007)

11. Yu, Q., Terzopoulos, D.: A decision network framework for the behavioral animation of virtual humans. In: Proceedings of the 2007 ACM SIGGRAPH/Eurographics Symposium on Computer Animation, pp. 119–128. Eurographics Association (2007)

12. Haumann, D.R., Parent, R.E.: The behavioral test-bed: obtaining complex behavior from simple rules. Vis. Comput. **4**(6), 332–347 (1988)

13. Renault, O., Magnenat-Thalmann, N., Cui, M., Thalmann, D.: A vision-based approach to behavioral animation (1990)

14. Noser, H., Thalmann, D.: Sensor-based synthetic actors in a tennis game simulation. Vis. Comput. **14**(4), 193–205 (1998)

15. Peters, C., O'Sullivan, C.: Bottom-up visual attention for virtual human animation. In: 16th International Conference on Computer Animation and Social Agents, pp. 111–117. IEEE (2003)

16. Ondřej, J., Pettré, J., Olivier, A.H., Donikian, S.: A synthetic-vision based steering approach for crowd simulation. ACM Trans. Graph. (TOG) **29**, 123 (2010). ACM

17. Goldenstein, S., Karavelas, M., Metaxas, D., Guibas, L., Aaron, E., Goswami, A.: Scalable nonlinear dynamical systems for agent steering and crowd simulation. Comput. Graph. **25**(6), 983–998 (2001)

18. Treuille, A., Cooper, S., Popović, Z.: Continuum crowds. ACM Trans. Graph. (TOG) **25**, 1160–1168 (2006). ACM

19. Alur, R., Courcoubetis, C., Henzinger, T.A., Ho, P.: Hybrid automata: an algorithmic approach to the specification and verification of hybrid systems. In: Hybrid Systems, pp. 209–229 (1992)

20. Harel, D., Marron, A., Wiener, G., Weiss, G.: Behavioral programming, decentralized control, and multiple time scales. In: Lopes, C.V. (ed.) SPLASH Workshops, pp. 171–182. ACM (2011)

21. Shimony, B., Nikolaidis, I., Gburzynski, P., Stroulia, E.: On coordination tools in the picos tuples system. In: Proceedings of the 2nd Workshop on Software Engineering for Sensor Network Applications, SESENA 2011, pp. 19–24. ACM, New York (2011)

22. Kugler, H., Plock, C., Roberts, A.: Synthesizing biological theories. In: Gopalakrishnan, G., Qadeer, S. (eds.) CAV 2011. LNCS, vol. 6806, pp. 579–584. Springer, Heidelberg (2011)

23. Reynolds, C.W.: Flocks, herds and schools: a distributed behavioral model. In: Stone, M.C. (ed.) SIGGRAPH, pp. 25–34. ACM (1987)

# The Event Coordination Notation:
# Behaviour Modelling Beyond Mickey Mouse

Jesper Jepsen[1] and Ekkart Kindler[2(✉)]

[1] Alumnus of DTU Compute, Kgs. Lyngby, Denmark
jepsen.jesper@gmail.com
[2] DTU Compute, Technical University of Denmark, Kgs. Lyngby, Denmark
ekki@dtu.dk

**Abstract.** The *Event Coordination Notation* (*ECNO*) allows modelling the desired behaviour of a software system on top of any object-oriented software. Together with existing technologies from *Model-based Software Engineering* (*MBSE*) for automatically generating the software for the structural parts, ECNO allows generating fully functional software from a combination of class diagrams and ECNO models. What is more, software generated from *ECNO* models, integrates with existing software and software generated by other technologies.

ECNO started out from some challenges in behaviour modelling and some requirements on behaviour modelling approaches, which we pointed out in a paper presented at the second BMFA workshop [1]; the integration with pre-existing software was but one of these requirements.

Different ideas and concepts of ECNO have been presented before – mostly with neat and small examples, which exhibit one special aspect of ECNO or another; and it would be fair to call them "Mickey Mouse examples".

In this paper, we give a concise overview of the motivation, ideas, and concepts of ECNO. More importantly, we discuss a larger system, which was completely generated from the underlying models: a workflow management system. This way, we demonstrate that ECNO can be used for modelling software beyond the typical Mickey Mouse examples. This example demonstrates that the essence of workflow management – including its behaviour – can be captured in ECNO: in a sense, it is a domain model of workflow management, from which a fully functioning workflow engine can be generated.

**Keywords:** Workflow engine · Meta-modelling · Behaviour modelling · Event Coordination · Code generation

## 1   Introduction

Long before the advent of *Model-based Software Engineering* (*MBSE*) and one of its main driving forces, the *Model-driven Architecture* (*MDA*) [2], there was an endeavor to better understand and distill the nature of communication and

© Springer International Publishing Switzerland 2015
E. Roubtsova et al. (Eds.): BM-FA 2009-2014, LNCS 6368, pp. 133–164, 2015.
DOI: 10.1007/978-3-319-21912-7_6

interaction in concurrent systems – with pioneering work of Petri [3], Hoare [4,5], Harel [6], and Milner [7] developing modelling notations for behaviour and identifying the fundamental concepts of communication and coordination, which are still valid to date. Today, there exist a plethora of modelling notations for modelling the behaviour of distributed, concurrent, or cooperating systems based on theses concepts.

With the advent of Model-based Software Engineering, models received even more attention – with the promise that a software system (or at least major parts of it) could be automatically generated from these models. Using technologies like the Eclipse Modeling Framework (EMF) [8] can save a lot of programming, making software development significantly faster and the resulting software more reliable. Most of the automatically generated code, however, concerns the structural parts of the software or standard functionality, but not the actual behaviour.

In view of the fact that notations for modelling behaviour have been out there for a quite a long time, it might appear a bit surprising that the use of behaviour models lags a bit behind in Model-based Software Engineering. There are different reasons for that. One reason is that the structural models, such as class diagrams, typically, lack a natural mechanism for "hooking" in behaviour on a higher level of abstraction. The only mechanism they provide for "hooking in" behaviour is method invocation – which is quite different from the communication mechanisms proposed by Hoare [4] and Milner [7]. Other reasons why behaviour modelling lags behind were pointed out in our contribution to the second BMFA workshop [1]: e.g. lack of mechanisms for integration with existing software which would allow for a smooth transition from programming software to modelling it.

Starting from these issues and challenges, we gradually developed a notation for modelling behaviour, which could overcome these problems: the *Event Coordination Notation (ECNO)* [9]. *ECNO* is a modelling notation that allows modelling the behaviour of a system on top of structural models (such as class diagrams) on a high level of abstraction based on some of the basic communication mechanisms proposed by Hoare and Milner. Still, the software can be generated from these models fully automatically. With the publication of the ECNO technical report [9], which covers the motivation, philosophy as well as all the details of ECNO's modelling concepts and notations and with the publication of the ECNO Tool, ECNO has reached a major milestone, which we report on in this paper.

The basic mechanism of ECNO for integrating behaviour models with structural models are *events*[1]; and events are a first class modelling concept in ECNO. The *life-cycle* of an object, basically, defines when an object can participate in which kind of events. We call this the *local behaviour* of the object; it, roughly, corresponds to what Harel and Marelly [10] call *intra-object behaviour*.

---

[1] In Milner's terminology, our events would be called *actions*, and in Hoare's terminology events would be channels or channel names.

ECNO provides different ways for defining the local behaviour of objects; the default way for modelling the life-cycle of objects in ECNO, however, is a simple form of Petri nets, which we call *ECNO nets*.

The more interesting part of ECNO, however, is the coordination of the behaviour of different objects that need to join in on the execution of events. ECNO provides *coordination diagrams* for defining which partners need to participate in an event, in a given situation. We call this the *global behavior*, whereas Harel and Marelly [10] would call it inter-object behaviour. The mechanisms used in coordination diagrams are similar to the communication mechanisms of Hoare and Milner, but – as we will see later – coordination diagrams are more general in that many partners can be required, and more than one event might be jointly executed. Moreover, the partners that are required to participate in an event, can depend on the current situation and the underlying object structure. We call the particular combination of objects and events that meet the requirements of the coordination diagram and are executed together an *interaction*.

Altogether, ECNO allows modelling the desired behaviour of software systems on a high level of abstraction (on top of structural software models), from which fully functioning software can be generated fully automatically. To achieve this, ECNO uses a carefully balanced and adjusted set of concepts and, on the technical sided, was designed so that it integrates with different MBSE and object-oriented technologies.

In this paper, we give an overview of the concepts of ECNO and provide some motivation and philosophical background. We informally introduce the main idea and concepts of ECNO by a simple, but complete, example in Sect. 2. In Sect. 3, we give a more systematic account of ECNO's basic concepts and introduce some of ECNO's more advanced concepts.

Up to now, our published papers on ECNO used neat and small examples particularly tuned to explain some concepts of ECNO. And it is fair to call them "Mickey Mouse examples". In order to demonstrate that ECNO reaches "beyond Mickey Mouse", this paper shows that ECNO can be used for modelling the concepts of workflow management, including their behaviour, from which a workflow engine can be generated fully automatically. This model, is discussed in Sect. 4; it was developed in a 5-month master's project [11]. Even though, we consider this a "beyond Mickey Mouse example", we do not call it case study; the reason is that ECNO actually evolved from an ad-hoc notation that we used to capture the essential concepts of business process models, which we called *AMFIBIA* for "*A Meta-Model for Integrating Business Process Aspects*" [12]. Though ECNO has significant extensions and a much more thought through and balanced combination of concepts as compared to AMFIBIA, a real case study for evaluating ECNO would need to come from a domain different from workflow management.

Most concepts of ECNO are actually not new, considered in isolation. The novelty of ECNO is the combination of concepts and its integration with MBSE technologies. In Sect. 5, we discuss the contributions of ECNO and relate them to existing work and concepts.

Naturally, this paper cannot cover all the details of ECNO. We refer to the ECNO technical report [9] and some earlier publications [13–16] for more details on ECNO – in particular concerning some more technical aspects and the ECNO Tool itself. The ECNO Tool and its documentation are available from the ECNO Home page: http://www2.compute.dtu.dk/~ekki/projects/ECNO/index.shtml.

## 2    ECNO: An Example

In this section, we give a brief and informal overview of the concepts and notations of ECNO by formalizing the behaviour of *Petri nets* by means of ECNO [16]; to be precise, we formalize the semantics of *P/T-systems* [17]. One reason for choosing Petri nets as our example here is that the modelled workflow engine will use *workflow nets* [18,19] for modelling the control aspect of business processes. Since workflow nets are a restricted class of Petri nets, we can re-use the understanding of this Petri net semantics later on when discussing the model of the workflow engine in Sect. 4.2.

Another reason for choosing Petri nets as our example is that it is neat and concise and allows us discussing the most important concepts of ECNO. Even though the example is neat, it might twist your mind a bit. The reason is that on the one-hand side, we use ECNO models for defining the semantics of Petri nets, which means that Petri nets occur on the instance level; but, ECNO itself also uses another version of Petri nets called ECNO nets for modelling the behaviour, which means that Petri nets occur also on the modelling level. The Petri nets used on these two level should not be confused with each other.

### 2.1    Petri Nets

Figure 1 shows a simple example of a Petri net, which models the mutual exclusion of two processes by a semaphor: there are two agents or processes, which cyclically run through the phases *idle*, *pending* (*pend*), and *critical* (*crit*). As indicated by the name, the two processes should never be in their critical section at the same time. This is achieved by each agent acquiring the *semaphor* (*sem*) when entering the critical section. The semaphor is returned again when the agent exits the critical section. In a Petri net, the possible states are represented by *places* which are graphically shown as circles or ellipses. A black dot, called a *token*, on a place indicates that the agent currently is in this state. In P/T-systems, it is possible that there is more than one token on a place, but this situation does not occur in our example. Figure 1 shows that, initially, both processes are idle (represented by the tokens on places *idle1* and *idle2*) and that the semaphor is available (represented by the token on place *sem*). The distribution of tokens on the places of the Petri net represents the current state of the system; it is called the *marking* of the Petri net.

The possible state changes are defined by the *transitions* of the Petri net, which are graphically represented by squares. The *arcs* from a place to a transition indicate on which places there needs to be a token for the transition to

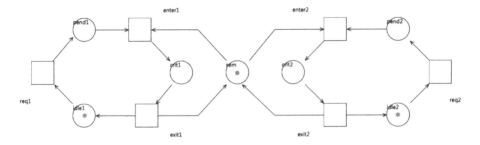

**Fig. 1.** A Petri net modelling mutual exclusion

be *enabled*. In the marking of the Petri net of Fig. 1, for example, the transition *req1* is enabled, since there is a token on the place *idle1*, which is the only place with an arc to transition *req1*. Likewise, transition *req2* is enabled since there is a token on *idle2*. All the other transitions are not enabled in this marking. An enabled transition can *fire*: if and when a transition fires, it *removes* one token from each place from which an arc is pointing to the transition; at the same time the transition *adds* one token to each place to which it has an arc pointing to.

## 2.2   Formalizing Petri Nets

Next, we formalize the syntax and semantics of Petri nets in a software engineering way by providing models [16]; actually, we formalize the *abstract syntax* of Petri nets only. The abstract syntax is defined by a class diagram[2], which represents the concepts of Petri nets and their relation among each other. The behavior is defined by a *coordination diagram* on top of the class diagram later.

Figure 2 shows the class diagram formalizing the concepts or the abstract syntax of Petri nets. We omit some constraints, though. The main concepts of Petri nets are Places and Transitions, and Arcs connecting them.

Next, we discuss how to define the behaviour of Petri nets (their semantics) by some ECNO models. In ECNO, the behaviour is modelled in two parts: the *local behaviour* or the life-cycle for each *element* (in ECNO, objects that have an explicit life-cycle are called elements); and the *global behaviour* which defines how to coordinate the local behaviours of the different elements with each other by so-called *coordination diagrams*.

We start with the discussion of ECNO coordination diagrams for modelling the behaviour of Petri nets, with some informal hints to the local behaviour, which we model later. Figure 3 shows the coordination diagram that defines the global behaviour of Petri nets. It shows the main elements of the class diagram from Fig. 2 again – with some additions. The main concept of ECNO that enable us to coordinate behaviour are *events* which can have different types (*event types*): for our Petri net example, the relevant event types are fire, add and

---

[2] Actually, it is an Ecore model, which is a kind of lightweight version of UML class diagrams supported by EMF [8].

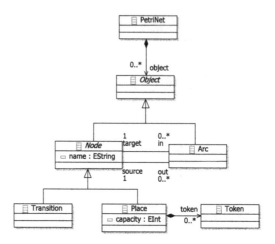

**Fig. 2.** Abstract syntax of Petri nets: Class diagram

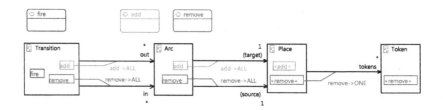

**Fig. 3.** Coordination diagram: Global behaviour of Petri nets

remove, which correspond to firing a transition, and the corresponding removal and addition of tokens from and to places. The event types are explicitly defined in the coordination diagram, shown as rounded rectangles. The rest of the coordination diagram defines how different elements coordinate their behaviour via events by annotating the underlying class diagram with *coordination annotations*, which we explain below.

Since the semantics of Petri nets is about firing transitions, we start explaining the coordination diagram at the transition. The *element type* Transition is associated with three event types: fire, add, and remove. Technically, this can be seen by the boxes inside the element types with the respective labels referring to the respective event types, which are called *coordination sets*. We will see later in Fig. 4 that the local behaviour of the element type Transition requires that three events of event types fire, add, and remove must be executed together for a Transition element. The *coordination annotations* attached to the references *out* and *in* respectively, require that all the arcs starting at the Transition (*out*) need to participate in an add event, and that all the arcs ending at the Transition (*in*) need to participate in a remove event whenever a Transition participates in such an event.

**Fig. 4.** Local behaviour of a Transition    **Fig. 5.** Local behaviour of a Token

As we will see later, when defining the local behaviors of the different element types, an Arc can always participate in add and remove events. The relevance of the Arc is that the coordination annotation attached to the reference *target* requires that the Place to which the arc points to participates in the add event, too. Likewise, the coordination annotation attached to the reference *source* requires the Place at which the arc starts to participate in the remove event, too. This way, the coordination diagram guarantees that every place with an arc to a transition is involved in a remove event, and every place with an arc from a transition is involved in an add event – initially triggered by a transition participating in a fire event.

The local behaviour of a Place when it participates in an add event adds a new token to this place. The place does not require other associated elements to participate in the add event. Therefore, the coordination set for add is not attached to any coordination annotation. Note that the label of that coordination set is enclosed between two plus signs, which indicates a subtlety of ECNO, which we will discuss later in Sect. 3.5: *counting events.*

The local behaviour of a Place when participating in a remove event does nothing, but the coordination annotation requires that one of the Place's tokens participates in the remove event. This participating Token will then take care of removing itself from the place.

In ECNO, the local behaviour of an element defines when the element can participate in an event – and what effect that will have on the element. ECNO uses a simple form of Petri nets for that purpose again[3], which we call *ECNO nets*; the ECNO nets (model level) for the different element types of Petri nets (instance level) are shown in Figs. 4, 5, 6 and 7. Note that most of these ECNO nets are very degenerated Petri nets (transitions not connected to any places, which means that they are enabled anytime).

Figure 4 shows the local behaviour of the Transition. It shows that a transition element can join a fire event any time (from the transition's point of view), but it requires the remove and add events to be part of that interaction too – this way, in combination with the global behaviour and the local behaviour for the other element types, making sure that the respective tokens are ready for removal and also removing and adding the respective tokens when executed.

Figure 7 shows the local behaviour of the Arc. There are two transitions, which can be executed anytime, which means that the Arc can participate in the events add and remove anytime. Since the transitions are independent of

---

[3] Note that these Petri nets are used on the modelling level now.

import dk.dtu.imm.se.ecno.example.petrinets.PetrinetsFactory;

final PetrinetsFactory factory = PetrinetsFactory.eINSTANCE;

**Fig. 6.** Local behaviour of a Place              **Fig. 7.** Local behaviour of an Arc

each other, an arc can even participate in both events in parallel. Actually, the participation of an Arc in any of these events does not have any local effect on the Arc at all. The Arc is a mediator only which propagates the respective events from the transition to the respective places as defined by the coordination diagram in Fig. 3.

Figure 6 shows the local behaviour of the Place. Again, there are two transitions in this ECNO net, which are enabled all the time. The first transition is bound to the add event. Note that there is an *action*, a Java code snippet, attached to this transition. This action is executed when the add event is executed: it creates a new token and adds it to the place itself (self) by using the API which is automatically generated from the underlying class diagrams.

Figure 5 shows the local behaviour of the Token. This is the only ECNO net in our example where the firing of the transition is restricted. Actually the single token on the place makes sure that a token can be removed only once in its life-time – the very semantics of a token in Petri nets. The action (Java code snippet) attached to the transition actually removes the token from the place (its owner) when the Token participates in a remove event.

Together, the models for the local behaviour (Figs. 4, 5, 6 and 7) and for the global behaviour (Fig. 3) define the semantics of P/T-systems. Starting from a fire event on a Transition element, the transition will also be required to participate in an add and remove event, which then will require the connected Arcs, Places and Tokens to participate. This combination of elements and events is called an *interaction*. Figure 8 graphically shows an example of one interaction that is possible in that Petri net in the given marking. The interaction is shown as an octagon containing all instances of events; the

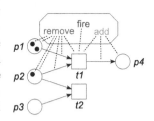

**Fig. 8.** Interaction: t1

dashed lines show which events are associated with which elements. Executing the interaction shown in Fig. 8 corresponds to firing transition t1 with the topmost token on place p1. Note, that there would be one other interaction possible in this situation (which is not shown here).

# 3    ECNO: Concepts

In this section, we give a more systematic overview of the terms and concepts of ECNO. We start with the core concepts, which we have seen in the example already. In the end, we give an overview of ECNO's more advanced concepts in order to give a more complete picture of ECNO.

## 3.1    Object-Oriented Modelling

ECNO is based on object-oriented models, in particular, *class diagrams* and *object diagrams*. In order to present a consistent overall picture, we briefly rephrase the needed concepts from object-orientation. ECNO and its tool are independent from any specific object-oriented technology. As a default however, the ECNO Tool uses the Eclipse Modeling Framework (EMF) [8] as its underlying technology. Therefore, we use EMF's terminology instead of UML's [20].

Basically, ECNO assumes that there are *classes* and *references* between them along with their *multiplicity*. Later, we also use *inheritance* on classes. Classes, can have *attributes*, but attributes are not specifically exploited by ECNO. In some of our class diagrams, we use *compositions*, which are a special case of references. These are typically relevant when a bunch of objects is serialised to a file. Like attributes, compositions are not directly exploited in ECNO, however. Classes and references are defined in the scope of a *Package*.

We have seen an example of a class diagram or a package in Fig. 2, which actually is an EMF *Ecore diagram* already.

An *object diagram* is an instance of a class diagram, which shows a specific situation of a system. An instance of a class is an *object* and an instance of a reference is a *link* – or vice versa, the type of a link of an object is a reference of the object's class.

## 3.2    ECNO: Basic Concepts

Next, we discuss the basic concepts of ECNO, which we have seen in the example already.

**Elements and Element Types.** ECNO aims at modelling the behaviour of a system on top of a class diagram. To this end, ECNO extends the notion of objects and classes of object-orientation. Note that an ECNO model does not need to define behaviour for all classes of the underlying class diagram. Not all classes have ECNO behaviour, some might be used as data only. In order to make this difference explicit, we call objects that have behaviour in ECNO *elements*, and we call the classes for which ECNO defines behaviour *element types*.

**Life-Cycle (Local Behaviour).** In a sense, an ECNO element is an object with an explicitly defined *life-cycle*. The life-cycle of the element is defined by a model which defines the *local behaviour* for a specific element type. So, an ECNO element type consists of a class from object orientation and a local behaviour; and there are some more concepts, which we discuss later. In this paper, the local behaviour is defined by a special version of Petri nets, which we call *ECNO nets*. In our example, the element types were defined by the class diagram of Fig. 2 and the ECNO nets of Figs. 4, 5, 6 and 7, by using the same name for the classes and the ECNO nets.

**Events and Event Types.** The life-cycle of an element defines when (i.e. in which situations) the element could participate in some *event*, and how the state of the element changes, when the element participates in that *event*. To be precise, we distinguish between *event types*, and an instance or occurrence of an event at a specific time at runtime when an interaction is executed. The *event types* are defined in ECNO's coordination diagrams, where they are represented as rounded rectangles. The ECNO nets refer to these event types for defining the local behaviour. For simplicity, we call an instance of an event type just an *event* in the rest of this paper. The relation between an event and an event type is similar to the relation between objects and classes. Still the nature of events is fundamentally different from the nature of objects: An event is inherently volatile and – at least conceptually – has no duration; when the execution of the interaction is finished, all its events "evaporate"; only their effects – defined by the life-cycles of the elements participating in the events – stay.

**Coordination and Interactions.** An *interaction* is the joint participation of some elements in some events. Conceptually an interaction is executed instantaneously[4]. What constitutes a combination of elements and events that make up a legal interaction is defined by the local behaviour of the elements as well as the *coordination annotations*. As explained already, the local behaviour defines, whether an element could participate in an event at a given time; it can also require that some events need to be executed together (see Fig. 4). The coordination annotations define which combinations of elements and events are valid. Basically, each coordination annotation formulates a requirement of the following nature: if an element of some type participates in an event of some type, one or all elements to which there exists a link of a certain reference need to participate in that event too. We have seen in Fig. 3 that, for a Transition to participate in an add event, all Arcs which go out from this transition must participate in the add event too. Together, these requirements might require that many elements participate in a valid interaction – once one element participates in some event. In practice, the possible interactions will be computed starting from one element participating in an event of some type, until all the requirements of all coordination annotations of the involved elements are met. The interaction of

---

[4] In practise, executing an interaction takes time. We will see later that the instantaneous execution of interactions is mimicked by executing them transactionally in the sense of the ACID principle [21]; in particular, interactions are executed "atomically" and "in isolation".

our example shown in Fig. 8 was computed starting from the transition t1 and a fire event. Note that, in general, there might be more than one possible interaction for a given element and event. And it might happen, that there is no such combination at all – in which case the overall behaviour would not allow the element to participate in that event at that time.

The coordination annotations are defined in an ECNO *coordination diagram*, which is based on an underlying class diagram. Note that coordination diagrams are also used to define the event types. The defined event types can then be used in the coordination annotations as well as in the ECNO nets for the local behaviour.

**Element State and Situations.** As discussed above, the coordination annotations together with the local behaviour for the elements define which interactions are possible in any given situation. The local behaviour and, in particular, the *actions* (Java snippets attached to the transition of the ECNO net, cf. Fig. 6) define what each element would do and how its state would change when the interaction is actually executed. Note that the *state* of an element consists of two parts: the state of the underlying object (i.e. all its attributes and links) as well as the state of its life-cycle (the marking of the ECNO net in our case). A *situation* consists of the state of all objects (e.g. represented as an object diagram) plus the state of the life-cycle for each object.

Above, we have roughly sketched which interactions would be valid in a given situation. A formal definition for the fragment of ECNO that we have discussed so far, can be found in Chap. 4 of the ECNO technical report [9].

**Controllers and GUI.** One question, however, was not answered yet: when will a possible interactions be computed and executed? Actually, the ECNO models do not define that at all. The ECNO models specify which interactions could be executed (are valid) in a given situation – and the ECNO execution engine will make sure that only valid interactions are executed. It is left to some *controllers* on top of the ECNO engine to decide when valid interactions are computed and then scheduled for execution. Typically, the execution of interactions is triggered by the user by clicking on some button in some Graphical User Interface (GUI); and the ECNO Tool comes with some predefined controllers and a default GUI for that purpose. These controllers are automatically instantiated for new elements, when the ECNO engine becomes aware of them. These controllers can also be programmed manually and registered with the ECNO engine, which then can compute and execute interactions on elements as they see fit. To this end, ECNO comes with a programming framework for implementing own controllers and for configuring them for an ECNO application. For details, see Sect. 5.5 of the ECNO technical report [9].

In our simple example, some element types and some event types, are specifically marked as *GUI types*. From this information, the ECNO code generator generates a simple GUI with standard controllers, where the user interactively can trigger enabled interactions on the GUI elements.

## 3.3   ECNO: Event Synchronisation and Parameters

Next we discuss some more advanced concepts that concern events, in particular, the synchronization of different events and *event parameters*, a concept which did not occur in our example yet.

**Life-Cycle: Choices.** As discussed above, each element has a life-cycle or a local behaviour, which in our example are defined by ECNO nets. But, there could be other formalisms for the local behaviour of elements; actually, the local behaviour can also be programmed. Basically, the *local behaviour* associated with an element, defines in any given situation, in which *choices* the element could participate. In ECNO nets, the possible choices are defined by the transitions of the ECNO net; these choices define which events would be involved in the choice by the *event binding* associated with the respective transitions. Moreover the choice defines the element's state changes when the choice is taken (executed); in ECNO nets, that would be defined by the change of the marking of the ECNO net by firing the transition, as well as by the *action* associated with the transition, which could change some of the attributes and links of the underlying object, as defined by some Java code snippet. In ECNO nets, transitions can also have an additional *condition*, which can refer to the parameters of the events (see below) and the attributes of the object in order to define additional pre-conditions for firing the respective choice. The interfaces for the local behaviour of an element as well as for choices form the backbone in the ECNO framework and allow the ECNO engine to compute valid interactions and execute them independently from a specific modelling notation for the local behaviour.

**Synchronizing Different Events.** Typically, the transitions of an ECNO net are associated with exactly one event type. But, it is possible that an event binding for a transition refers to more than one event type (in the ECNO net of Fig. 4, the binding refers to three event types fire, remove, and add). In that case, the same element would be required to participate in two or more events at the same time within the same interaction. This way, it is possible that an element participating in one event requires the element to participate in some other events too, which is then also propagated to other elements as defined by the coordination annotations. Basically, this corresponds to the synchronization of two or more different events.

**Event Parameters.** In general, event types can have parameters, which are defined for each event type with a name and a data type. The local behaviour can assign values to these parameters in the event bindings, and the parameters of the involved events can be used in the condition and action associated with the event. In contrast to methods of classes, an event is not owned by an element. The relation of all participants to an event is completely symmetric: there is no "caller" or "callee" of an event; there are only participants in an event. In principle, any

participant of an interaction can contribute a value to an event it is participating in. This could result in different elements contributing different values.
The default behaviour of ECNO's event parameters is that an interaction is valid
only, if all values contributed to the same parameter are actually the same (in the
sense of Java's equal()). We call this kind of event parameter *exclusive* parameters. And the ECNO execution engine will make sure that valid interactions
meet this condition.

In some cases, however, we would like to allow all participants that engage in
an event to contribute a value; and the contributed values should not be required
to be equal. We call this kind of event parameter a *collective* parameter. In that
case, when accessed in a condition or action, the value of a parameter would
return a collection of all the values contributed by the different partners. This
can, for example, be used, to get hold of all the partners involved in the same
event, by each partner assigning itself to this parameter.

The parameters are assigned to the events in the event bindings, by providing an expression for the respective parameter. This expression could refer
to attributes of the element or the underlying object (self) and also refer
to other event parameters. The parameters of an event e can be accessed by
e.parameter, where parameter is the name of the parameter. In order to refer
to an event, event bindings are represented as an assignment, assigning the
bound event to a name: In the binding shown in Fig. 4, we could refer to the
instance of the fire event by f, the variable the event is assigned to. When using
an expression for assigning a parameter to an event, which refers to other parameters, there is one complication: There could be an assignment of a parameter
that depends on an other parameter. In such cases, the ECNO engine makes
sure that these assignments are done in the order respecting the dependencies –
in case of cyclic dependencies, the interaction would be considered invalid. The
value of an event parameter, can be accessed in event bindings, in conditions and
in actions, by referring to the respective event and the name of the parameter
as discussed above.

Actually, it is this completely symmetric way of dealing with contributing
values to an event parameters, which helps us doing away with the invocation
based way of coordinating behaviour. Parameters are not passed in a specific
direction; they are just shared among different participants. It is perfectly possible that different parameters of the same event are contributed by different
partners of an interaction.

### 3.4 ECNO: Inheritance

ECNO also has a concept of inheritance. Actually, there are different forms
of inheritance in ECNO: There is inheritance on element types, which we call
*behaviour inheritance*. And there is inheritance on event types, which even comes
in two flavours: *specialisation* and *extension*.

Even though inheritance on event types is probably more interesting, we focus
on behaviour inheritance in this paper. For details on inheritance on events, we
refer to the ECNO technical report [9].

If the underlying classes of two element types have an inheritance relation in the object-oriented model, the corresponding element types in an ECNO model can also have an inheritance relation between them. In ECNO, however, one element type can inherit from at most one other element type, which gives rise to a linear inheritance hierarchy – multiple inheritance on element types is not supported by ECNO.

The behaviour of an element of an element type that inherits from an other element type (and indirectly from more), basically consists in running all the life-cycles of the element's type hierarchy in parallel and synchronizing them on the same events. This way, a sub-type restricts the behaviour of the life-cycle of its super types. In addition, a sub-type can introduce event types not known or not used by its super types; in that case, the sub-type will actually add new behaviour concerning the new event types since the super type will not synchronize on events it does not know. Typically, the top-level element type will define some overall life-cycle; and sub-types will just add some additional constraints on when the sub type can participate in the event, and what happens when the event is executed. Due to the synchronization of all the life-cycles of the element type hierarchy, it could easily happen that some events are blocked completely. Developing a methodology and modelling guidelines that avoid inadvertently blocking some events, is planned for the future.

Generally, we feel that synchronizing the life-cycles of the element type hierarchy provides a more faithful notion of inheritance since the sub-types cannot arbitrarily change the behaviour – the behaviour of the super types is still accounted for in the sub-types, which, for example, is not true in Java, where sub-classes can completely change the behaviour of a method by overriding it.

In some cases, however, sub-types might want to change the behaviour that was defined by the super type. To this end, ECNO also provides a mechanism to partially or completely override the local behaviour of super types. And in the actions, the local behaviour of sub-types has options to determine in which order the actions of the life-cycles on the element's type hierarchy should be executed – the default is starting with the action of the sub-types and continuing all the way up in the type hierarchy. But, we do not discuss the details here (see Chap. 4.2.1 of [9] for more information).

In addition to the local behaviour, sub-types can also add new coordination sets and new coordination annotations for an element type that inherits from another element type. These additional coordination sets and annotations are taken into account for computing valid interactions of course. Whether and to which extend this is needed and would need some extensions, is yet to be seen, since all of our examples make very limited use of this possibility.

## 3.5    ECNO: More Concepts

In order to get an overview, we give a brief account of some subtle additional concepts of ECNO, which we do not discuss in full detail though.

**Coordination Sets and Priorities.** In our example, each element type had at most one coordination set for each event type. In general, an element type can have more than one coordination sets for the same event type. For the coordination, this means that one of these coordination sets could be chosen for coordinating an event of that type with other elements. So, only the coordination annotations for one of the coordination sets of that event type needs to be taken into account. This way, the requirements for coordinations with respect to one event type is a disjunction (choice between the different coordination sets) of conjunctions of coordination annotations (all coordination annotations attached to the coordination set).

In some cases, we would like to give one coordination set preference over some others, if both of them would result in viable interactions. To this end, different coordination sets can be given a priority. Then, an interaction in which a coordination set with a higher priority is enabled will be given the preference. Section 6.1 of [9] and [16] show an application of this feature when defining the semantics of so-called Signal-Event nets – as an extension of the semantics for P/T-systems that we discuss here.

**Parallel Behaviour.** Sometimes, we want to allow an element to participate in two events in parallel. In our Petri net example, the ECNO net for the Place (Fig. 6) allows the place to participate in and add and a remove event at the same time. This way, a transition with a loop to some place can remove and add a token to the same place at the same time (in the same interaction). In ECNO nets, two transitions with there associated events can fire in parallel when the transitions are completely independent of each other or because there is more then token available at the places they have in common. In some cases, such as defining the semantics of Petri nets, it makes sense that the local behaviour of an element exhibits such parallel behaviour too. Therefore, ECNO supports behaviour where more than one choice is allowed to be executed at the same time, which we call *parallel behaviour*.

**Counting Events.** In the default case of ECNO, if an element participates in an event of the required type already, it will not participate in another event of that type, if another element also requests this: both requests will be joint on a single event. This way, we can be sure that the computation of valid interactions always terminates.

In some cases, however, we want an element to participate as many times in the event as request exists from other elements to do so. In the semantics of Petri nets for example, we would like to add a token as many times as there are arcs from the transition to the place. In order to achieve this, it is possible in ECNO for an element type to declare an event type as *triggering* or *counting event*, graphically indicated by the event type being enclosed between two plus symbols in the respective coordination sets (see element types Place and Token in Fig. 3). This makes sure that elements of that type participates in these events as many times as it is triggered by other elements. In that case, an interaction does not only take care of that an element participates in events of the respective type – it also takes care of it participating in the correct number of times.

In case of cyclic requirements, counting events can, however, result in requesting an unbounded number of participations, and consequently the computation of valid interactions might not terminate anymore (this would be ECNO's counterpart of infinite loops). Therefore, the modeller needs to take great care when making use of counting events for an element type.

### 3.6    Execution Engine

Above, we have discussed the concepts of ECNO and how they define possible interactions in any given situation. The possible interactions in a given situation are calculated by an ECNO execution engine – typically triggered by the controllers associated with the elements. The controllers will also issue the execution of the interactions calculated by the engine; of course, it might happen that an interaction becomes invalid due to some changes made by other interactions or some other programs running concurrently. Therefore, the interaction might not be valid anymore, when its execution is issued. The execution engine will actually take care of that interactions that became invalid after they were computed are invalidated and not executed at all. In addition, all interactions are executed in a transactional way according to the ACID principle. The ECNO execution engine can also be used to save the complete state of a running ECNO application to a file and later start the ECNO application again from there.

In the latest official release, the state (current situation) of an ECNO application is saved in a file; but it was demonstrated in a masters project that the state of an ECNO application can also be persisted in databases [22].

## 4    ECNO: Modelling a Workflow Engine

In this section, we discuss the ECNO models of a workflow engine, which is inspired by the ideas of AMFIBIA [12]; which distinguishes the core concepts of business processes, and separates them from the concepts of specific aspects of a business process such as control, information, and organization. Note that we discuss only the most relevant excerpts of these models. This ECNO Workflow Engine and all its models are deployed together with the ECNO Tool, so that you can have a look at the actual models in all their details yourself, and you can play with the generated workflow engine with some example processes (see detailed instructions in the ECNO technical report [9]).

### 4.1    Core Model

We start with discussing the core concepts of business process models and their behaviour in this section. These concepts are independent from the different aspects of business process models and independent from the formalisms used for modelling the different aspects.

Figure 9 shows the class diagram with the core concepts of our workflow meta-model. The most important concepts are shown in the two rows at the bottom (shaded in light yellow). The two top rows (shaded in grey) show some more technical infrastructure, which allows us structuring and accessing business process models and their different aspects, registering them with the engine, and maintaining the runtime information. In our discussion, we focus on the concepts at the bottom. Actually, the diagram is also split vertically: the left-hand side shows the concepts of the business process models (modelling time); the right-hand side shows the concepts of instances of business processes (runtime). Having meta-models for the modelling concepts for business process models as well as for the runtime information and clearly separating the runtime information from the model was one of the main principles of AMFIBIA already. Note that runtime information can refer to the information of the models, but not the other way round: The process models "do not know" which instances of them are running, but instances "know" the modelling concepts they are an instance of.

At the heart of AMFIBIA [12] and also of our ECNO Workflow Engine are four concepts: Process, Task, Case, and Activity, where Case represents one running instance of a Process (indicated by the reference process) and Activity represents one running instance of a Task (indicated by the reference task). On the modelling side, the main concepts are *processes* and *tasks*: a business *process* model may consist of any number of *tasks*, which, at runtime, are reflected by *cases* and their *activities*.

Note that the core concepts do not yet represent in which order the tasks (actually the corresponding activities) are supposed to be executed. Neither do the core concepts represent who is allowed to initiate or execute activities, or which data are needed for or are produced by the activities. All this is represented by models that represent different aspects of a business process. In the ECNO workflow engine, the three main aspects from AMFIBIA are covered: *control*, *organisation*, and *information*. We discuss the concepts for some of these aspects later in Sect. 4.2.

The core concepts do not mention any of the concrete aspects yet. They just provide the infrastructure so that a Process can consist of different parts that represent the concepts relating to its aspects – in the models as well as at runtime. The respective concepts are shown in the left-most column concerning models, and in the right-most column concerning the runtime information for the running instances: a process model refers to the models for the different aspects of that process; likewise the case and the activity contains the runtime information for the different aspects. Note again, that the runtime information can refer to the models, but not the other way round.

Note also that all the concepts for aspects are interfaces only. This means that specific concrete versions of them need to be defined when defining an aspect.

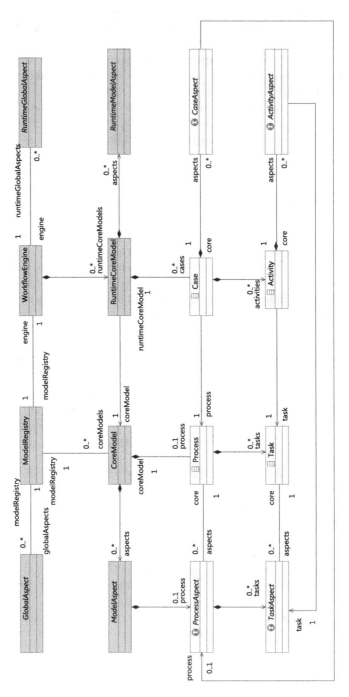

**Fig. 9.** BPM: Core concepts (Color figure online)

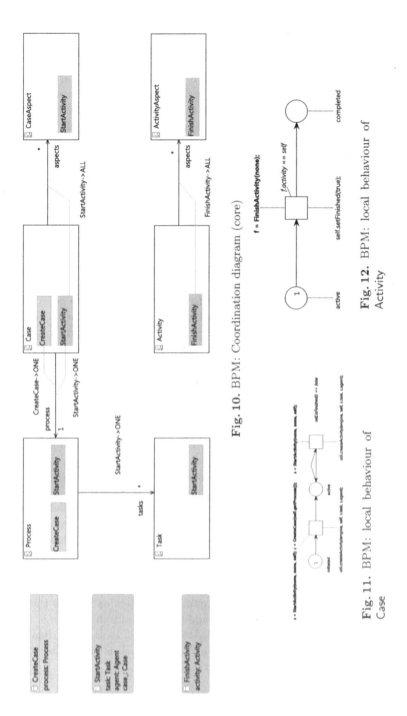

**Fig. 10.** BPM: Coordination diagram (core)

**Fig. 11.** BPM: local behaviour of Case

**Fig. 12.** BPM: local behaviour of Activity

Now, let us have a brief look at the behaviour concerning the core concepts. Figure 10 shows the coordination diagram for the core elements. This diagram defines the event type CreateCase for creating a new instance of a process, which is a Case for the respective process; moreover, the diagram defines the event types StartActivity and FinishActivity, which represent starting and finishing an activity within a case. Note that there is a slight asymmetry between the event types StartActivity and FinishActivity: the event StartActivity is triggered from a Case, whereas FinishActivity is triggered from the Activity itself. The reason is that, when starting an activity, the activity does not exist yet; therefore, it needs to be created from somewhere else, the Case. The Activity can, however, take responsibility for its own termination. Note that the CreateCase is dealt with in a slightly different way: the Case, actually, seems to trigger itself. This is a minor hack: the workflow engine always keeps one fresh instance of a case for each process ready, which is activated when the first activity of the case is started; the StartActivity will then by synchronized with the CreateCase event, which in turn will activate this case and create another fresh instance of a case for that process for the next case to be started. Conceptually, this reflects the fact that starting the first activity of a case, actually, starts the case.

The coordination diagram of Fig. 10 also shows the necessary coordinations for these event types, most of which are straight-forward. The most important coordinations concern the runtime part: the StartActivity and FinishActivity require all the aspects of the respective concept to participate in that event. This way, the coordination makes sure that activities are started and finished only when all aspects are ready for that. With the three aspects that we cover here, an activity can be started only when the control allows to start it (control aspect), all the needed data are ready (information aspect), and there is an agent available who is allowed to perform this activity (organisation aspect).

Most of the life-cycles of the core concepts are trivial – meaning that all events are possible anytime (there are some minor twists, though, which we do not discuss here). The most interesting local behaviours are the ones for Case and Activity, which are shown in Figs. 11 and 12, respectively.

We start discussing the life-cycle of the Case. Remember that there is always one fresh case, which is ready for being activated by starting one of its initial activities. The case is activated by a CreateCase event, which actually is jointly executed together (synchronized) with the StartActivity event that starts the first activity of the case at the same time. After that, the Case can participate in further StartActivity events without synchronizing it with another CreateCase event. In a running case, StartActivity events can happen as long as the case is not finished, which is represented by an additional condition.

Figure 12 shows the life-cycle of the Activity. This is almost trivial, making sure that every activity can finish only once, which is similar to the local behaviour of tokens in the ECNO semantics of Petri nets.

## 4.2   Models for Aspects and Formalisms

Next, we discuss some of the models relating to the different aspects of business processes. Note that we restrict this discussion to the control aspect and a part of the organisation aspect. The ECNO workflow engine covers the information aspect too, but we do not discuss this aspect here.

We start with the discussion of the control aspect as well as one formalism for modelling the control aspect of business processes: Petri nets or actually workflow nets. Note that AMFIBIA set out to separate the concepts of an aspect from the realization of these concepts in a concrete formalism. Anyway, we discuss the general concepts of the control aspect together with a concrete modelling formalism here.

Figure 13 shows the general concepts of the control aspect as well as how these concepts can be captured by the Petri nets formalism – actually by *workflow nets* [19,23]. The classes in the top row (in light yellow) represent the concepts from the core model again (as see in Fig. 9 already). The classes in the two rows below (in light blue) represent the general concepts of the control aspect, and the classes below that (in magenta) show the concepts of Petri nets implementing the concepts of the control aspect. Like before, the classes on the left-hand side represent the modelling concepts, whereas the classes on the right-hand side represent the runtime concepts.

The class TaskC represents the control aspect of a task (it implements Task Aspect), which in Petri nets is realized as a Transition. On the runtime side, the class ActivityC represents the control aspect of an activity (implementing ActivityAspect), which in turn refers to the control aspect of the case CaseC. The most important part of the control aspect is that a case has a concept of a State, which determines which activities are possible to be started in the current situation. In Petri nets, the State is realized as a Marking, which is represented by a set of tokens associated with some places of the Petri net. The model for Petri nets here, roughly, resembles the model of Petri nets that we had seen in Sect. 2.1. The most important difference is that tokens are not contained in places anymore, but are part of the marking; instead, each token refers to the place it belongs to. The reason for detaching tokens from places in this model is that tokens represent runtime information, which the actual model should not know about. This leaves the question of how the initial marking of the Petri net is represented in the model itself. To this end, we exploit a speciality of workflow nets: they always start in a specific marking, exactly one token on a so-called start place. So, the model does not need to represent the initial marking; we just need to represent the start place and the finish place of the net. This is reflected by the references from the PetriNet to the start and finish place. Transitions that are enabled when a single token is added to the start place correspond to the initial tasks of a process, which implicitly start the process (as discussed above).

The more interesting part of the models for the control aspect concerns the behaviour at runtime. The corresponding coordination diagram is shown in Fig. 14. Starting an activity requires the control aspect of the case (CaseC) to

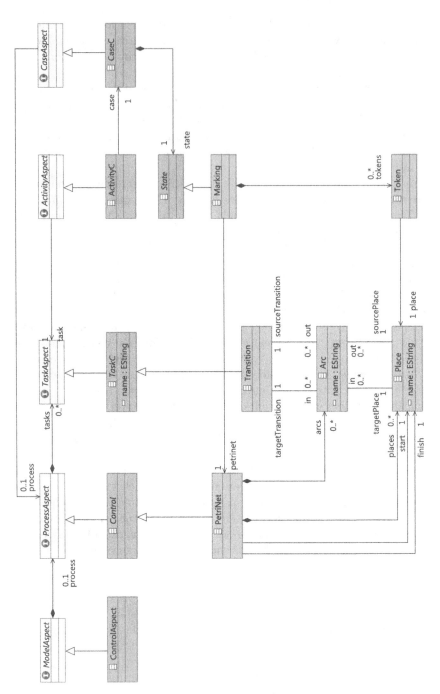

**Fig. 13.** BPM: Concepts for control and Petri net formalism

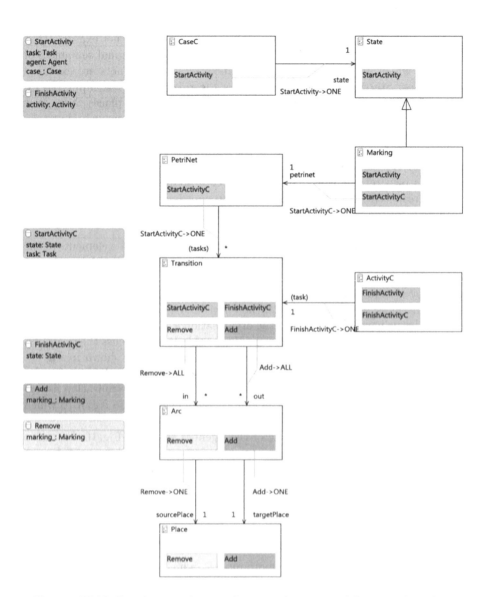

**Fig. 14.** BPM: Coordination diagram for control aspect and Petri net formalism

coordinate the event StartActivity with its State, which will require a synchronisation with another event StartActivityC; this event represents the control aspect of the event StartActivity. The state, in turn, will need the model for the control aspect – in our case the Petri net – to participate in the StartActivityC event, which will require a Remove event on a Transition to be part of the coordination. The Remove is used and handled in a similar way to the Petri net example that we had discussed in Sect. 2.1. Note that in contrast to the original semantics of Petri nets which fires a transition instantaneously, workflow nets are executed in two steps: Starting the activity removes the tokens from the input places, whereas finishing the activity adds the tokens to the output places. Note that this way, in workflow nets a transition does note fire instantaneously, but take time; this reflects the fact that activities in workflows take time.

The start of an activity needs to be issued from the case since an instance of the activity is created only upon starting it. By contrast, the activity can take care of its own termination. The ActivityC coordinates a FinishActivityC event with the respective transition, which in turn coordinates it with an add event which adds all the tokens to the postset of the transition – similar to the Petri net semantics that we had discussed earlier.

The only interesting local behaviours are the life-cycles of the elements of the Petri net. Since these are similar to the ones discussed in Sect. 2.1, we do not discuss them here. All the other local behaviours are quite simple. Most importantly they synchronize the StartActivity event with the StartActivityC event, and likewise the FinishActivity event with the FinishActivityC event.

Next, let us have a brief look at the organisation aspect. Since the underlying class diagram for this aspect is quite simple, we skip it and discuss the coordination diagram for the organization aspect right away, which is shown in Fig. 15. Basically, the organisation aspect for the case, CaseO, delegates the StartActivity event to one of the (possibly) involved Agents; likewise the organisation aspect of an activity ActivityO delegates the FinishActivity event to the Agent to which this activity was assigned.

The ECNO net for the life-cycle of the Agent is shown in Fig. 16. From the organisation point of view, an agent can start any activity as long as it does so on its own behalf, and the organisation model allows the agent to do so, which is represented by the additional conditions, which are attached to the transitions of the ECNO nets.

## 4.3   Workflow Engine and GUI

From the models above and a few more models, which are similar, a fully functioning workflow engine can be generated fully automatically. The only part that needed to be implemented manually was the GUI – in particular, the worklist which allows the agents to log in and to select, start and finish work items. The implementation of this GUI, however, is straight-forward. We do not discuss it here (see [9,11] for details), since all behaviour comes from the ECNO models.

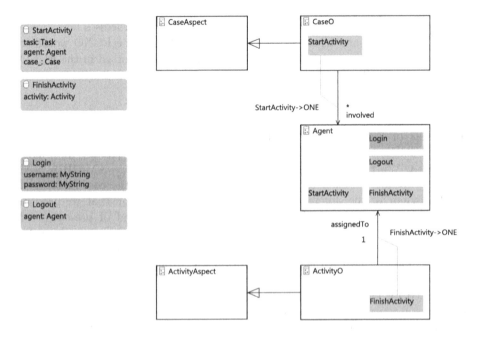

**Fig. 15.** BPM: Coordination diagram for organisation

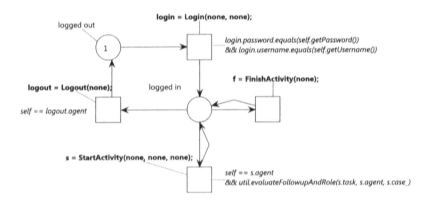

**Fig. 16.** BPM: local behaviour of Agent

The workflow engine can then be started with some process models, which cover the control, organisation, and information aspect. Up to now, there is only a simple tree editor for creating and editing such process models, since the focus of this project was on the feasibility and not the usability of its editors. Once the workflow engine is started, the different agents can log on, and via the GUI start cases, activities, and inspect, add, and change the data involved in an activity, and then finish the activity. For lack of space, we cannot discuss the use of the workflow engine and the execution of some example processes here. Some example processes are deployed together with ECNO and the ECNO workflow engine; the installation and the use of the examples are discussed in the ECNO technical report [9].

# 5  Related Work

The ideas of ECNO have evolved over many years and started out from a meta-model that distilled the essence of business process modelling notations: AMFIBIA [12]. For capturing the behaviour of these concepts, AMFIBIA used a simple ad-hoc notation for the local behaviour and for the coordination of the behaviour of the different elements. The ad-hoc notation that we used in AMFIBIA was later formalized and implemented in a kind of pre-cursor of ECNO, which we called MoDowA [24,25]. The idea of ECNO goes back to the ad-hoc notations of AMFIBIA and MoDowA; ECNO is more general and the too tight integration with aspect-orientation was dropped, so that ECNO – at its core – is not explicitly aspect-oriented anymore. Moreover, inheritance was introduced for elements and for events, which needed some careful tuning; for that reason, there is a complete Chap. 4 that is devoted to the discussion of inheritance in the ECNO technical report [9]. Starting out from the challenges of behaviour modelling [1], we then defined the core concepts of ECNO [13–15] with minor variations, which now seem to converge.

As pointed out in our earlier work [15] already, none of the concepts used in ECNO are particularly new or original; the contribution of ECNO is more in the careful combination of its concepts and, on the technical side, its integration with existing object-oriented technologies.

ECNO's coordination mechanism via events resembles the synchronization of actions in process algebras [4,5,7]. One difference, though, is that ECNO's synchronization is not restricted to bi-lateral synchronizations and that the partners required to participate in an event might dependent on the dynamically changing underlying structure of the system. Also this aspect has been seen before in process algebras like ACP [26], the chemical abstract machine [27], or the $\Pi$-calculus [28]. What is new, however, is that, in ECNO's coordination mechanism, different of these synchronization mechanisms work together, combining these coordination requirements transitively, which allows us to define much more complex interactions.

The proposal of behavioral programming [29] exploits the idea of synchronizing events for programming concurrent behaviour (b-threads). The idea of behavioural programming is very similar in spirit to ECNO – with a focus on programming. But, in behavioural programming possible synchronizations on the same event are global and not driven by the dynamic relation to other objects; moreover, behavioural programming does not allow synchronizing different events or transitively combining synchronizations into more complex interactions, nor does it come with an inherent notion of joint atomic execution when synchronizing on events.

Another major concern in the design of ECNO was the clear separation between coordination aspects and computation aspects of a system. Actually, ECNO is about coordination only, but ECNO's concept of actions provides a way to interface with the computational aspects by invoking methods or functions. This idea, however, is not new either: Harel and Pnueli [30] had proposed the distinction between transformational and reactive systems. ECNO takes care of the reactive aspect of the system by defining possible interactions – the transformational aspect is left to the underlying programming language (Java in our case) for the actions by invoking methods.

Another major concern of ECNO is the distinction between local behaviour and global behaviour [1]. Also this idea is not really new: Harel and Marelly [10] distinguish between intra-object behaviour and inter-object behaviour, which correspond to local and global behaviour, respectively. The only difference is the way this behaviour is represented. Concerning the local behaviour, this is mostly a question of syntactic sugar. For inter-object behaviour (global behaviour), Harel and Marelly use a set of Live Sequence Charts (LSCs) [31], which are an extension of Message Sequence Charts [32]. This is a scenario-based and temporal approach, where the focus of inter-object behaviour is the behaviour over time. In ECNO, the coordination annotations focus on the needed partners for a single interaction only: it is about behaviour at a time. Therefore, both approaches have a different focus. It might be interesting to combine both of them; this might in particular be interesting since ECNO does not have a way to define what must happen in a system – it defines what can happen only. LSCs [31] allow to characterize both kinds. But a detailed investigation of such a combination would require further research.

As discussed above, the ideas of ECNO started out from an ad-hoc notation in which aspects were an explicit modelling concept and therefore, ECNO has some relation to aspect-oriented programming [33,34] or aspect-oriented modelling [35,36]. Actually, from the philosophical angle, the original ideas were close to the Theme approach [37] and closer to the idea of subject-oriented programming [38]. Anyway, the explicit notion of aspects was removed in ECNO again. A bit of the original subject-oriented idea survived in one of the two different concepts of inheritance on event types, which we did not discuss here. And by using some specific modelling patterns, ECNO can be used for modelling in an aspect-oriented way: In a way, events of ECNO can be considered to be join points of AspectJ [39]. The difference, though, is that events are an explicit modelling concept [40], whereas join points are formulated on top of a program. This way, events are a concept of the domain, whereas join points are programming artifacts (which of course could have a counter-part in the domain). The coordination annotations of ECNO then correspond to pointcuts. Though stripped of an explicit notion of aspects, ECNO still shares some philosophy with aspect- or subject-orientation: joining events together via coordination annotations into interactions.

The local behaviour of elements could be modelled in many different ways. We could use traditional automata or StateCharts [6]. We mainly use a special form of

Petri nets [3, 41], which we call ECNO nets. Initially, the reason for using ECNO nets was mostly a practical one: we could use our own framework for Petri net tools, the ePNK [42], for easily implementing a graphical editor for ECNO nets. And the ePNK is based on EMF [8], which is the object-oriented technology that happens to be the default object-oriented technology of ECNO. But, it turned out to be useful that Petri nets have a natural notion of concurrent or parallel firing of transitions, when it comes to parallel behaviour (see Sect. 3.5). Therefore, simple automata are not sufficient for modelling the local behaviour of elements. Like Petri nets, StateCharts have a notion of parallel behaviour, which makes them an other good candidate for modelling local behaviour, too. Our main concern with StateCharts would be that they might be too powerful: modellers might be tempted to put too much into the local behaviour of elements, since StateCharts allow nested complex states. But, this is up to future evaluation and a question of methodology, which is yet to be worked out in full detail.

At last, ECNO has some similarities with *agent-based software engineering* and *Multi-Agent Systems* (MAS) [43, 44]; but, at least in its basic form, ECNO would probably not qualify as an approach towards agent-based software engineering. This, however, depends on which level we look at things: From our point of view, ECNO is more a notation and technique[5] whereas agent-based software engineering is more a way of thinking. Anyway, some of the principles underlying ECNO were proposed by the proponents of agent-based software engineering. The two most important shared principles are: getting rid of the thread-oriented way of thinking, and giving agents control over what they do or to which kind of request they react or – as we would say in ECNO – in which events they participate. In addition, in agent-based software engineering, agents have attitudes and are pro-active and take initiative. Even disregarding the more social notions of initiative and attitude, ECNO elements are not even active – remember that ECNO models describe what can happen in a given situation, but they do not describe what must happen. Therefore, ECNO's elements are technically not agents. But, by adding controllers on top of elements, elements can be turned active. This way, ECNO might be a notation and technique in which agent-based designs or agent-based thinking can be formulated and implemented. But, this is up to others to judge.

Speaking of agents, we should mention another approach, which uses Petri nets for defining local behaviour: Renew [45]. Renew also uses a mechanism for synchronizing different parts of a system with each other following some fixed relations between these parts. But, theses synchronisations need to follow some very specific containment structures following the so-called nets-within-nets paradigm [46]. By contrast, ECNO models can exploit the dynamic structure of the underlying object-oriented model for defining the required partners, which was one of its express goals.

Altogether, ECNO has many different flavours. On a first glance and depending on ones background, ECNO might appear as just another process algebra, just another notation for aspect-oriented modelling, just another agent-based

---

[5] The methodology part of this technique is yet to be worked out in detail.

approach, just another form of transactions, just another ... – and there might be some truth to that. But, we believe that it is the combination of these different things and a carefully adjusted set of concepts that makes ECNO what it is: A way of clearly separating coordination from computation, and of separating coordination from local behaviour.

## 6  Conclusion

In this paper, we have given an overview of ECNO and motivated some of its concepts and definitions. Moreover, we have discussed an ECNO model of a workflow engine, which demonstrates that ECNO can be used for "beyond Mickey Mouse examples". From this ECNO model, a complete workflow engine can be generated fully automatically [11]. Together with the other examples [9], this shows that ECNO can be used for a wide range of different applications.

Modelling the workflow engine consisted in providing a domain-specific language (DSL) for workflow models; this DSL was defined by class diagrams concerning the abstract syntax of the DSL; on top of these class diagrams ECNO models defined the actual behaviour (semantics) of this DSL. In a similar way, ECNO was used for defining the semantics for Petri nets – again a meta-model was provided for Petri nets; ECNO models on top of these meta-models defined the semantics of Petri nets. This shows that ECNO can be used to define and implement also the semantics of a DSL. Actually, we believe that the semantics of ECNO can be defined in ECNO itself, which however is yet to be worked out in detail.

ECNO shows that there are mechanisms beyond method invocation for integrating behaviour models with structural models. The implementation of the ECNO framework and tool shows that interactions can be executed in a transactional way, and this way be executed in a multi-threaded or concurrent environment without explicitly thinking about threads or modelling them. Since ECNO is independent of a specific underlying object-oriented technology, it can also be used for integrating software using different technologies.

What is still missing is a coherent methodology with modelling guidelines and best practices for properly using ECNO, which we plan to work out in the future. In order to gain more experience and to work out this methodology, we will need some more examples of realistic size. The currently published version of ECNO and the corresponding ECNO Tool[6], are a good basis for working on some more realistic examples.

## References

1. Kindler, E.: Model-based software engineering: the challenges of modelling behaviour. In: Aksit, M., Kindler, E., Roubtsova, E., McNeile, A. (eds.) Proceedings of the Second Workshop on Behavioural Modelling - Foundations and Application (BM-FA 2010), pp. 51–66 (2010) (Also published in the ACM electronic libraries)

---

[6] see http://www2.compute.dtu.dk/~ekki/projects/ECNO/index.shtml.

2. OMG: MDA guide v1.0.1. (2003). http://www.omg.org/cgi-bin/doc?omg/03-06-01
3. Petri, C.A.: Kommunikation mit Automaten. Technical report Schriften des IIM, Nr. 2, Institut für instrumentelle Mathematik, Bonn (1962)
4. Hoare, C.: Communicating sequential processes. Comm. ACM **21**(8), 666–677 (1978)
5. Hoare, C.: Communicating Sequential Processes. Prentice-Hall, Upper Saddle River (1985)
6. Harel, D.: Statecharts: a visual formalism for computer systems. Sci. Comput. Program. **8**(3), 231–274 (1987)
7. Milner, R.: Communication and Concurrency. International Series in Computer Science. Prentice Hall, Upper Saddle River (1989)
8. Budinsky, F., Steinberg, D., Merks, E., Ellersick, R., Grose, T.J.: Eclipse Modeling Framework. The Eclipse Series, 2nd edn. Addison-Wesley, Reading (2006)
9. Kindler, E.: Coordinating interactions: The Event Coordination Notation. Technical report DTU Compute Technical report 2014–05, DTU Compute, Kgs. Lyngby, Denmark (2014)
10. Harel, D., Marelly, R.: Come Let's Play: Scenario-based Programming Using LSCs and the Play-engine. Springer, Heidelberg (2003)
11. Jepsen, J.: Realizing a workflow engine with the Event Coordination Notation. Master's thesis, Technical University of Denmark, DTU Compute (2013) IMM-M.Sc.-2013-101
12. Axenath, B., Kindler, E., Rubin, V.: AMFIBIA: a meta-model for the integration of business process modelling aspects. Int. J. Bus. Process Integr. Manag. **2**(2), 120–131 (2007)
13. Kindler, E.: Integrating behaviour in software models: an Event Coordination Notation - concepts and prototype. In: Proceedings of the Third Workshop on Behavioural Modelling - Foundations and Application (BM-2011) (2011)
14. Kindler, E.: The Event Coordination Notation: execution engine and programming framework. In: Störrle, H., Botterweck, G., Bourdellès, M., Kolovos, D., Paige, R., Roubtsova, E., Rubin, J., Tolvanen, J.P. (eds.) Fourth Workshop on Behavioural Modelling - Foundations and Application (BM-FA 2012), Joint proceedings of co-located events at ECMFA 2012, pp. 143–157 (2012)
15. Kindler, E.: Modelling local and global behaviour: Petri nets and event coordination. Trans. Petri Nets Other Models Concur. **6**, 71–93 (2012)
16. Kindler, E.: An ECNO semantics for Petri nets. Petri Net Newslett. **81**, 3–16 (2012). Cover Picture Story
17. Reisig, W.: Place/Transition systems. In: Brauer, W., Reisig, W., Rozenberg, G. (eds.) Petri Nets: Central Models and Their Properties. LNCS, vol. 254, pp. 117–141. Springer, Heidelberg (1987)
18. van der Aalst, W.: Exploring the process dimension of workflow management. Computing Science Reports 97/13, Eindhoven University of Technology (1997)
19. van der Aalst, W., van Hee, K.: Workflow Management: Models, Methods, and Systems. Cooperative Information Systems. The MIT Press, Cambridge (2002)
20. OMG: OMG Unified Modeling Language (OMG UML), Superstructure, V2.1.2. Object Management Group, 140 Kendrick Street, Needham, MA 02494, USA (2007) OMG Document number: formal/2007-11-02
21. Gray, J., Reuter, A.: Transaction Processing: Concepts and Techniques. Morgan Kaufmann, San Mateo (1993)
22. Nielsen, H.E.: A database integration for the Event Coordination Notation. Master's thesis, Technical University of Denmark, DTU Compute (2014)

23. van der Aalst, W.: Verification of workflow nets. In: Azéma, P., Balbo, G. (eds.) ICATPN 1997. LNCS, vol. 1248, pp. 407–426. Springer, Heidelberg (1997)
24. Schmelter, D.: Eine Technik zur Entwicklung und Ausführung aspektorientierter Modelle. Master's thesis, Department of Computer Science, Software Engineering Group, University of Paderborn, Paderborn, Germany (2007)
25. Kindler, E., Schmelter, D.: Aspect-oriented modelling from a different angle: modelling domains with aspects. In: 12th International Workshop on Aspect-Oriented Modeling (2008)
26. Bergstra, J.A., Klop, J.W.: Process algebra for synchronous communication. Inf. Control **60**(1–3), 109–137 (1984)
27. Berry, G., Boudol, G.: The chemical abstract machine. In: POPL, pp. 81–94 (1990)
28. Milner, R., Parrow, J., Walker, D.: A calculus of mobile processes (Parts I & II). Inf. Comput. **100**(1), 1–40 & 41–77 (1992)
29. Harel, D., Marron, A., Weiss, G.: Behavioral programming. Commun. ACM **55**(7), 90–100 (2012)
30. Harel, D., Pnueli, A.: On the development of reactive systems. In: Apt, K. (ed.) Logics and Models of Concurrent Systems. Series F: Computer and System Science, vol. 13, pp. 477–498. Springer, Heidelberg (1985)
31. Damm, W., Harel, D.: LSC's: Breathing life into message sequence charts. In: Ciancarini, P., Fantechi, A., Gorrieri, R. (eds.) FMOODS 1999. IFIP, vol. 10, pp. 293–311. Springer, Boston (1999)
32. ITU-T Recommendation Z.120: Message sequence charts (MSC). ITU (1996)
33. Kiczales, G., Lamping, J., Mendhekar, A., Maeda, C., Lopes, C.V., Loingtier, J.M., Irwin, J.: Aspect-oriented programming. In: Moreira, A. (ed.) ECOOP 1997. LNCS, vol. 1743, pp. 220–242. Springer, Heidelberg (1997)
34. Mens, K., Lopes, C., Tekinerdogan, B., Kiczales, G.: Aspect-oriented programming workshop report. In: Bosch, J., Mitchell, S. (eds.) ECOOP 1997. LNCS, vol. 1357, pp. 483–496. Springer, Heidelberg (1998)
35. Brichau, J., Haupt, M.: Survey of aspect-oriented languages and execution models. Technical report AOSD-Europe-VUB-01, AOSD-Europe (2005)
36. Chitchyan, R., Rashid, A., Sawyer, P., Garcia, A., Alarcon, M.P., Bakker, J., Tekinerdogan, B., Clarke, S., Jackson, A.: Survey of aspect-oriented analysis and design approaches. Technical report AOSD-Europe-ULANC-9, AOSD-Europe (2005)
37. Clarke, S., Baniassad, E.: Aspect-Oriented Analysis and Design: The Theme Approach. Addison-Wesley, Reading (2005)
38. Harrison, W., Ossher, H.: Subject-oriented programming (a critique of pure objects). In: OOPSLA, pp. 411–428. ACM (1993)
39. Kiczales, G., Hilsdale, E., Hugunin, J., Kersten, M., Palm, J., Griswold, W.G.: An overview of AspectJ. In: Lindskov Knudsen, J. (ed.) ECOOP 2001. LNCS, vol. 2072, pp. 327–353. Springer, Heidelberg (2001)
40. Douence, R., Noyé, J.: Towards a concurrent model of event-based aspect-oriented programming. In: European Interactive Workshop on Aspects in Software (EIWAS 2005) (2005)
41. Reisig, W.: Petri Nets. EATCS Monographs on Theoretical Computer Science, vol. 4. Springer, Berlin (1985)
42. Kindler, E.: The ePNK: an extensible Petri net tool for PNML. In: Kristensen, L.M., Petrucci, L. (eds.) PETRI NETS 2011. LNCS, vol. 6709, pp. 318–327. Springer, Heidelberg (2011)
43. Wooldridge, M.: Agent-based software engineering. IEE Proc. Softw. Eng. **144**(1), 26–37 (1997)

44. Jennings, N.R., Sycara, K.P., Wooldridge, M.: A roadmap of agent research and development. Auton. Agent. Multi-Agent Syst. 1(1), 7–38 (1998)
45. Kummer, O., Wienberg, F., Duvigneau, M., Schumacher, J., Köhler, M., Moldt, D., Rölke, H., Valk, R.: An extensible editor and simulation engine for Petri nets: RENEW. In: Cortadella, J., Reisig, W. (eds.) ICATPN 2004. LNCS, vol. 3099, pp. 484–493. Springer, Heidelberg (2004)
46. Valk, R.: Petri nets as token objects: an introduction to elementary object nets. In: Desel, J., Silva, M. (eds.) ICATPN 1998. LNCS, vol. 1420, pp. 1–25. Springer, Heidelberg (1998)

# New Ways of Behaviour Modelling: Protocol Modelling

# Protocol Modelling

## A Modelling Approach that Supports Reusable Behavioural Abstractions

Ashley McNeile$^{(\boxtimes)}$ and Nicholas Simons

Metamaxim Ltd., 48 Brunswick Gardens, London W8 4AN, UK
{ashley.mcneile,nick.simons}@metamaxim.com

**Abstract.** We describe a behavioural modelling approach based on the concept of a "Protocol Machine", a machine whose behaviour is governed by rules that determine whether it accepts or refuses events that are presented to it. We show how these machines can be composed in the manner of mixins to model object behaviour and show how the approach provides a basis for defining reusable fine-grained behavioural abstractions. We suggest that this approach provides better encapsulation of object behaviour than traditional object modelling techniques when modelling transactional business systems.

We relate the approach to work going on in model driven approaches, specifically the Model Driven Architecture initiative sponsored by the Object Management Group.

**Keywords:** Behavioural modelling · Reuse · Protocols · State machines · Mixins · Executable modelling

## 1 Introduction

### 1.1 Background and Purpose

The modelling ideas described in this paper have their origins in work done by the authors in the late 1980s to develop a scheme for generating code from models. Since that early work we have developed a series of tools that implement the approach and have refined the ideas and their formal basis. Our motivation has been to develop suitable abstractions for describing the behaviour of a class of systems normally termed "transactional business systems". This class includes such familiar applications as accounting, order processing, workflow, stock control, etc.

This paper explores a possible formal basis for the ideas. We believe that this formalisation will help others in the modelling community to understand and assess our work, and provide a basis to extend and improve it. We also compare aspects of our approach with more traditional object-oriented modelling (as supported, for instance, by the Unified Modelling Language, UML) and explain how ours differs and why it may be better.

This paper originally appeared in *Software & Systems Modeling*, 5(1):91–107, 2006 and is reproduced here by kind permission of Springer-Verlag.

© Springer International Publishing Switzerland 2015
E. Roubtsova et al. (Eds.): BM-FA 2009-2014, LNCS 6368, pp. 167–196, 2015.
DOI: 10.1007/978-3-319-21912-7_7

## 1.2    Structure of the Paper

In Sect. 2 we introduce the underlying concepts of Events, Protocol Machines and Protocol Systems. These are the basis for the rest of the paper.

In Sect. 3 we show how these basic concepts can be used to model the behaviour of objects, and in Sect. 4 how the behavioural metadata of objects is defined. This section includes an example illustrating a graphical notation for metadata.

Section 5 explains how the ideas can be used to build semantically complete object models, capable of execution. Section 6 describes how the approach supports reuse of behavioural metadata.

Section 7 discusses the differences between our approach and other forms of object based modelling. We note that our focus on modelling behaviour is aligned to some of the aims of the Object Management Group's "Model Driven Architecture" (MDA) initiative, and we relate our work to other work in the MDA field.

Finally, Sect. 8 gives a short history of implementations of the ideas described in this paper.

## 2    Underlying Concepts

This section describes the three concepts that form the basis of the approach described in this paper. These concepts are:

– events,
– protocol machines, and
– protocol systems.

### 2.1    Events

Our focus has been on modelling the behaviour of event driven systems. Our modelling approach uses a core behavioural abstraction that we refer to as a "protocol machine". Before describing the concept of a protocol machine in detail, we start with the notion of an "event".

An "event" (properly an "event instance"[1]) is the data representation of an occurrence of interest in the real world business domain. Examples of such real world occurrences are *Customer Fred places an order for 100 widgets to be delivered on 12th August* or *Policy holder Jim makes a claim for £250 against policy number P1234.* These occurrences are considered to be atomic and instantaneous in the domain.

An event represents such an occurrence as a set of data attributes. Every event is an instance of an event-type, and the type of an event determines its metadata (or attribute schema), this being the set of data attributes that completely define an instance of the event-type. In a banking system, for instance, an

---

[1] We will use "event" for event instance throughout this paper. Where we need to refer to an event type we will use the explicit term.

event-type might be "Withdraw" with metadata (Account Id, Date and Time, Amount).

This approach to modelling events is identical to that used in other event based modelling approaches such as Jackson System Development [8] and Syntropy [15]. From a more formal standpoint, our treatment of events corresponds to that described by Jackson and Zave [9].

We use meaningful, natural language names for Event-types to aid their identification with the real world occurrences that they represent. For the same reason, we use natural language names for attributes in the metadata of an event-type.

## 2.2   Protocol Machines

A "protocol machine" is a conceptual machine that has a defined repertoire of events that it understands, and the ability to accept, refuse or ignore any event that is presented to it. Protocol machines have the property that large, complex protocol machines can be assembled from small, simple ones. We are interested in using them to build models of systems that comprise objects and, in this use, the smallest protocol machines are more fine-grained than objects. The largest, however, represent whole systems.

The use of the term "protocol" in this context is borrowed from UML, as used in the concept of a "protocol state machine" [13]. In UML, protocol is used to mean an allowable sequence of operation (method) invocations in the life of an object. Although we are talking about sequencing of events rather than operations, the intent (namely to define allowable sequences) is the same so we use the same term.

**Type.** A protocol machine has a "machine-type" which is a fixed, immutable property of the machine. The machine type, $M$, of a machine instance, $m$, can be determined using a type function:

$$M = \tau(m)$$

(Note: Throughout this paper we use upper case to denote a type and lower case to denote an instance.)

**State.** A protocol machine has a stored "local state" which only it can alter, and only when moving to a new state in response to an event.

Machines can be nested. If a machine $m1$ is immediately nested in machine $m2$, then:

- The local state of $m1$ is a subset of the local state of $m2$.
- Only $m1$ can alter that part of the local state of $m2$ that is also the local state of $m1$.

In addition, a machine has a "state environment", being stored state that the machine can access but cannot alter. The state environment of $m1$ is defined as the union of:

– the local state of $m2$ that is not local state of $m1$, and
– the state environment of $m2$.

A machine that is not nested inside another has an empty state environment, and is called a "closed machine". This is summarised in Fig. 1.

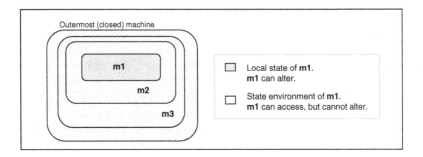

**Fig. 1.** Machine Nesting

**Repertoire.** A protocol machine has a set called its "repertoire" that determines the events that it is able to understand[2]. The only requirement of a repertoire is that when an event is presented to a machine, it must be possible to determine whether or not that event is represented in the repertoire. Exactly how this determination is made is defined in Sect. 3.3 in terms of "binding". For the present we shall take it that the repertoire of a machine is a set of event-types. The machine can understand any event with a type that belongs to its repertoire.

As we describe later in Sect. 5.4, the repertoire of a machine can change. However, it must always be possible to determine the repertoire of a machine when the machine is in a stable state.

When machines are nested, the repertoire of an inner machine is always a subset of the repertoire of the machine within which it is embedded. This is required for consistency, as it makes no sense for a machine to ignore an event that another machine nested inside could understand.

**Behaviour.** The behaviour of a protocol machine is entirely event driven. Events are presented to the machine one at a time by its environment.

---

[2] More formally: an event-type is included in the repertoire of a protocol machine if there is some state of the machine in which it would be capable of accepting or refusing it.

The machine has no capability to process more than one event at a time, and is stable between events. Presenting an event to a machine also presents it to every embedded machine.

The behaviour of a machine is defined as follows:

a. When presented with an event that is not represented in its repertoire, the machine ignores it.
b. When presented with an event that is represented in its repertoire, it will either accept it or refuse it.
c. Acceptance of an event is not possible unless the quiescent values of the machine's local state and of its state environment both before and after the event meet constraints specified by the machine.
d. By accepting an event, the machine is allowing (but not requiring) its new quiescent state to be designated as its new stable state.

**Quiescence and Stability.** A machine is quiescent when, if starved of further events (no further events presented to it), it cannot undergo any further change of local state. Informally, this just means that the processing that the machine performs to update its local state in response to an event is complete.

When a machine reaches quiescence after being presented with an event, one of the following must take place:

– Its new quiescent local state is designated as its new stable state; or
– The new quiescent local state is abandoned, and the machine remains at the stable state that pertained before the last event.

Whichever of these takes place, it applies to the machine itself and to all embedded machines. The decision as to which happens is, in general, not made by the machine itself. This is discussed later in Sect. 5.2.

Only after a new stable state has been established can a new event be presented to the machine.

**Determinism.** Protocol Machines are deterministic in the following sense. The new quiescent state that a machine reaches as a result of being presented with an event is completely determined by:

– the last stable value of its own local state,
– the last stable value of its state environment, and
– the event-type and the values of the attributes of the event presented to it.

This also means that whether or not a machine accepts an event is similarly deterministic, and therefore that executions of a protocol machine based model are repeatable.

To ensure that this degree of determinism is achieved requires that:

a. The algorithm by which a machine updates its local state is deterministic[3].

---

[3] This rules out, for instance, using multiple threads of processing in the algorithm if this can cause indeterminism by introducing race conditions.

b. When a machine accesses its state environment in the course of update, it will always obtain the last stable value, not yet reflecting any update for the current event.          .

c. A machine does not begin to update its own local state until all embedded machines have reached their new quiescent states, and access to the state of an embedded machine yields its new quiescent state.

The last of these means that, using the terminology defined above, if machine $m2$ is performing updates to its local state for an event $e$:

– $m2$ cannot start to alter its own local state before $e$ has been presented to $m1$ and $m1$ has reached quiescence.
– $m2$ has access to this new quiescent state of $m1$.
– $m2$ also has access to its own state environment in its last stable state, i.e., not reflecting any updates for $e$.

The scheme is shown pictorially in Fig. 2.

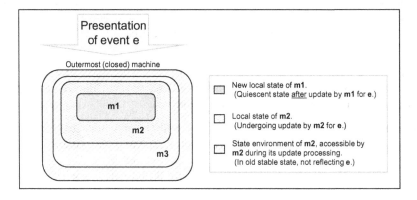

**Fig. 2.** State Update Discipline

## 2.3   Protocol Systems

We are interested in building executable models by putting together protocol machines.

In this section we describe, in general, how a set of protocol machines can be composed in parallel to form another protocol machine. We call a machine formed in this way a "protocol system". A protocol system has no stored state or behavioural capacity beyond that provided by the machines that constitute it.

In the following sections we describe how a protocol system behaves and show how it conforms to the definition of a protocol machine. For ease of reading across, the headings mirror those used in Sect. 2.2 to describe a protocol machine.

**Type.** A system has a system-type which is a unique, immutable property of the system. The type of a system has associated metadata which determines a fixed set of machine types to which any constituent machine must belong.

The system-type, $S$, of a system, $s$, can be determined using a type function:

$$S = \tau(s)$$

As a system is itself a protocol machine, its system-type is also its machine-type.

**Repertoire.** The repertoire of a system is the union of the repertoires of its constituent machines.

**State.** The local state of a system is the union of the local states of the constituent machines.

The state environment of each constituent machine is the union of:

- the local states of all the other constituent machines, and
- the state environment of the system.

**Behaviour.** When an event is presented to a system it is presented, in some order, to all of the constituent machines of the system.

The disposition (ignored, refused or accepted) of an event presented to a system is determined by, and only by, the responses of the constituent machines in the system. This determination is made as follows:

a. If the event is not represented in the repertoire of the system, the system ignores it.
b. If any constituent machine refuses the event, the system refuses it.
c. Otherwise the system accepts the event.

Note that this definition of the semantics of composition bears a close resemblance to the parallel composition operator, $P \parallel Q$, in Hoare's Communicating Sequential Processes [5]. We explore some aspects of this resemblance in an earlier paper, State Machines as Mixins [2].

**Quiescence and Stability.** It follows from the definition of quiescence for a protocol machine that the system is quiescent when:

- all constituent machines that could update their local state as a result of the last event presented to the system have done so, and
- all of its constituent machines are quiescent.

Once a system is quiescent a determination of its new stable state is made, as described in Sect. 5.2.

**Determinism.** A protocol system is deterministic, shown inductively as follows:

a. By assumption, the constituent machines are deterministic. So the only source of non-determinism in the system is in different choices of the order in which the constituent machines are presented with an event and perform their update.
b. As any constituent machine, while in progress of updating its local state, cannot see updates made for the current event by any other constituent machine, the ordering of updates does not influence the result of the updates.

This induction requires that elementary machines (those not defined in terms of other machines) are deterministic. This is addressed in Sect. 4.3.

## 3   Modelling Objects

This section describes how the concepts of events, protocol machines and protocol systems can be used to construct models that have a notion of object.

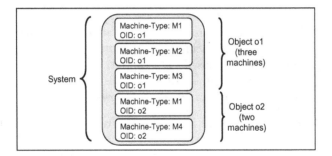

**Fig. 3.** Object Composition

### 3.1   Object Identifiers

Our aim is to be able to model a population of objects as a protocol system. We do not want each object instance to require its own machine type, so we have to be able to accommodate multiple instances of a given machine type in a system and identify them as different individuals.

To provide for unique identification of machines in a system, and to tie every machine to the object whose partial description it represents, we require that every constituent machine of a system has a property called its "object identifier", or OID. The OID is a fixed, immutable property of the machine. The combination of the OID and machine-type properties of a machine must be unique in a system.

The collection of all machines sharing a given OID represents an object, so the relationship between objects and machines is one to many[4], as shown in Fig. 3.

Figure 3 shows a system containing two objects, one comprising three machines and the other two machines. The combination of machine-type and OID yields a unique identifier for each machine. Note that machine type $M1$ is used by both objects.

## 3.2   Repertoire Specification

In Sect. 2.2 we introduced the idea of a repertoire, and suggested that the repertoire of a machine type can be thought of as a set of event-types.

With the introduction of objects the use of a simple event-type as a repertoire entry is not sufficient, and needs to be qualified in two ways as described below.

The first need for qualification results from having multiple machines of the same type in a system. When an event is submitted to a system it will be relevant to some objects and not others. Thus a "Withdraw" occurrence in a banking domain will be for a particular account. Other accounts are not affected by it and should ignore it.

From the objects' point of view the event instance corresponding to the Withdraw is in the repertoire of one particular account, and should be ignored by other accounts. To allow the repertoire to be used to determine that an event is to be ignored because it is for a different object, the entries in the repertoire of the machine are made to include the OID of the machine. Concretely, we express this by specifying an entry in the repertoire of a machine using both the event-type and the OID:

$$(E, o, \dots)$$

Here $E$ is an event-type and $o$ is the OID of the machine. The ellipsis indicates that we are now going to add more to the entry, because of the second need for qualification.

The second need for qualification is more subtle. It is required because, in some cases, event-type is not a unique determinant of the meaning of an event to a machine. Ambiguity can occur when an event instance can be presented to two machines of the same type.

Consider the case of a "Transfer" event that moves money from one bank account to another. Clearly an instance of Transfer has a different effect in the two accounts: in one (the source) it causes a reduction in the balance but in the other (the target) it causes an increase. It may also be that the Transfer is subject to different protocol rules in the two accounts: for instance, if an account is in a "frozen state", this may mean that it cannot serve as the source of a Transfer but may not affect its ability to act as a target.

---

[4] An alternative formation, having one machine per OID, is also possible but adds complexity with no apparent advantage.

If both accounts are represented by a machine of the same type, it is necessary for the machine to know both the event-type (Transfer) and its role in the event (Source or Target) to determine its behaviour. To ensure lack of ambiguity, the role (e.g., Source or Target) that an object can play when engaging in an event is added to the event-type and OID to create an unambiguous repertoire entry thus:

$$(E, o, R)$$

Here $R$ is a role name. To keep the formalisation uniform, and without loss of generality, we assume that all repertoire entries use this triple form, even if the role name is not required for disambiguation.

As would be expected, the roles that an event-type can play are specified in its metadata. The metadata for the Transfer event-type might be as shown in Fig. 4. This shows the attributes of the Transfer event and an indication, in parentheses, of the type of value that each attribute is allowed to take.

```
Transfer:
    Source (OID),
    Target (OID),
    Amount (Currency).
```

**Fig. 4.** Event Metadata

We shall use the names of the OID valued attributes, "Source" and "Target" in Fig. 4, as the names of the roles associated with the event-type. For example, the entry (Transfer, 12345, Source) in a machine's repertoire signifies that the machine will understand, and either accept or refuse but will not ignore, an event that wants to transfer funds, using the account corresponding to OID 12345 as the source of the transfer.

### 3.3  Binding

When an event is presented to a machine its treatment by the machine depends on whether the event is represented in the repertoire of the machine. We use the term binding to describe whether or not an event is represented in the repertoire of a machine.

When an event is created, some of its attributes (as defined by the event-type's metadata, see Fig. 4) take OIDs as their values. Suppose an event instance $e$ of event-type $E$ containing an attribute $R$ with OID value $o$ is presented to machine $m$. We say that the attribute is "bound" to $m$ if $m$'s repertoire contains the entry $(E, o, R)$.

Based on this, we can define the possible levels of binding between an event $e$ and a machine $m$ as follows:

a. If $e$ has no OID valued attributes, the binding between $e$ and $m$ is undefined.

b. If any OID valued attribute of $e$ is bound to $m$, $e$ is bound to $m$.

c. If all OID valued attributes in $e$ are bound to $m$, $e$ is fully bound to $m$.

d. If no OID attribute of $e$ is bound to $m$, $e$ is not bound.

The phrase "an event $e$ is represented in the repertoire of a machine $m$" introduced in Sect. 2.2 we now formally define to mean "$e$ is bound to $m$". Thus a machine $m$ will ignore an event $e$ that is presented to it unless $e$ is bound to $m$.

### 3.4   Single Binding Rule

Consider an event of type $E$ that has two OID valued attributes ($R1$ and $R2$) with the same OID value, $o$. There is the risk here that the model contains a machine that has both $(E, o, R1)$ and $(E, o, R2)$ in its repertoire, and that this machine will accept and react in two different ways to the event. This could give rise to non-deterministic behaviour.

To prevent this, we require that a given OID may appear as the value of at most one attribute in a given event instance, so that it is not possible for two attributes of the same event instance to bind to the same machine. Having an event instance that binds twice with a given machine is avoided by using another event-type that only binds once. Thus a "Suicide" event would be used in place of "Murder" if the murderer and victim are the same person.

### 3.5   Object Types

The scheme described so far does not place any restriction on the combinations of machine types that may be used to form an object. If a system has $n$ machine types, any of the $2^n - 1$ combinations could be used. We now describe a more restricted, but much more useful, formulation in which there is a fixed number of predefined object types.

To do this we ensure that every system only allows a predetermined combination of machine types to share the same OID. Each combination of machine types allowed is specified as a set called an "object type". The set of object types supported by a system of type $S$ is denoted by $\Omega(S)$ and is part of the metadata associated with the system-type.

## 4   Machine Metadata

Ultimately any protocol machine is defined in terms of "elementary machines": machines that are not defined (as systems) in terms of other machines.

The properties and behaviour of an elementary machine are determined by the metadata associated with its machine-type. This metadata determines:

a. The repertoire of the machine.

b. The initialized value of the local state of a newly instantiated machine.

c. The tests that the machine applies to the quiescent states before and after an event to determine whether or not it accepts the event.

d. The updates that it makes to its local state as the result of an event.

It is not the purpose of this paper to describe the details of a concrete modelling language, but some aspects of the metadata definition are described below.

## 4.1   Machine Meta-Repertoire

The metadata of an elementary machine type M defines the set of event-type/ role combinations $(E, R)$ that any machine of type $M$ can understand. This set is called the "meta-repertoire" of $M$ and is denoted by $\Lambda(M)$.

When an elementary machine is instantiated from metadata and given an OID, $o$, the machine's repertoire entries in the form $(E, o, R)$ are created from the OID and the meta-repertoire in the obvious way.

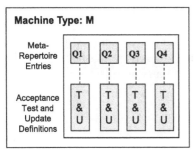

**Fig. 5.** Metadata Structure

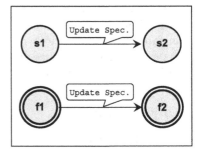

**Fig. 6.** Transition Notations

## 4.2   Machine Behaviour

For each entry in the meta-repertoire of a machine, the machine's metadata must provide:

– A definition of the tests that determine whether or not an event instance that matches the repertoire entry is accepted, and

– The updates to the machine's local state that are performed if it is.

The metadata for a machine can be thought of as having the logical structure shown in Fig. 5.

This picture depicts a structure for the metadata for a machine type, M. The upper boxes represent the entries of the meta-repertoire of $M$, so: $\Lambda(M) = \{Q1, Q2, Q3, Q4\}$. Each member of $\Lambda(M)$ has the form $(E, R)$ described in Sect. 4.1.

The lower box for a given meta-repertoire entry defines how a machine of type M handles an event that matches the meta-repertoire entry. The handling is defined by:

a. Tests to be applied to the quiescent states before and after an event that determine whether or not the event can be accepted by the machine. These tests have as their domain the local state and the state environment of the machine.
b. The algorithm that defines the update to be applied to the local state of the machine as a result of the event.

## 4.3    A Graphical Notation

In principle, the metadata for the test and update definitions (the lower boxes in Fig. 5) can take any convenient form: for instance a programming language. However, the following graphical form is attractive and works well in practice.

The graphical notation uses state transitions. There are two variants of the notation, as shown in Fig. 6.

In both variants, the circles represent states of the machine, and the transition represents the effect of an event. In both cases, the diagram represents a successful event acceptance scenario.

In the upper variant, the states "s1" and "s2" are values of a distinguished stored variable (the "state variable") in the local state of the machine. The semantics of the upper diagram is:

a. The scenario is applicable if the value of the state variable in the quiescent local state of the machine before the event is "s1".
b. The scenario results in a set of updates, specified by **Update Spec**, being applied to the local state of the machine.
c. In addition to the updates specified by **Update Spec**, the scenario results in the machine's state variable being set to "s2" after the event, this being the only mechanism whereby the state variable can be changed.

In the lower variant, the circles (this time with a double outline) represent values that are computed by the machine, using a distinguished function called the machine's "state function". This is a function on the local state and state environment of the machine that returns an enumerated type, of which "f1" and "f2" are two possible values. Again, the diagram represents a successful event acceptance scenario, but with the following semantics:

a. The scenario applies if the value returned by the state function in the quiescent state of the machine before the event is "f1" and the value returned by the state function in the quiescent state after the event is "f2".
b. The scenario results in a set of updates, specified by **Update Spec**, being applied to the local state of the machine.

One or more scenarios can be used to specify the lower box metadata in Fig. 5 for a given entry in the meta-repertoire of a machine. An event presented to the machine is accepted if there is a corresponding scenario specified against the repertoire entry for the event that is successful according to the semantics defined above.

The rule that a machine must be deterministic (as specified in Sect. 2.2) requires that the scenarios are designed so that a given machine cannot have more than one successful scenario for a given event. This is most easily arranged by requiring that, where more than one scenario is specified for a given repertoire entry, the starting states of the scenarios are mutually exclusive.

Also note the following:

- The two variants are not mixed within a given machine-type. A machine type is either "stored state" in which case it has a single, distinguished, state variable as part of its local state and only uses upper variant scenarios; or it is "derived state" in which case it has a single, distinguished, state function that returns its state value and only uses lower variant scenarios.
- The success scenario diagrams for a single machine type can be "stitched together" to form a single graphical state transition diagram that represents the behaviour of the machine.

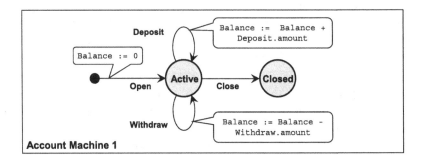

**Fig. 7.** Simple Bank Account

### 4.4   Example

Figure 7 shows a state transition diagram for a machine that represents a simple bank account.

Each arrow represents a scenario for a different meta-repertoire entry, and each is labelled with the meta-repertoire to which it belongs: **Open**, **Deposit**, **Withdraw** or **Close**[5]. This machine uses a stored state and thus uses the upper variant described in Fig. 6. The current state (**Active** or **Closed**) is stored as part of the local state of the machine and changes to its value are driven by the transitions as shown in the diagram.

Now suppose that an account can be frozen and that, while frozen, funds cannot be withdrawn. Figure 8 shows a machine that specifies this behaviour.

---

[5] Strictly speaking these meta-repertoire entries should be specified in the form $(E, R)$. In these examples the role, $R$, is not required for disambiguation and we have omitted it for ease of reading.

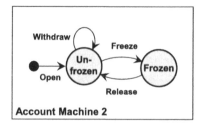

Account Machine 2

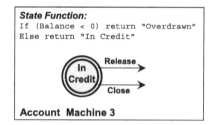

**State Function:**
If (Balance < 0) return "Overdrawn"
Else return "In Credit"

Account Machine 3

**Fig. 8.** Account Freezing          **Fig. 9.** Release\Close Control

This machine type, then, is added to the set that defines the Account object type.

This machine also uses a stored state and specifies four scenarios. The machine performs no updates to its local state, apart from the state variable update implicit in the transitions.

As the **Withdraw** event is subject to scenarios in both **Account Machine 1** and **Account Machine 2**, it can only be accepted if allowed by both: in other words, if the Account is both **Active** (in **Account Machine 1**) and **Unfrozen** (in **Account Machine 2**).

Suppose that additionally we want to specify that an account cannot be released (from a frozen state) or closed if it is overdrawn. A third machine with the metadata shown in Fig. 9 is added to the Account object type.

This machine specifies two scenarios, corresponding to the two arrows, one for **Release** and one for **Close**. The scenarios state that these events cannot take place unless the Account state as returned by the machine's state function before the event is **In Credit**. This machine uses the lower variant from Fig. 6 but, as we are not interested in the state after the events, no ending state is needed on the scenarios. Note that the state function refers to the Balance maintained by **Account Machine 1**, which forms part of **Account Machine 3**'s state environment.

Finally, suppose that the account is subject to an overdraft limit of £50. We add a fourth machine, shown in Fig. 10.

In this machine, the overdraft limit rule is expressed as a constraint on the state that results from a **Withdraw** event. If the state after the event is not as specified by this machine, the event is refused. So no withdrawal can be made that results in a violation of the £50 overdraft limit.

As a final note, a state function may be more complex than shown here. In a previous paper, Mixin Based Behaviour Modelling [3], we describe a model of marriages in which the marital status of a **Person** (**Single** or **Married**) is computed by detecting the presence of a valid **Marriage Contract**, another object type in the model.

## 4.5   State Spaces

Generally, the number of machines required to model the behaviour of an object is the number of separate "state spaces" that the object possesses. For instance,

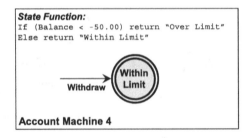

**Fig. 10.** Withdraw Control

a model of **Person** might have two state spaces, (**Single** or **Married**) and (**Working** or **Unemployed**), and would therefore require two machines to model its event protocol.

This is only a guideline. Sometimes it is appropriate to use more than one machine for a state space to improve model readability or to render machines more re-usable across different object types.

### 4.6   Proto Machines

To support the instantiation of new machines when a new object is created, it is assumed that a system has an inexhaustible supply of "proto-machines", being machines that have a type but no OID.

Proto-machines are in an initial state. The initial state of an elementary machine is specified by the machine's metadata. In particular, stored state variables are initialised to a value that corresponds to the starting pseudo-state (the black dots in Figs. 7 and 8). The initial state of a system is a system with no constituent machines. Proto-machines have no repertoire, so ignore all events.

The way in which proto-machines are used to create new objects is described in the following section.

## 5   Protocol Models

A "protocol model" is a protocol machine built out of other protocol machines by combining them recursively as systems[6]. A protocol model is privileged in having the following two capabilities, not shared by its constituent machines:

- The capability to determine whether or not a new quiescent state becomes a new stable state, and
- The capability to bring new objects into existence.

To qualify for this privilege, a protocol model must be closed (in the sense defined in Sect. 2.2) and requires that every event that is presented to it is fully bound to it, otherwise the result of presentation is undefined.

---

[6] Subject, of course, to the constraint that a system is not defined directly or indirectly in terms of itself.

## 5.1   Full Binding

The implication of full binding is that every OID valued attribute of an event is represented in the repertoire of at least one elementary machine in the model (see Sect. 3.3).

Consider, for example, the Transfer event in Fig. 4. Full binding means that when an instance of the Transfer event type is created, Accounts exist for both OIDs specified in the event. This does not mean that the event is necessarily accepted, as one or both Accounts involved in the transfer might refuse the event.

However it does mean that no OID in the event can be ignored and in this sense, the full binding requirement ensures that the behavioural semantics of a model is complete. This is a prerequisite for meaningful execution.

## 5.2   Determination of Stability

After an event has been presented to a model and the model has reached a new quiescent state, it is able to determine a new stable state for itself. It does this as follows:

a. If the event was accepted by the model, the new quiescent state becomes the new stable state.
b. If the event was refused, the new stable state is the same as the one that pertained before presentation of the event.

This determination defines the new stable state of the model itself and of all nested machines.

## 5.3   OIDs in Models

A model does not itself have an OID but every other machine in the model does have one. This is because every machine in a model, with the exception of the model itself which is at the top of the nesting, belongs to a system and so requires an OID as described in Sect. 3.1. In particular, every elementary machine in a model has an OID[7].

Because a constituent machine of a system can itself be a system, there can be many systems in a model, each having its own set of OIDs. This recursion can be used, for instance, to model an object that structurally owns a homogeneous population of further objects, as an Order owns Order Lines[8].

The OIDs of a model must satisfy the following rule: Given an OID, even one not currently used by any machine in the model, it must be possible to determine the system to which the OID belongs. In other words, there must be an "object ownership" function, $\omega$, which gives the system $s$ to which an OID $o$ belongs: $s = \omega(o)$.

---

[7] We ignore the case of a model that consists of a single elementary machine.
[8] UML refers to this kind of ownership relationship as "aggregation".

## 5.4  Object Creation

A new object is created when an event containing an OID that does not currently exist (i.e. there are no machines in the model with that OID) is presented to a model. This is done before the level of binding between the event and the model has been determined.

Suppose an event contains an OID valued attribute with value $o$, and that no object exits in the model with this OID. The event creation mechanism must ensure that $\omega(o)$ exists at the time the event is presented. The model then creates a new object in the system $\omega(o)$ with OID $o$.

Object creation is done by assigning the OID $o$ to a set of proto-machines in $\omega(o)$. The object creation mechanism must ensure that the set of types of the proto-machines selected to instantiate the object is a member of $\Omega(\tau(\omega(o)))$, the set of object types allowed in $\omega(o)$.

When an elementary proto-machine is given an OID, it also acquires a repertoire as described in Sect. 4.1. Because the repertoire of a system is the union of the repertoires of its constituent machines (see Sect. 2.3) the new repertoire entries percolate up the nesting hierarchy and contribute new entries to the repertoire of the model. Only after the model repertoire has been re-established is the level of binding of the event with the model determined.

## 5.5  Attribute Typing

The metadata for an event-type includes a "type" for each attribute of the event. Giving an event attribute a type is an instruction to the mechanism that handles event instance creation concerning the allowable values that may be loaded into the attribute. This mechanism is normally a user interface, although it could also be software.

For a non-OID valued attribute the type is a primitive value type such as String, Integer, Real, Date, Boolean, etc. with the obvious meaning for what may be loaded at event creation time.

For OID valued attributes we have so far specified the type as "OID" (for instance in Fig. 4) indicating that the attribute references an object. However, this gives no indication of what type of object is an appropriate addressee of the event, and therefore no guarantee that the event will be bound. A better scheme is to type event attributes that reference objects with a machine-type. In the next section, we show how it is then possible to ensure that events are properly (fully) bound to a model.

First, we define what is meant by giving an OID valued attribute a type. Suppose an attribute $R$ of an event type $E$ is given type $M$ (a machine-type). Suppose that an instance $e$ of type $E$ is created, and that the attribute $R$ is given the OID value $o$. To honour the type, $M$, of the attribute, the event creation mechanism must ensure that there is a machine of type $M$ with OID $o$ in the model. Moreover, this must be the case whether $o$ is an existing object or a new object created according to the description in Sect. 5.4.

If a new object is to be created, and there is more than one object-type that meets the type match criterion given above, which one is chosen is undefined by the model and must be determined externally. This determination is normally by user choice at event creation time.

## 5.6   Design Time Binding

With OID valued attributes typed in this way, it is possible to ensure at design time (i.e., based on metadata of a model) that events are always fully bound to a model. We now describe a recipe for doing this.

First we define the meta-repertoire, $\Lambda(O)$, of an object type $O$ as follows:

$$\Lambda(O) \equiv \{Q \mid (Q \in \Lambda(M)) \wedge (M \in O) \wedge M \text{ is elementary}\}$$

To guarantee that an attribute $R$ in event-type $E$ will be bound to a model $X$, we choose the type $M$ for the attribute as follows:

a. Let $\Sigma$ be the set of all system-types used in the metadata of $X$. Define $\Omega(X)$, the set of object types in $X$, as: $\Omega(X) \equiv \{O \mid (O \in \Omega(S)) \wedge (S \in \Sigma)\}$
b. Define the set $O(E, R, X)$ of all object types in $X$ that have $(E, R)$ in their meta-repertoire: $O(E, R, X) \equiv \{O \mid (O \in \Omega(X)) \wedge ((E, R) \in \Lambda(O))\}$
c. For the type of $R$ in $E$, find a machine-type $M$ such that any object using a machine of type $M$ has $(E, R)$ in its meta-repertoire: $\forall O \in \Lambda(X), M \in O \Rightarrow O \in O(E, R, X)$

This construction of the attribute type for $R$, combined with the assurance provided by the event creation mechanism that any value loaded into $R$ must conform to type, guarantees that the attribute $R$ will be bound to the model. So if this construction is carried out for all the OID valued attributes of an event type, event instances of that type will be fully bound.

In step c of the construction it is possible that no machine-type $M$ with the property required exists. In this case it is possible to create one as follows[9]:

i. Create a new elementary machine type $M'$ with $\Lambda(M') = \{\}$. Any machine of type $M'$ will have an empty repertoire so will ignore all events presented to it. Hence adding $M'$ to an object-type has no effect on the behaviour of objects of that type.
ii. Add the machine-type $M'$ to all object-types in $O(E, R, X)$ (from step b above). Use $M'$ as the type for the attribute.

## 5.7   Example

We now expand the banking example introduced earlier to illustrate the effect of having an event bound to multiple objects.

---

[9] In practice, the need to create a machine type that has no behaviour is an indication that a model contains poorly chosen behavioural abstractions.

```
Open:
    Customer (Customer Machine 1),
    Account (Account Machine 1),
    Account Name (String).
```

**Fig. 11.** Metadata for Open

Consider the **Open** event, that opens a bank account for a customer with the metadata shown in Fig. 11.

This event has two OID valued attributes. The Account attribute is typed by the machine **Account Machine 1** (Fig. 7). The machine for Customer is shown in Fig. 12.

Suppose that an instance, $e$, of the **Open** event is created with value $o1$ for the Customer attribute and $o2$ for the Account attribute.

Assuming that $e$ is fully bound and successful (not refused) then $e$ must have been accepted by a machine of type **Customer Machine 1** with OID $o1$ and by a machine of type **Account Machine 1** with OID $o2$. Moreover, the $o1$ machine must have been in the state **Registered** and the $o2$ machine in the initial pseudo-state (the black dot on Fig. 7), otherwise the event would not have been accepted.

In the case of the Customer machine, there may not have been any change to the local state of the machine as a result of the event. The point here is that acceptance of an event by a machine signifies consent to the event being possible, and may or may not involve an update to the local state of the accepting machine. Designing the metadata of a protocol model is therefore about designing the "event consent schema" of each event type, across all the object types it involves. We emphasise this to dispel the possible misconception that an event-type only needs to appear in the metadata of a machine if an occurrence of the event actually alters the state of the machine.

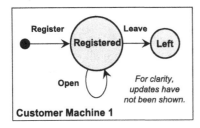

**Fig. 12.** Customer Machine

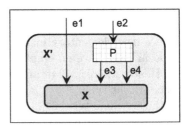

**Fig. 13.** Model Extension

## 5.8   Extended Models

It is possible to extend a model so that the effect[10] of one event is defined in terms of a set of generated events.

The general scheme is shown in Fig. 13. Here the model $X'$ is created by extending the model $X$ with:

- A new event type, $EP$.
- A process $P$ that handles instances of $EP$.
- Protocol metadata within $X$ that determines when events of type $EP$ can be accepted.

Events presented to $X'$ that are not of type $EP$ are presented directly to $X$ (as in the case of $e1$ in Fig. 13).

Events of type $EP$ are presented to a process $P$ that is in $X'$ but outside $X$, as shown in the case of $e2$. $P$ creates new events and presents them to $X$, as is the case with $e3$ and $e4$. The generated events are handled by $X$ exactly as though $X$ were a stand-alone model: $P$ is simulating an environment for $X$ by presenting it with events. This means that, while $P$ is active, $X$ determines acceptance and state stability for the generated events.

Note the following points about $P$:

- $P$ is specific to an event type and is used for every instance of that event type presented to $X'$.
- $P$ is not, itself, a protocol machine. When an event is presented to it, it must accept it.
- While $P$ is active, $X$ behaves like a model for all the events generated by $P$. This includes object creation in $X$ and determining acceptance or refusal of the generated events.
- $P$ has access to the attributes of $e2$ and to the interim stable states that $X$ reaches between the presentation of successive generated events.
- Once $P$ completes and $X$ reaches a quiescent state, the quiescent state of $X'$ is the same as that of $X$. In other words, $P$ does not contribute to this state.

Although presented to $X$, $e2$ must not itself cause any change to the state of $X$. Instead, the required updates are performed by the events created by $P$. This rule ensures that there is no possible indeterminacy in the processing of $e2$ resulting from different interleavings of the updates required for $e2$ itself with those required for the generated events.

A necessary condition for the acceptance of $e2$ by $X'$ is that every generated event is accepted by $X$. This is not a sufficient condition, as the metadata of $X$ may impose protocol constraints on the acceptance of $e2$ that are not guaranteed by the acceptance of the generated events.

$X'$ is responsible for determining state stability for events presented to $X'$. So the new quiescent state of $X'$ after presentation of $e2$ becomes the new stable

---

[10] Here "effect" of an event means the change to the total stored state of the model resulting from its acceptance.

state if, and only if, all generated events are accepted by $X$ and $e2$ itself is accepted by $X'$. Otherwise the new stable state of $X'$ is the stable state prior to presentation of $e2$.

As an example of the use of model extension, suppose that in a banking system separate events have been defined to:

- Register the new customer, and
- Open a current account, and
- Open a savings account.

Suppose also that, for most new customers, it is usual to do all three of these and do them together. It would be possible to use model extension to define a new "standard customer set-up" event that registers a new customer and opens the two accounts as a single event.

Model extension can also be used to create and send events to a number of objects.

## 6    Behaviour Reuse

One of the motivations for the approach to behaviour modelling described in this paper is to support the reuse of behavioural abstractions. The basis for this is that the same elementary machine type may be included in the definition of many object types. As the behaviour of a given machine type is specified by its metadata, this translates into a mechanism for reuse of behavioural metadata across many object types.

This style of object behaviour definition by combining the metadata of smaller elements that can be reused conforms to the pattern described by Bracha et al. as a pure mixin approach [6].

While this provides the foundation for behaviour reuse, its utility is limited without a means to define behaviour that abstracts from particular event-types, as the next section illustrates.

### 6.1    Approach to Re-Use

Suppose that the Account example described in Sect. 4.4 is to amended to support two different types of account: a Current Account and Savings Account. A Current Account allows overdrafts, and each Current Account has an overdraft limit agreed with the customer at the time the account is opened. Savings Accounts, on the other hand, do not allow overdrafts.

When a Current Account is opened its overdraft limit is specified as part of the open event, so the open event must include this as an attribute in its metadata. The open event for a Savings Account does not have this attribute and is therefore a different event-type.

It makes sense to want to use **Account Machine 1** (Fig. 7), which describes the basic mechanism for account balance maintenance, for both types of account. However, there is an apparent problem here: how do you represent the "open" event in this machine when there are two different kinds of open event, one for each of the two different kinds of account?

There are a number of possible mechanisms that might be considered, none of which is satisfactory:

- Include both event types in the definition of **Account Machine 1**. However, this pollutes the repertoire of each account type with an **Open** event that does not belong to it.
- Require that the set of events defined for the application be re-factored, for instance so that opening a current account is separated into two events: a generic open and another event that sets the overdraft limit. However, it is not proper that the vocabulary of event types should be driven or constrained by limitations of the modelling language.
- Take a similar line to that described above, but hide the internal configuration of events by using the Model Extension mechanism (see Sect. 5.8) to generate them. However, the consequent separation between the vocabularies of external and internal, generated, events dilutes the clarity of the protocols as statements about rules of the domain.

Instead of any of these, our route has been to build mechanisms into the modelling language that allow abstract events to be defined. Two mechanisms are involved:

- Conditional Repertoire Entries
- Repertoire Macros

These are described in the following sections.

## 6.2 Conditional Repertoire Entries

This is a mechanism that allows the behaviour of a machine to be influenced by its context, as defined by the other machines which belong to the same object.

Suppose that a machine type $M$ has an entry $Q = (E, R)$ in its meta-repertoire. We can define a new machine type, $M/\{Q\}$, which is the same as $M$ except that the entry $Q$ is absent from its meta-repertoire. This means that a machine of type $M/\{Q\}$ will ignore requests to participate as player of role $R$ in an event of type $E$. Otherwise the machine behaves exactly like one of type $M$.

Now we define $M//\{Q\}$, a machine in which $Q$ has been made a "conditional" entry in the meta-repertoire of $M$. The behaviour of a machine of this type depends on its context in a protocol system. Suppose that a machine $m$ of type $M//\{Q\}$ and with OID $o$ is present in a system $s$. Then:

a. If any other constituent machine of $s$ has the entry $(E, o, R)$ in its repertoire, resulting from a non-conditional entry $(E, R)$ in its meta-repertoire, $m$ behaves as though it had type $M$.
b. Otherwise $m$ behaves as though it had type $M/\{Q\}$.

The effect of this is that the meta-repertoire entry $Q$ in a machine of type $M//\{Q\}$ is "active" (i.e., causes the machine to accept or refuse events) if and only if the machine is part of an object that has at least one other machine whose meta-repertoire contains $Q$ as a non-conditional entry.

We will use underlining to denote a conditional meta-repertoire entry, thus: $\underline{Q}$.

## 6.3 Full Binding Revisited

With the introduction of conditional repertoire entries we need to revisit the discussion of full binding in Sect. 5.6 to check that the ideas set out there still work.

Suppose a machine type $M$ that has a conditional meta-repertoire entry $\underline{Q}$ is used by an object type $O$, so that $M \in O$. If no other machine type in $O$ contains $Q$ as a non-conditional entry, $Q$ is inactive in $O$ and so should not appear in the meta-repertoire, $\Lambda(O)$, of $O$.

With this observation it is clear that, provided conditional meta-repertoire entries are ignored when compiling the meta-repertoire of an object, the full binding recipe works as before. The definition of the meta-repertoire of an object type given previously in Sect. 5.6 is therefore amended to:

$$\Lambda(O) \equiv \{Q \mid (Q \in \Lambda(M)) \land (M \in O) \land M \text{ is elementary} \land Q \text{ is non-conditional in } M\}$$

## 6.4 Conditional Entries and Reuse

Returning to the example of the current and savings accounts, we now explain how conditional repertoire entries allow machine metadata reuse.

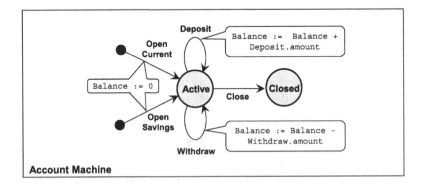

**Fig. 14.** Modified Bank Account

We start by assuming that we want to use a common machine to describe the basic account mechanism of maintaining a balance, as **Account Machine 1** did in our earlier example, but that we include both types of account opening event. The machine is described in Fig. 14.

This machine type allows either of the two (different) event types **Open Current** or **Open Savings** to be the first event in its lifecycle. Either event has the effect of initialising the balance and enabling deposits and withdrawals to take place until the close event. However, if used as it stands in the context of defining both the current and savings account objects, both objects will end up with both types of open event in their repertoire, and this is not appropriate.

To avoid this, we can create a reusable version of the machine by forming the machine:

**Account Machine**//{(**Open Current**, Account), (**Open Savings**, Account)}

in which the two entries for the open events are made conditional[11].

Note that the Current Account object must contain at least one (non-reusable) machine that includes **Open Current** non-conditionally in its meta-repertoire, otherwise **Open Current** would not appear in the meta-repertoire of Current Account at all. Assuming however, as is reasonable, that none of the machine types involved in defining the Current Account object contains **Open Savings** non-conditionally in its meta-repertoire, **Open Savings** will not be in the meta-repertoire of Current Account at all. A similar argument applies to Savings Account.

## 6.5    Repertoire Macros

While the conditional repertoire entry mechanism can support the creation of reusable machines by making it possible to "switch off" the entries in a machine's repertoire not relevant to the context of a particular object, we have not captured an idea of abstraction that would allow the distinction between two event types (such as the two open events) to be hidden where it is not required. The second mechanism, Repertoire Macros, is the basis for doing this.

Suppose a machine type has the metadata shown in Fig. 15.

Consider the relationship between the metadata for $Q1$ and an event instance that it processes. In particular we need to understand what information about an event the metadata needs to obtain from an event instance at run time. Because the metadata, by assumption, is specific to an event type and role (as specified in $Q1$) these are known to the metadata by design, and do not need to be obtained at run time. Therefore, only the values of event attributes need to be obtained at run time. This means that the metadata definitions for two meta-repertoire entries can be identical if:

– the event attributes referred to by the two metadata definitions are present in the metadata of both event types, and
– the processing required (i.e., both testing for event acceptance and performing local state update) defined by the two entries is the same.

---

[11] For concreteness in showing the meta-repertoire entries it is assumed that the both of the open events have an attribute called Account that takes the OID of the (new) Account being opened.

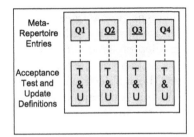
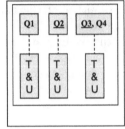
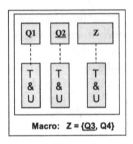

**Fig. 15.** Base Version

**Fig. 16.** Shared Metadata

**Fig. 17.** Repertoire Macro

Under these circumstances, the two entries can share a single lexical copy of the metadata. This is shown in Fig. 16. Figure 16 represents the same machine as Fig. 15 but recognises that the (conditional) meta-repertoire entry $Q3$ and the (non-conditional) entry Q4 have identical metadata and can share the same lexical copy. We now provide a simple compile-time lexical replacement (or macro) facility to re-write Fig. 16 as shown in Fig. 17.

Using this technique in the context of the **Account Machine** defined earlier, we can define a macro:

$$\textbf{Open} = \{(\textbf{Open Current}, \text{Account}), (\textbf{Open Savings}, \text{Account})\}$$

In this definition, **Open** is a macro name now defined in the meta-repertoire of **Account Machine**, but which is replaced by the two conditional meta-repertoire entries for the two types of open event at compile time. This macro definition is possible because the metadata treatment of the two open events in the context of the **Account Machine** is identical, as can be seen in Fig. 14. This is equivalent to noting that, at least in the context of Account Machine, abstraction from the particular types of open to a generic open is appropriate, and the Open macro can be viewed as naming this abstraction.

We can now restore Fig. 14 to the simpler form that it had in Fig. 7, with the single arrow for opening an account, supplemented by the macro definition that makes it re-usable across the different types of account.

## 7    Discussion

### 7.1    Behaviour Encapsulation

Most object-oriented modelling techniques, in particular the UML, do not have a primitive notion of an "event" as described here and typically events are modelled as objects. A "Transfer" event that moves funds between accounts would have its own class with responsibility for checking that a transfer can complete, i.e. that both the source and target accounts exist and are in a state to participate in the transfer. This checking might include a check that the source account is not frozen, as this might prevent the account from being used in this role.

Freezing an account would also prevent cash withdrawal, so the class that models the Withdraw event would need to include a similar check.

In this approach the behavioural states and the event protocol of an object are implicit in the tests that transactions perform to determine whether or not they can proceed. This has two consequences:

– Each transaction can potentially take a different view on how the attributes of an object determine its state. So that there is no guarantee, for instance, that Transfer and Withdraw determine whether or not the account is frozen in the same way. If they do it in different ways, the behaviour of the system becomes incoherent.
– Because event protocols are embedded in the transactions and not the object, sub-classing the object does not sub-class the protocol. This means that sub-classing cannot be used to create behavioural variants of an object in the way that one might hope or expect.

We think that these are symptoms of poor encapsulation of behaviour. Neither of these issues can arise in protocol based modelling as the protocol of an object is a property of the object itself, by virtue of the protocol machines used to define it.

## 7.2   MDA

Our focus on model execution is driven by a belief that execution at the model level has value in providing a means of validating models early in the systems development lifecycle. The idea that models embody behavioural semantics that potentially support model execution is also part of the vision of the Model Driven Architecture initiative sponsored by the Object Management Group. In this section we relate our work to some of the stated aims of MDA and compare the protocol machine approach with other approaches that also aspire to address these aims.

**MDA and Model Execution.** The OMG characterises MDA as follows: *Fully-specified platform-independent models (including behaviour) can enable intellectual property to move away from technology-specific code, helping to insulate business applications from technology evolution and further enable interoperability* [12]. (The underlining is ours.)

Moreover, Richard Soley, CEO of OMG, says that one of the aims of MDA is that *Models are testable and simulatable* [14]. Oliver Sims, a member of various OMG Task Forces who served for several years on the OMG Architecture Board, says that *The aim [of MDA] is to build computationally complete PIMs [models]* [11]. As Oliver Sims points out, the term "computationally complete" means capable of being executed.

| Contract | Protocol |
|---|---|
| A "Contract" is specified in terms of pre- and post-conditions, with the following meaning: | A "Protocol" is specified using pre- and post-constraints, with the following meaning: |
| *If the pre-condition of a function is true before invocation, then the function must ensure that the post-condition is true after invocation. If, on the other hand, the pre-condition is not true, the result of invocation is unspecified.* | *If software that exhibits a protocol is presented with an event, then it will refuse to engage (i.e., will not undergo any permanent change of state) if either a pre-constraint is false before the event and/or a post-constraint is false after the event.* |
| Contracts are a mechanism for formal specification of a function, by placing conditions on what the function returns without constraining the choice of algorithm. | Protocols are a mechanism for specifying the behaviour of software by defining the relationships between the states of the software and its ability to accept events. |

**Fig. 18.** Contracts versus Protocols

**Other MDA Approaches.** Here we compare our approach to other work currently being promoted under the MDA banner. There are two main camps of MDA, both of which take the UML as their basis, and we consider each in turn below.

The first camp is based on "Design By Contract" [4], and uses the Object Constraint Language (OCL) [7] to specify contracts in terms of pre-and post-conditions on operations invoked in objects. The claim is that adorning a UML structural (class) model with contracts enables behaviour to be captured formally [1].

While the language of Design by Contract (pre- and post-conditions) is very similar to that used in this paper for protocols (pre- and post-constraints), it seems clear to us that Contracts and Protocols are conceptually different (see Fig. 18). In particular, the language of contracts does not bring with it any new primitives with behavioural semantics to raise the level of abstraction at which behaviour is described. This means that a model that expresses behaviour as contracts will either not be executable (and therefore not simulatable or testable) or will not be at a level of abstraction above a programming language.

The second camp is that termed "Executable UML", which is based largely on the work of Shlaer and Mellor [17]. In this approach, state machine descriptions of object life-cycles are adorned with definitions of the processing performed by the object expressed in a high level imperative language, the Action Language [16].

This work bears superficial resemblance to ours in its use of state transition diagrams as a means of describing object behaviour and in its aim of providing model executability. Moreover, the state machines do provide some level of explicit definition for the behavioural states of an object. However, the state machine semantics in Executable UML are different from ours, in that a state machine may ignore an event but cannot refuse one. Without the ability to refuse events, state machines cannot describe event protocols in situations where an event must be accepted by multiple objects, which is usual in transactional business systems. This leads to the need to model transactions (events) as classes in their own right, containing behaviour rules that check event acceptability across multiple contexts. This approach has the encapsulation weaknesses that we outlined in Sect. 7.1.

Two other points where the Executable UML approach differs from that described in this paper are also worth noting:

- The approach advocates a single state machine per class. An object with multiple state spaces, such as the Person example in Sect. 4.5, would need to be modelled using more than one class.
- There is no concept of a calculated state, as described in Sect. 4.3. This means, in general, that state spaces such as (In Credit or Overdrawn) can only be handled by generating internal events that have no domain meaning to drive the machine between these states.

Finally, the Executable UML technique offers no mechanism for behaviour reuse which, in the literature describing the method, is explicitly discouraged.

## 8   Implementations

The ideas presented in this paper have emerged from 15 years of work building and using tools that support the behavioural design of transactional business systems.

Our focus in this work has been to provide tools that allow behavioural models, described as protocol machines, to be executed and tested early in the development lifecycle. This early testing reduces the risk that severe behavioural problems are found at late stages of development, when rectification can be very expensive. The executable models can be viewed as a form of prototype, and the testing and exploration of model based prototypes provides a vehicle for users and other stakeholders to engage in the modelling process even if they have no understanding of the notations and concepts used to build the model.

All of these tools are aimed at exploring and validating behaviour with users. The user interface for driving model execution is therefore designed to be understandable by people who do not know anything about the modelling concepts used. In particular, the user interface presents object instances without revealing their internal machine level structure or requiring the user to understand this structure.

The first version of the tool, built in 1989, used the concepts and notations of Jackson System Development [8], an early object-based modelling approach developed in the 1970s. This tool only allowed one machine per object and had no support for behaviour reuse. Also, this version had a primitive user interface that required OIDs to be constructed and entered explicitly by the user.

In 1993 we moved to using state transition diagrams as the basic notation for defining protocols. This allowed a more intuitive style of user interface, as it became possible to grey out the event-types incapable of being accepted by an object because they violate a pre-constraint. A new approach to binding events to the model was introduced based on selecting object instances from user interface lists rather than entering OIDs; and OIDs became completely hidden from the user. This tool also supported multiple machines per object and extended the notion of state transition diagrams by allowing states to be calculated, as described in Sect. 4.3. However, there was only limited support for machine re-use.

The most recent tool, ModelScope [10], developed in 2002, improved the metadata language and added support for the event abstraction ideas described in Sect. 6, greatly increasing the capabilities for behavioural reuse.

# References

1. Kleppe, A., Warmer, J., Bast, W.: MDA Explained: The Model Driven Architecture: Practice and Promise. Addison-Wesley Longman Publishing Co., Inc., Boston (2003)
2. McNeile, A., Simons, N.: State Machines as Mixins. J. Object Technol. **2**(6), 85–101 (2003)
3. McNeile, A., Simons, N.: Mixin Based Behaviour Modelling. In: 6th International Conference on Enterprise Information Systems, vol. 3, pp. 179–183 (2004)
4. Meyer, B.: Object-Oriented Software Construction. Prentice Hall PTR, Englewood Cliffs (2000)
5. Hoare, C.: Communicating Sequential Processes. Prentice-Hall International, Englewood Cliffs (1985)
6. Bracha, G., Cook, W.: Mixin-based Inheritance. In: ASM Conference on Object-Oriented Programming, Systems, Languages, Applications, pp. 179–183 (1990)
7. Warmer, J., Kleppe, A.: The Object Constraint Language: Getting Your Models Ready for MDA, 2nd edn. Addison-Wesley Longman Publishing Co., Inc., Boston (2003)
8. Jackson, M.: System Development. Prentice Hall, Englewood Cliffs (1983)
9. Jackson, M., Zave, P.: Domain Descriptions. In: Proceeding of IEEE International Symposium on Requirements Engineering, pp. 56–64 (1993)
10. Metamaxim Ltd., ModelScope. Metamaxim Website: http://www.metamaxim.com. Accessed Feb 2004
11. Sims, O.: MDA: The Real Value. OMG Website: http://www.omg.org/mda/presentations. Accessed Feb 2004
12. Object Management Group. How Systems Will Be Built. OMG Website: http://www.omg.org/mda. Accessed Jan 2004
13. Object Management Group. UML 2.0 Superstructure Final Adopted Specification. OMG Document reference ptc/03-08-02, August 2003
14. Soley, R.: MDA: An Introduction. OMG Website: http://www.omg.org/mda/presentations. Accessed Feb 2004
15. Cook, S., Daniels, J.: Designing Object Systems: Object-Oriented Modelling with Syntropy. Prentice-Hall, Englewood Cliffs (1994)
16. Mellor, S., Balcer, M.: Executable UML: A Foundation for Model-Driven Architectures. Addison-Wesley Longman Publishing Co., Inc., Boston (2002)
17. Shlaer, S., Mellor, S.: Object Life Cycles - Modeling the World in States. Yourdon Press/Prentice Hall, Englewood Cliffs (1992)

# Integrating Protocol Contracts with Program Code – A Leightweight Approach for Applied Behaviour Models that Respect Their Execution Context

Marco Konersmann[(✉)] and Michael Goedicke

paluno - The Ruhr Institute for Software Technology,
University of Duisburg-Essen, Essen, Germany
{marco.konersmann,michael.goedicke}@paluno.uni-due.de

**Abstract.** In the domain of information systems, behaviour is typically described without a formal foundation. These systems could benefit from the use of formal behaviour modeling. However, the perceived costs for integrating a formal behaviour modeling approach seems to be higher than the expected benefits. A framework for formal behaviour modeling and execution could help bringing the benefits of formal modeling to this domain when it imposes a low barrier for integrating the approach. To achieve this, we present our approach for designing and executing behaviour models which are encoded with well-defined source code structures. In our approach the model is statically represented in the program code. Therefore the model does not exist as a first class citizen, but is extracted from the code at design time and run time. These models can be integrated within a context of arbitrary other program code, that does not follow the semantics of the model type. They therefore impose only a small barrier for their use.

## 1 Motivation

The domain of information systems is driven by platforms that are defined in industry standards. These platforms typically describe the structure of information systems that use the platform, including structural specifications for data models, logical components, and user interfaces. The specifications are most often accompanied by specifications for security, logging, monitoring, and other cross cutting concerns.

Formal behaviour models are not broadly used in the domain of information systems. Although the domain includes some problems that require complex behaviour descriptions, great parts of information systems are not modeled by behaviour models. The benefit of formal behaviour models – the ability to formally reason about the behaviour and the ability to model small, interacting behavioural components – is often considered not necessary, or the costs for using formal behaviour models is considered too high for their benefits. Therefore, the widely used platforms for information systems do not include formal behaviour models, but rely on the underlying imperative programming language

© Springer International Publishing Switzerland 2015
E. Roubtsova et al. (Eds.): BM-FA 2009-2014, LNCS 6368, pp. 197–219, 2015.
DOI: 10.1007/978-3-319-21912-7_8

for behaviour specifications. Another property of information systems is, that they are often long-living systems, which are and have been subject to evolution. Therefore changing the complete behaviour towards a formal model implementation is infeasibly expensive.

For behaviour specifications to be more broadly used in information systems, we believe that a framework needs to be available, which imposes a low barrier for its integration. We identified the following criteria for a solution for formal behaviour models in the information system domain:

- **Ease of Application Integration.** As it is not expected that the complete behaviour of an information system is changed at once, it is desirable that behaviour models can easily be used for increasingly many parts of the software in an evolutionary fashion. This includes that arbitrary application program code can be called from the model to get or set external information.
- **Ease of Platform Integration.** It is desirable that a solution is easily integratable into the standard platforms for information systems.
- **Integrated Editor.** The model specifications should be editable in the typical editors for information systems, e.g. IDEs like Eclipse[1].
- **Ease of Development Tool Integration.** The tools used for developing information systems today are very much focused on program code and text based files. This includes e.g. code repositories, collaboration tools, or code metric tools. It is desirable that a solution for behaviour models in information systems integrate well with these tools. Therefore, the key model information should be readable and editable with text editors. Ideally, it should also be debuggable in an IDE.
- **Possibility to Monitor.** The model should be easy to monitor.
- **Possibility to Debug.** It should be possible to debug the model. Ideally this can be done within an IDE.

Our approach for a formal behaviour model framework that can be used in information systems is to integrate model specifications into the source code of programs. With this approach, the models can be reliably extracted from the code. We call this approach Architecture-Carrying Software (ACS) [5]. In ACS we integrate static structure models, including component models and behaviour models with source code that complies with component frameworks. Other models, including quality information and deployment information, are planned to be added. Currently, the behaviour model included in ACS is a batch-oriented state machine (see [1]). This batch-oriented model is, however, not well suitable for information systems, because often one wants to interactively influence the behaviour of a subsystem.

In this paper we present an alternative behaviour model integrated with source code. The integrated model type is that of Protocol Contracts [6,7]. The model allows for interactive behaviour, which makes it better-suited for information systems. In the following, we will first explain briefly the conceptual foundations of our work in Sect. 2. Section 3 describes the integration of Protocol Contracts with Java source code at design time. The execution runtime and

---

[1] http://www.eclipse.org.

the corresponding run time model are described in Sect. 4. The idea behind a model editor for integrated Protocol Contracts is introduced in Sect. 5. We discuss our approach in Sect. 6, before we present future work in Sect. 7 and related work in Sect. 8. We conclude in Sect. 9.

## 2    Conceptual Foundations

In this section we introduce the conceptual foundations for this paper. First we briefly introduce our approach for integrating model information with source code. Then we describe Protocol Contracts, before we describe the integration of Protocol Contracts with source code in Sect. 3.

### 2.1    Architecture-Carrying Software

The idea of Architecture-Carrying Software (ACS) [5] is to represent architectural models in source code with sophisticated code structures. *Architecture-Carrying* means that the software itself carries its architecture information, without the need for adjacent models that are separate from the code.

The code structures that represent models in ACS only define architecturally relevant code. Therefore they include interfaces to execute arbitrary other, non-architectural code.

These code structures are not meant to be directly changed with source code editors, but with model editors. These model editors allow to edit the architecture in a representation that software architects are comfortable with, e.g. UML or formal specification languages. The editor extracts the architecture from the underlying code base and presents a model to interact with. Changes to the model are reflected by changes to the underlying code base. The model view is volatile. It only exists as long as the model editor is in use. With ACS, the architecture model is available at compile time as source code structures and at run time via reflection mechanisms.

The code can still be viewed and edited with text editors. The source code representing models should be edited with respect to the ACS code structure definitions. The source structures define so-called entry points where external code is meant to be integrated. Code that does not represent the models can still be edited freely.

Currently, the only behaviour model included in ACS is a batch-oriented state machine (see [1]). This batch-oriented model is, however, not suitable for many applications, because usually one wants to interactively influence the behaviour. In this paper, we present our ongoing work how we extend ACS with Protocol Contracts.

### 2.2    Protocol Contracts

Protocol Contracts [6,7] describe event-driven, state-based behaviour of object models. In a Protocol Contract, events are presented to protocol models. Protocol Models react to events by accepting them and changing their state, or by refusing them. In the following, we will briefly introduce Protocol Contracts as they are described in [7]. An example of a protocol model is shown in Fig. 1.

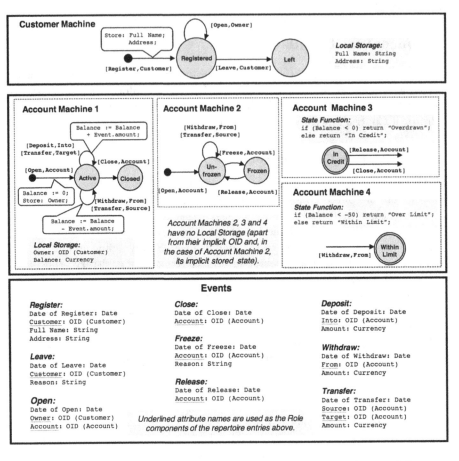

**Fig. 1.** An example system specified as Protocol Contract (Source: [6])

**Events.** Events in Protocol Contracts are typed. An event type has a name and attributes. Event attributes are also typed. Attribute types are the usual primitive types of programming language. This especially includes integers, floating point numbers, booleans, and strings. In addition, attributes can have the type of an object. An example is the event of the type *Deposit* in Fig. 1. This event type defines an attribute *date of deposit* of the type *Date*, an attribute *amount* of the type *Currency*, and an attribute *into*, which is a reference to an object to be affected by this event. An event type is instantiated to an event instance (also called *event* in this paper) by setting attribute values.

**Protocol Machines.** Protocol machines describe a deterministic behaviour contract for objects. They can be built up either by states and rules how to change the states in reaction to events, or by comprising other protocol machines. The first are called *elementary machines*.

Elementary machines have a stored state. The stored state consists of typed variables, including an implicit state variable (just state variable from now on). The variables work analogously to attributes in objects of object-oriented programming languages like Java. The state variable represents a finite set of possible states, that a protocol machine can be in. The value of a state variable can be determined by the sequence of events, that the machine accepted (so called topological states), as it is known from UML state machines [9, page 535 ff.], or by a state function that is evaluated when a event is presented to the machine.

Non-elementary machines are built by nested non-elementary and eventually by elementary machines. They build their stored states based on the stored states of the nested machines. A nested machine can read and write its own stored state. It can read the stored state of all other machines in its environment. The environment of a machine is built by the stored states of its parent machines and all of their parents' nested machines.

Protocol machines have a repertoire, that describes which events are accepted or rejected. Events that are neither accepted nor rejected are ignored. Repertoire entries include:

1. an event type,
2. a reference to an object that is represented by this machine (the OID),
3. a role in which the machine accepts the event type,
4. a boolean expression based on the machine's stored state, that has to evaluate to true before the event is processed (the "test")
5. a term that expresses the update to the machine's stored state when the event is processed

The role is important when an event references several similar machines. E.g. the event *Transfer* (see Fig. 1) transfers money from one bank account to another. This event references one account in the role *source*, and another account in the role *target*.

An event is accepted by a machine, if (1) it has a repertoire entry for the given event type, (2) it represents exactly one object that is referenced by the event, (3) in the role stated by the object reference in the event, and (4) the test is evaluated to true. If the test evaluates to false, the event is rejected. In any other case the event is ignored.

Non-elementary machines reject an event when any nested machine rejects the event. When all nested machines ignore the event, the non-elementary machine ignores the event. When at least one nested machine accepts the event and all other nested machines accept or ignore the event, the event is accepted.

**Protocol Systems.** Protocol systems compose protocol machines in terms of Communicating Sequential Processes (CSP) [4]. Protocol systems themselves have no stored state, event types, and referenced object. Their repertoire and their references to objects are built by their composed machines. A protocol machine that is composed by a protocol system has read access to the attributes of all other protocol machines within the system. Protocol systems can themselves be subject to composition by other protocol systems.

**Protocol Models.** Protocol models are protocol machines that are not nested or composed by any other protocol machine or system. They describe the complete, self-enclosed behavior of the objects they represent.

## 3   Model Integration

For adding new behaviour models to ACS the following artefacts are necessary:

1. a meta model of the model type to integrate,
2. integration mechanisms for a specific framework or language,
3. a runtime to execute the model,
4. an editor to inspect and change the model in a model view.
5. a monitor to show the executed model

The meta model of protocol contract comprises a design time meta model and a run time meta model. This is due to the fact, that instances of protocol machine specifications are created at run time. Therefore elements exist at run time, that are not modeled explicitly at design time. In the following we present the meta model for the design time (Sect. 3.1) and integration mechanisms for Protocol Contracts in the Java programming language (Sect. 3.2).

The execution runtime, including the run time meta model, is described in Sect. 4. An editor, which may also serve as a monitor and for debugging purposes, is described in Sect. 5.

### 3.1   Design Time Meta Model

The ACS prototype is implemented in Java and based on Ecore models [11]. Therefore, the meta model is implemented in Ecore. In this section, we describe the design time meta model for our implementation of Protocol Contracts, which is based on the description from McNeile and Simons [7].

**Machine Types.** There are two machine types represented in our meta model: The *Protocol Machine* and the *Protocol System*. In our model (Fig. 2) a *Protocol-System* always composes at least two machines. Using this notation, a hierarchy of machines can be built. The inner nodes and the root of the tree are *Protocol-Systems*. The leafs are *ProtocolMachines*.

The *ProtocolMachine* contains *MachineAttributes*, *MachineRoleAttributes*, one *Statetype*, *Roles*, *EventTypes*, and *RepertoireEntries*. The *MachineAttributes* and *MachineRoleAttributes* specify the local storage of a machine. The first

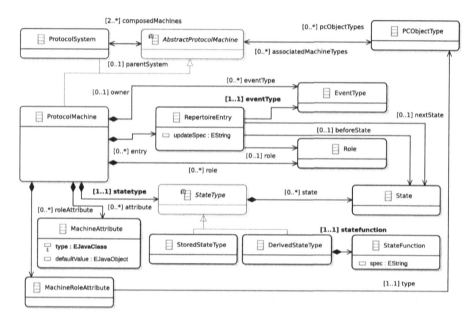

**Fig. 2.** Machine types in the Protocol Contracts meta model

define value-based attributes. The latter define references to OIDs in Protocol Contracts. The attributes are typed, and may define a default value, which is null, when not specified. The *Statetype* defines the type of the machine, i.e. whether the machine defines topological states (*StoredStateType* in our model), or a state function (*DerivedStateType* in the model). Both types may have a number of *States*. However, the *DerivedStateType* also has a *StateFunction* which contains an attribute *spec* of the type EString (an Ecore representation of a Java String), specifying its function in terms of Java source code. The repertoire, that each machine contains, is formed by the *RepertoireEntries* in our model. The *EventType* and *Role* of the repertoire entry are represented as references of the contained elements of a machine. This allows to reuse *EventType* and *Role* elements. Repertoire entries can also reuse Event Type and Role elements of their machines. This introduces a dependency on the model level towards these other machines. The *updateSpec* defined by repertoire entries represent the update of the local storage during transitions. Each entry knows its *beforeState* and the *nextState*, if applicable. This represents the precondition and the update of the state variable of stored state machines, and the pre- and postcondition for derived state machines.

Figure 3 shows the part of the meta model that defines event types. The class *EventType* may contain typed *EventAttributes*. The *EventType* may contain *Role2ObjectEntities*, which bind the *Role* in an event type to a *PCObjectType*. The *PCObjectType* is the type of an OID. This e.g. represents the type Customer in the example in Fig. 1.

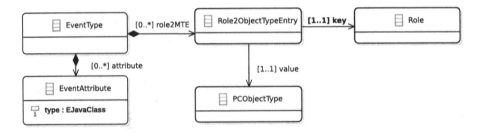

**Fig. 3.** Event Types in the Protocol Contracts meta model

## 3.2   Integration Mechanisms

For describing Protocol Contracts as model type for ACS, source code structures for the design time meta model elements have to be defined. In the following sections, we describe the source code structures that represent Protocol Contracts in Java code. Elements that represent the instantiation of machines and events are runtime artefacts and therefore not represented in the code.

**Protocol Machine.** A protocol machine is represented in Java code as a Java package that includes a class, which implements a marker interface *IProtocol-Machine*. We call this class the *Protocol Machine Class* (or just *Machine Class*). Listing 1.1 shows the Machine Class template. A marker interface is an interface without any operations, that only exists to mark classes. Only one Machine Class is allowed within a Java package. Other classes that define the protocol machine (as shown in the following) also reside within this package or subpackages[2]. Other classes, unrelated to the protocol machine, may also reside in that package, although we do not recommend that.

The Machine Class also includes a reference to the object type that is represented by the machine. It is an attribute in the class definition marked with a *MachineOID* annotation. The object type of the OID is a simple Java class. The type of the attribute is that class. The variable is named *oid* for convenience.

**Machine Attributes and Machine Role Attributes.** Machine attributes and machine role attributes are represented in a separate class, called *Variable Class*. The Variable Class contains the local storage (excluding the state variable) and the corresponding get and set methods. The methods are also represented in interfaces: one interface for get methods, the *Read Interface*, and one interface for set methods, the *Write Interface*. These interfaces are entry points for reading and changing the attributes. The Variable Class implements these interfaces. A third interface, the *Context Interface*, defines the environment of the machine. For a single protocol machine, the Context Interface extends the Read Interface

---

[2] This is actually a recommendation, not a requirement. For protocol machines with more than 3 or four states, we found it practical to use subpackages for structuring reasons.

```
public class $MachineName implements IProtocolMachine {

    @MachineOID
    $PCObjectTypeName oid;

    @MachineContext(
        localState = $MachineNameVariable.class,
        localStateRead = IReadableVariable.class,
        localStateWrite = IWritableVariable.class)
    IContext context;
}
```

**Listing 1.1.** The source code structure for a Protocol Machine Class with the reference to a Machine Attribute Class

and the Write Interface of the machine. The Machine Class contains a variable, with the type of the Context Interface as a reference to its environment, the machine context. Due to the interface and class structure described above, the Context Interface allows for reading and writing the local storage of the machine, and for reading the local storages of its environment. An annotation on the variable for the machine context states the Read Interface, the Write Interface, and the Variable Class. Listing 1.1 shows how the Machine Class is built with the Variable Class (here and in the following listings, a dollar sign denotes a variable in a template). The reference to the OID is a reference to the underlying object, and allows for executing operations of this object. It is therefore a reference to model-external code.

**States and OIDs.** States are represented as a Java class that extends the abstract class *AbstractPCState* (see Listing 1.2). The name of the state is represented by the class name. The class extends the abstract class *AbstractPCState*. That abstract class has a type parameter that represents the OID type of the machine. *AbstractPCState* has an *oid* reference to an arbitrary object. This is the interface of the states to model-external code. This can be used within transition code to execute arbitrary operations in the context.

**State Variable.** The state variable in Protocol Contracts can be built in two ways. In stored state protocol machines, the state variable is determined by the initial state and the updates. In derived state protocol machines, the state variable is derived using a state function.

The state variable of stored state machines does not have a static representation. Therefore no source code structure exists for that state. Machine Classes of derived state protocol machines contain a method *getCurrentState()* to evaluate the state variable. The method returns *Class< ? extends AbstractPCState>*,

```
public class $StateName extends AbstractPCState<$PCObjectTypeName> { }
```

**Listing 1.2.** The source code structure for a state

i.e. the reference to the class that represents the current state. The method's body implements the state function.

**Roles and Event Types.** Roles are represented as classes implementing the marker interface *IRole*. An event type is represented in the source code as *Event Type Class*. This is a class implementing the marker interface *IEventType*. Event types contain two types of meta data: (1) event attributes, and (2) roles and object references.

Event attributes are represented as object variables in the class with the corresponding type. The attribute *name* is represented by the name of the variable. The variable is complemented by a get and a set method.

*PCObjectTypes* are represented as Java classes. Therefore, roles and object references can be represented by variables with the corresponding class as variable type, and the role as variable name. These variables are also complemented by corresponding get and set methods. Listing 1.3 shows the source code structure for an Event Type Class.

**Repertoire Entries.** Repertoire entries define the following data: (1) an event type, (2) a referenced object, (3) a role for which the event type is accepted, (4) a test, and (5) an update specification. In the source code these are represented as annotated methods (*Repertoire Entry Methods*), as shown in Listing 1.4. The methods are contained by State Classes or a Protocol Machine Class. The test is defined by the class that implements the method. When a State Class implements the method, that state is the necessary source state. When a Protocol Machine Class of a stored state machine implements the method, the source state is the initial pseudo state. When a Protocol Machine Class of a derived state machine implements the method, the before state is empty. The method's parameters are a reference to an Event Type Class object (event), a reference to an object of the Context Interface (context), and a reference to the Role class. The parameter event represents the event type. The context parameter is used for the update specification and is a reference to the machine's context. The next state of the repertoire entry is given as parameter of an annotation as class reference.

Both, the Machine Class and the State Class have an attribute *oid* that is the reference to the object defined by the machine. Here the attribute acts as an interface to non-architectural code. Within the update specification, operations

```
public class $EventTypeName implements IEventType {

    $PCObjectTypeName $roleName;

    $AttributeType $attribtueName;

    // getters and setters
}
```

**Listing 1.3.** The source code structure for event types, including event attributes and roles

```
@RepertoireEntry(nextState = $StateName.class)
public void $eventTypeName($EventTypeName event, IContext context, $RoleName role){
    // Update Specification
}
```

**Listing 1.4.** The source code structure for repertoire entries

to the OID can be called. The semantics of the executed operations of the OID are not part of the model.

**Protocol Systems.** The source code representation of a protocol system is a *Protocol System Class*, or shortly *System Class* (see Listing 1.5). Such a class implements the marker interface *IProtocolMachine*, just as Protocol Machine Classes. In addition, Protocol System Classes are annotated with the annotation *ProtocolSystem*, which takes a list of classes as parameter, that extend the IProtocolMachine interface. One package may only contain either one Protocol System Class or one Protocol Machine Class. Subpackages may contain further Protocol Machines or Systems.

```
@ProtocolSystem({ $MachineName.class, ... })
public class $ProtocolSystemName implements IProtocolMachine {

    @SystemEnvironment
    ISystemContext context;
}
```

**Listing 1.5.** The source structure for Protocol Systems

Protocol Systems influence the environment of their referenced protocol machines and systems. To represent this influence, each Protocol System Class is accompanied by a *System Context Interface*. This interface extends the Read Interfaces of its composed protocol machines and the System Context Interfaces of its composed protocol systems. The System Context Interface is an attribute of the Protocol System Class, annotated with an annotation *SystemEnvironment*.

When a protocol machine is composed by a protocol system, the machine can read variables from all machines composed in the system. To reflect this, the machine's Context Interface replaces the extension of its Read Interface with the System Context Interface of the highest Protocol System in the composition hierarchy (see Fig. 4).

**Protocol Models.** Protocol models are protocol machines that are not nested or composed by any other protocol machine or system. This can be evaluated from the machine context. Thus no explicit source code structures exist for protocol models.

## 3.3   Example

To show the functionality of our meta model and source code structures, we implemented a desktop example. Our example is an implementation of the Bank

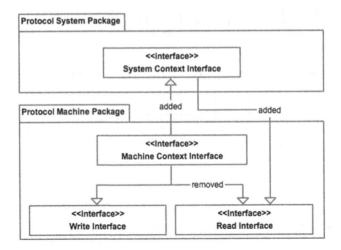

**Fig. 4.** The given interface and class structure ensures that the variables of all composed machine are readable by every machine in the system, and that each machine can only alter its own variables.

Model example given in [6]. The model of the example system is shown in Fig. 1. We will here only show parts of the example that differ enough to show the different working concepts. We therefore show here our implementation of account machine 1, a protocol machine with stored states; account machine 4, a protocol machine with derived states; and the account system, a protocol system.

**Account Machine 1.** Account machine 1 (AM1) is a protocol machine with stored states. All of the classes for AM1 are placed in the same Java package. Figure 5 gives an overview of the classes and interfaces in the package. The Protocol Machine Class for AM1 is depicted in Listing 1.6.

The Protocol Machine Class of AM1 defines one repertoire entry from the pseudo state — here represented by the containment relationship from the Protocol Machine Class to the method — to the State *Active*. The body of the method *open* shows the update specification.

Figure 6 shows the class structure of the machine attributes for AM1 (without the influence of the system, that composes the machine). The interfaces shown in this figure contain get and set methods according to their task. The implementing class is shown in Listing 1.7.

The Event Type Class of Open is shown in Listing 1.8. It contains the attributes and roles prescribed by the specification in in terms of attributes, get methods, and set methods.

The State Class of the state *Active* is shown in Listing 1.9. It includes repertoire entry methods for all accepted events as described in Fig. 1. Our source code structure however does not allow to create an entry with the same update and target state, but with multiple event types and roles without copies of the update specification. We need multiple methods to represent this structure.

R Ⓒ Account
M Ⓒ AccountMachine1
M Ⓒ AccountMachine1VariablesImpl
O Ⓒ AccountObject
S Ⓒ Active
E Ⓒ Close
S Ⓒ Closed
O Ⓒ CustomerObject
E Ⓒ Deposit
R Ⓒ From
M ⓘ IContext
R Ⓒ Into
M ⓘ IReadableVariables
M ⓘ IWritableVariables
E Ⓒ Open
R Ⓒ Source
R Ⓒ Target
E Ⓒ Transfer
E Ⓒ Withdraw

**Fig. 5.** The package structure of protocol machine for Account Machine 1. The annotations mean: (E) Event Type Classes; (M) Machine Class, Variable Class and interfaces; (O) Referenced Object classes; (R) Role Classes; (S) State Classes. The c in a circle denotes a class. The i in a circle denotes an interface.

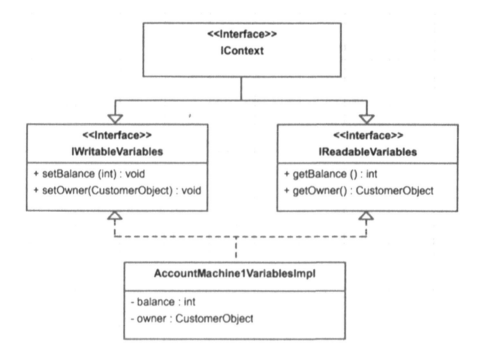

**Fig. 6.** The class structure for the machine attributes of Account Machine 1

```
public class AccountMachine1 implements IProtocolMachine {

    @MachineOID
    AccountObject oid;

    @MachineContext(
        localState = AccountMachine1VariablesImpl.class,
        localStateRead = IReadableVariables.class,
        localStateWrite = IWritableVariables.class)
    IContext context;

    @RepertoireEntry(nextState = Active.class)
    public void open(Open event,
            IContext context, Account role) {
        context.setBalance(0);
        context.setOwner(event.getCustomer());
    }
}
```

**Listing 1.6.** The implementation of the Machine Class for Account Machine 1

```
public class AccountMachine1VariablesImpl
        implements IReadableVariables, IWritableVariables {
    int balance;

    CustomerObject owner;

    // getters and setters
}
```

**Listing 1.7.** The machine attribute class of Account Machine 1

```
public class Open implements IEventType {
    Date dateOfOpen;

    AccountObject account;

    CustomerObject owner;

    // getters and setters
}
```

**Listing 1.8.** The Event Type Class of the event type *Open* of Account Machine 1

Some classes are not shown in detail here. The Role Classes implement the Interface IRole, but do not contain any methods or attributes. The Event Type Classes that are not shown are built accordingly to the Event Type Open in the obvious way.

**Account Machine 4.** Account Machine 4 (AM4) is a protocol machine with a derived state. Thus its structure differs slightly from AM1. Figure 7 gives an overview of the classes and interfaces in the package. The package does not contain Role Classes or Event Type Classes, because the machine relies on the classes already stated by AM1. The Protocol Machine Class for AM4 is depicted in Listing 1.10. It especially contains the State Function Method *getCurrentState*, which shows the implementation of the state function in Java. All other classes are built in the ways already stated and do not include anything surprising.

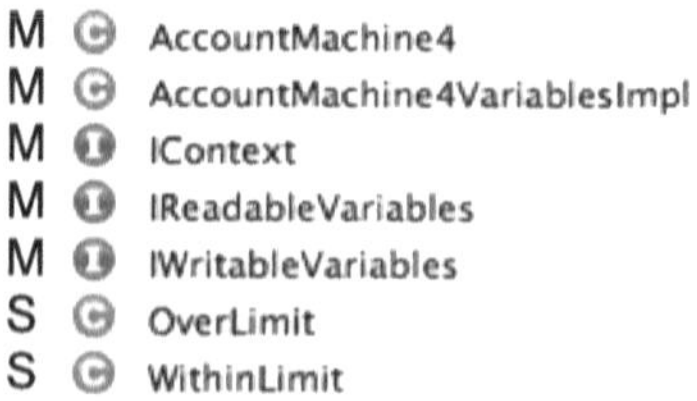

| | | |
|---|---|---|
| M | Ⓒ | AccountMachine4 |
| M | Ⓒ | AccountMachine4VariablesImpl |
| M | ⓘ | IContext |
| M | ⓘ | IReadableVariables |
| M | ⓘ | IWritableVariables |
| S | Ⓒ | OverLimit |
| S | Ⓒ | WithinLimit |

**Fig. 7.** The package structure of protocol machine for Account Machine 4. The annotations mean: (M) Machine Class, Variable Class and interfaces; (S) State Classes. The c in a circle denotes a class. The i in a circle denotes an interface.

```java
public class Active
            extends AbstractPCState<AccountObject> {

    @RepertoireEntry(nextState = Active.class)
    public void transfer(Transfer event,
            IContext context, Target role) {
        oid.notifyMoneyReceived("You received money:" + event.getAmount());
        context.setBalance(
            context.getBalance() + event.getAmount());
    }

    @RepertoireEntry(nextState = Active.class)
    public void deposit(Deposit event,
            IContext context, Into role) {
        oid.notifyMoneyReceived("You received money:" + event.getAmount());
        context.setBalance(
            context.getBalance() + event.getAmount());
    }

    @RepertoireEntry(nextState = Active.class)
    public void transfer(Transfer event,
            IContext context, Source role) {
        context.setBalance(
            context.getBalance() - event.getAmount());
    }

    @RepertoireEntry(nextState = Active.class)
    public void withdraw(Withdraw event,
            IContext context, From role) {
        context.setBalance(
            context.getBalance() - event.getAmount());
    }

    @RepertoireEntry(nextState = Closed.class)
    public void close(Close event,
            IContext context, Account role) {
    }
}
```

**Listing 1.9.** The *Active* state of Account Machine 1

```
public class AccountMachine4 implements IProtocolMachine {

    @MachineOID
    Account oid;

    @MachineContext(
        localState = AccountMachine4VariablesImpl.class,
        localStateRead  = IReadableVariables.class,
        localStateWrite = IWritableVariables.class )
    IContext context;

    public Class
            <? extends AbstractPCState<AccountObject>>
            getCurrentState() {
        if (context.getBalance() < -50)
            return OverLimit.class;
        else
            return WithinLimit.class;
    }

    @RepertoireEntry(nextState = WithinLimit.class)
    public void withdraw(Withdraw event,
            IContext context, From role) {
    }
}
```

**Listing 1.10.** The implementation of the Machine Class for Account Machine 4

**Bank System.** The protocol system *Account System* (AS) composes AM1 to AM4 (AM2 and AM3 are not shown in this paper). Following the source code structures defined in Sect. 3.2, the AS consists of one Protocol System Class (Listing 1.11) and the System Context Interface, which is an interface without any own operations. Figure 8 shows how the class structure is influenced by the system. IContext of AM1 no longer extends the Read Interface of AM1, but the ISystemContext of the AS. The ISystemContext extends the Read Interfaces of all composed machines (only AM1 and AM4 are shown in this figure). Therefore each machine has read access to all variables in the environment.

```
@ProtocolSystem({ AccountMachine1.class, AccountMachine2.class,
                  AccountMachine3.class, AccountMachine4.class })
public class BankAccountSystem implements IProtocolMachine {
    @SystemEnvironment
    ISystemContext context;
}
```

**Listing 1.11.** The source code of the System Class of the Bank Account System

## 4    Execution Runtime

The Protocol Contracts meta model is executable. The runtime is in a prototype state. It is divided into a *bytecode to model extractor*, and a *protocol model executor*. The bytecode to model extractor parses bytecode to read the protocol model structures encoded as presented in Sect. 3.2 using code reflection mechanisms. From these structures it builds the design time model, on which the run time model is based. The protocol model is then available as Ecore model in memory.

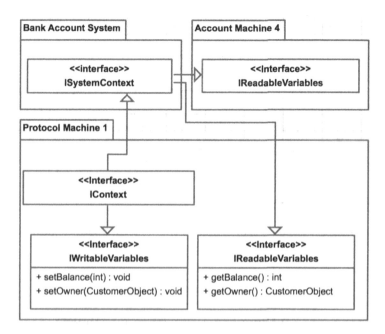

**Fig. 8.** The composition by the Account System has an influence on the source code structure of the Account Machine 1. IContext no longer extends IReadableInterface, but the ISystemContext. The ISystemContext extends the Read Interfaces of all composed machines (only AM1 and AM4 are shown in this figure). Therefore each machine has read access to all variables in the environment.

The protocol model executor manages the model. i.e. it provides interfaces for clients to interact with the protocol model. For executing the model, an instance of event classes can be created, filled with attribute values and presented to the execution runtime. The execution runtime uses the model information at run time, e.g. to create machine instances, switch the stored states, and uses calls to the operations of the source code structures for executing update specifications. It then reports about the acceptance of the event, which can be *accepted*, *ignored*, or *refused*.

These calls enable the source code structures to contain interfaces to model-external code. The update specification of a repertoire entry may contain calls to the underlying object using the attribute *oid*. The update specification is encoded as Java method, which is called by the runtime in an inversion-of-control pattern. When the control flow hits the underlying object, the model-external code is executed.

### 4.1  Run Time Meta Model

At run time, instance of machines, events, and related model elements are created. Figure 9 shows the elements for instantiating machines. Protocol systems

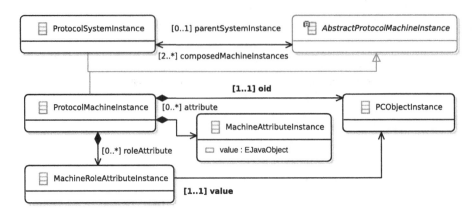

**Fig. 9.** Protocol machines instantiation in the Protocol Contracts meta model

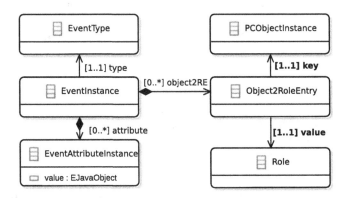

**Fig. 10.** Event instantiation in the Protocol Contracts meta model

and protocol machines each have model elements for their instantiation. They are build analogously to their type specification. *ProtocolMachineInstances* contain *MachineAttributeInstances*, which represent the actual values of the value types in the local storage. *MachineRoleAttributeInstances* represent the references to OIDs in machine instances, which are related to a role. All elements have relations to their respective type elements. This is not shown in the figure for readability reasons.

Event instances (see Fig. 10) are represented as *EventInstance* elements. They reference their type. They contain *EventAttributeInstances*, value-based attributes, and *Object2RoleEntries*, which map OIDs as *PCObjectInstances* to roles.

## 4.2   Monitoring and Debugging

The execution runtime offers a web service to register a monitor for a running protocol model. The monitor can be informed about the current system state (including the design time mode, and the runtime model), and about incoming events. A debugging interface allows to change values of machine attributes. The monitoring and debugging interfaces are currently in a prototype state.

## 5   Model Editor

The editor is divided into a *source code to model extractor/adapter* to extract the model from source code, and the model editor. The extractor/adaptor uses the Java Development Tools (JDT)[3] to parse code structures for building an Ecore model of the protocol model described in the source code, while keeping the trace links to the code. Technically, these trace links are java objects that relate source code elements to model objects, while providing methods to translate the one into the other. When the model is changed in the editor, the changes are reflected in the code, following the trace links. Therefore the source code is not overridden, but changed. The editor itself is a standard Ecore editor in Eclipse. The extractor/adaptor is not fully implemented yet.

## 6   Discussion

Our integration of Protocol Contracts follows several design decisions. The main variation points are the meta model and the integration mechanisms. The meta model was designed to be close at the description in [7]. As some parts of the example were not completely described, we cannot be sure that the meta model is in a final version.

Two attributes in the model are strings without semantics. The attribute *spec* in the class *StateFunction*, and the attribute *updateSpec* in the class *RepertoireEntry*. Both contain Java source code that is part of the model definition. This might seem inconsequent. These method bodies are, however, entry points for model-external code. The operations called upon the OID objects are not semantically encoded in the model.

The work presented in this paper are part of the research project ADVERT[4] that aims at using Architecture-Carrying Software for solving evolution challenges in long-living software. We plan to integrate the meta model for Protocol Contracts with the meta model for architecture descriptions from this research project. Therefore we also expect slight changes to the meta model for integration purposes.

The integration mechanisms presented in this paper are designed for Java programs. The model execution is event-based. One could possibly create other

---

[3] https://eclipse.org/jdt/.
[4] http://advert-project.org.

integration mechanisms that better integrates with already existing event-based communication frameworks. In the research project mentioned before, we provide integration paths to multiple runtime frameworks. Therefore we expect to create other integration mechanisms. These can, however, base largely on the mechanisms presented in this paper.

## 7   Future Work

As future work, we plan to further evaluate the concept and implementation, and integrate it in our framework for Architecture-Carrying Software. This includes that the Protocol Contracts are included into an existing architecture-modeling language. The architecture languages, on which ACS is based, typically have components and their interconnections as first-class entities. We intend to create a mapping from *oids* to component instances, and object types to component types. We can then define the behaviour of component types with Protocol Contracts. The interfaces to arbitrary code play an important role here, to allow for behaviour that should not be modeled on an architectural level. However, some details of the integration still have to be inspected.

Furthermore the source code to model extractor/adaptor has still to be developed. Blueprints for such components exist in the context of the ADVERT project for other model types. Therefore we expect no substantial difficulties in the development of this component. Also the execution runtime is currently in a prototype state. We need to test it with further examples to be more confident about its reliability.

The editor is currently in the work. Blueprints for this editor are also available. The editor is based on the standard reflective Ecore editor in the Eclipse IDE. Only the loading and the saving mechanisms will be overridden to extract the model from the code while keeping the trace links between model elements and the code, and to execute the changes on the code when the changes are saved.

## 8   Related Work

Related work to ours can be found for several aspects. Balz already created an integration for a behaviour model in his PhD thesis [1]. He integrates state machine models. His implementation of state machine models is working in a batch-like mode. I.e. a state machine is started and is executed until it terminates. The integration of Protocol Contracts is working interactively by generating events and presenting them to the protocol model.

Managing multiple representations of software design and specifically architecture has been subject to other fields of research. Related to the paper at hand is the field of Model-Driven Development (MDD) (e.g. [3,10]) and round trip engineering (e.g. [8]).

MDD concentrates on deriving code from models. The models and the code are two representations of the program that are independently subject to evolution and maintenance. Changes in the specification can be taken over automatically in the implementation. When the program changes in the implementation, these changes cannot be automatically taken over in the specification.

Round trip engineering (RTE) describes techniques to synchronize models and code. The models used in RTE are very detailed and technical, e.g. UML class diagrams. RTE thus allows for two-way synchronization, but does not bridge the gap between abstraction levels, as our approach does.

The work presented here can be seen as part of models@runtime [2]. We have models with a high abstraction level that are not tied to the underlying technology. We have a technology specific runtime to execute the models. In addition, we have defined interfaces between the model and arbitrary source code.

A runtime for Protocol Contracts already exists (see [6]). We did not find extensive information about that runtime. For our runtime we plan to allow for inspecting and debugging of running Protocol Contracts at run time. It is not clear from [6] whether this is possible with the already existing runtime.

## 9  Conclusion

For behaviour specifications to be more broadly used in information systems, we believe that a framework needs to be available, which imposes a low barrier for its integration. We identified six criteria that a possible solution has to fulfill to be a candidate for a broader use in this particular domain. In this paper we presented our proposal for a framework for developing and executing Protocol Contracts in the domain of information systems. We evaluated the functionality in a small desktop example. The evaluation shows that the meta model and source code structures are suitable to model Protocol Contracts. Our implementation meets the identified criteria:

- **Ease of Application Integration.** Our framework allows the Protocol Contract implementations to call external code during state transitions. This includes information interchange with program code outside of the model implementation. The oid objects represent conceptual interfaces between the model and the model-external code. This allows to integrate such a formal behaviour model incrementally into existing applications.
- **Ease of Platform Integration.** The framework is implemented in Java as a library. The Protocol Contract implementation consists of code following the necessities of this framework code and a dependency to the execution runtime implementation. It is therefore easy to embed into typical information systems implemented in Java. Model instances can be created from information system platform code, and platform functions can be called from within the models. This allows to integrate the formal modeling execution framework into information system platforms.

- **Integrated Editor.** We are currently developing an editor that is integrated with the Eclipse IDE, and reuses much of this IDE's concepts and code. However, the editor is not available yet.
- **Ease of Development Tool Integration.** The model specification is readable and editable without an explicit model editor. A text editor suffices, but a comprehensive Java editor is recommended to read and edit the code that represents the model. As the model specification is based only on program code, it can be easily managed with source code management systems and other Java tools.
- **Possibility to Monitor.** A monitoring interface for the execution runtime exists as a prototype, which allows to be informed about the current system state and about executed events.
- **Possibility to Debug.** A debugging interface for the execution runtime exists as a prototype, which allows to read and change machine attributes at run time. This is only a starting point. An extension of this interface should be able to also edit e.g. running machine instances and types. However, as the model is based on Java code, especially the update specifications of transitions and the state functions can be edited at run time with the standard Java debugging mechanism.

We see that all of the criteria are fulfilled to a certain extend. The fewest developed criterion is the integrated editor, which is in the work, but not available yet.

**Acknowledgements.** Parts of the meta model presented in this paper are based on the work of Noyan Kurt from the institute paluno at the University of Duisburg-Essen. The work presented in this paper is partially funded by the DFG (German Research Foundation) under the grant number GO 774/7-1 within the Priority Programme SPP1593: Design For Future Managed Software Evolution.

# References

1. Balz, M.: Embedding Model Specifications in Object-Oriented Program Code: A Bottom-up Approach for Model-based Software Development. Ph.D. thesis, Universitt Duisburg-Essen, Mai (2011)
2. Blair, G., Bencomo, N., France, R.: Models@ run.time. Computer **42**(10), 22–27 (2009)
3. Brown, A., Conallen, J., Tropeano, D.: Introduction: models, modeling, and model-driven architecture (mda) model-driven software development. In: Beydeda, S., Book, M., Gruhn, V. (eds.) Model-Driven Software Development, ch. 1, pp. 1–16. Springer, Heidelberg (2005)
4. Hoare, C.A.R.: Communicating sequential processes, vol. 178. Prentice-hall, Englewood Cliffs (1985). http://www.usingcsp.com/
5. Konersmann, M., Goedicke, M.: A conceptual framework and experimental workbench for architectures. In: Heisel, M. (ed.) Software Service and Application Engineering. LNCS, vol. 7365, pp. 36–52. Springer, Heidelberg (2012)

6. McNeile, A.T., Roubtsova, E.E.: Programming in protocols - a paradigm of behavioral programming. In: Gonzalez-Perez, C., Jablonski, S. (eds.) ENASE, pp. 23–30. INSTICC Press, Portugal (2008)
7. McNeile, A.T., Simons, N.: Protocol modelling: a modelling approach that supports reusable behavioural abstractions. Softw. Syst. Model. 5(1), 91–107 (2006)
8. Nickel, U.A., Niere, J., Wadsack, J.P., Zündorf, A.: Roundtrip engineering with FUJABA. In: Proceedings of 2nd Workshop on Software-Reengineering (WSR), Bad Honnef, Germany (2000)
9. OMG. OMG Unified Modeling Language (OMG UML), Superstructure, Version 2.4.1, August 2011
10. Stahl, T., Voelter, M., Czarnecki, K.: Model-Driven Software Development: Technology, Engineering, Management. Wiley, New York (2006)
11. Steinberg, D., Budinsky, F., Paternostro, M., Merks, E.: EMF: Eclipse Modeling Framework 2.0, 2nd edn. Addison-Wesley Professional, Singapore (2009)

# Decision Modules in Models
# and Implementations

Serguei Roubtsov[1]([⊠]) and Ella Roubtsova[2]

[1] Technical University Eindhoven, Eindhoven, The Netherlands
s.roubtsov@tue.nl
[2] Open University of the Netherlands, Heerlen, The Netherlands
ella.roubtsova@ou.nl

**Abstract.** We define a type of concern called a decision module. Decision modules can be seen as a specific subset of often changeable business rules, identified in requirements. We present decision modules as protocol machines in protocol models. The proven property of such protocol machines is their unidirectional dependency from other protocol machines. The composition technique used in protocol models allows for such local changes in a protocol machine that the behaviour of unchanged machines in the whole system is preserved.

We analyse different Java implementation techniques in order to find the possibility of building decision modules having the same properties as in protocol models. We implement decision modules using object composition, reflection, the publisher-subscriber design pattern, interceptors and aspects. The results of our experiments are illustrated with an example of a document submission system. We discuss the functionality of a generic library that we build for adopting the new style of locally changeable implementations with separated decision modules.

## 1 Introduction

Modules are useful instruments for handling complexity of software systems. Modules are created for various purposes giving birth to different approaches to modularisation. Among the goals of modularisation are traceability of requirements and ease of code modification, reuse, testing and support of system evolution.

The major goal of the modularisation technique presented in this paper is the support of system evolution. The system evolution starts with new requirements caused by new business ideas, changes in laws, regulations and business rules. "International Data Corporation (IDC) asked in a survey: How often do you want to customize the business rules in your software? 90 % of respondents reported they try to change it annually or more frequently. 34 % said monthly... A conventionally programmed software package can seldom be reprogrammed this often"[9].

New policies, laws and business rules result in instructions on what to do in a given situation. An instruction combines a description of the situation, the expected actions or events and the directives permitting or forbidding events

© Springer International Publishing Switzerland 2015
E. Roubtsova et al. (Eds.): BM-FA 2009-2014, LNCS 6368, pp. 220–249, 2015.
DOI: 10.1007/978-3-319-21912-7_9

in the described situation. A model or implementation of such an instruction usually combine states of system objects, as well as events and control flow constructions corresponding to the description. In this paper, we define such a combination as a decision module. If a business rule could be presented as a decision module in models and implementations and if this module could be locally changed without the necessity to change the rest of the model or implementation, then such a modularisation would ease system evolution. However, the separation of such modules is not a common practice in conventional modelling and implementation approaches.

The most commonly used modularization is the separation of object life cycles. This means that a domain concept is modelled as a class of objects. Each object is created, exists in some states, makes decisions on the basis of its states and recognised events. Eventually, the object is destroyed or deleted. Modularisation of object life cycles hides the states of objects and process control points inside objects. To implement a new policy, modify a program or generate a test, the control points inside life cycle modules have to be analysed. As a result, each modification of policies and business rules requires re-modelling and re-implementing all the life cycle modules contributing to the decisions made by these policies and business rules.

The research on business rules [4, 10] investigates the ways of modularisation of business rules and the methods of their integration. However, the business rules engines are usually based on the workflow concept and the Business Process Modeling Language (BPML). They integrate the entire control flow and, thus, do not provide the possibility for local changes of the business rules.

There is a modelling technique called Protocol Modelling that supports the separation of the modules called "behaviours" that derive own state from the states of different objects and combine event descriptions with control flow elements. Protocol Modelling is based on the CSP parallel event-based composition technique [8] extended for models with data [22]. This composition technique, implemented in a composition engine, supports separation and composition of both life cycle modules and "behaviours". The property of observational consistency proven in Protocol Modelling for modules and the system they form perfectly supports local changes of modules without the need to validate the rest of the model. Thus, the properties of "behaviours" facilitate model changing and testing. The same properties are desirable for the decision modules both in models and implementations. In this paper we intend to investigate *if it is possible to protocol model decision modules and implement them using the available object-oriented techniques in such a way that the implementations would have the same properties of "behaviours" as in executable protocol models.*

The rest of the paper is structured as follows.

Section 2 defines a decision module.

Section 3 presents related work.

Section 4 introduces a case study used for illustration of our modularization vision.

Section 5 shows how the decision modules are identified in requirements.

Section 6 identifies the decision modules in executable protocol models. It explains the composition of decision modules and life-cycle modules and recognizes the attractive properties of modules in Protocol Modelling.

Section 7 applies different software development techniques (object composition, reflection, the publisher-subscriber design pattern, interceptors and aspects) for implementation of decision modules and evaluates how the implementations preserve the desired properties of protocol models.

Section 8 discusses the advantages of the proposed approach for the modelling and implementation as well as tackling the obstacles in its adoption.

Section 9 concludes the paper and draws perspectives for the future work.

## 2   Definition of Decision Module

In this section, we give a notation independent definition of a decision module. Later in Sect. 6, a decision module will be defined as a protocol machine.

A model of a system is described as a set of interacting objects. A behaviour of an object is its description in terms of states and transitions. The behaviour of a system of objects is defined on the basis of the states and events of objects. However, a system has its own goals and the behaviour of the system is often different from the disjoint union of the individual behaviours of objects. Decision modules direct behaviours of objects in particular combinations of states towards system goals.

**Definition 1.** *A decision module represents a specification of an instruction on how to make the decision about allowing or forbidding certain events.*

- *The instruction is defined on a set of objects selected in a model. The type of each selected object contains specifications of its possible states and the events allowed in the specified states. All possible combinations of the states of selected objects and a subset of the union of all events of the set of selected objects are used for specification of a decision module.*
- *The instruction can be seen as an "if (case)"- construction*

$$if\ (State\ Function() = value)\ then\ allow\ Event;$$

*The domain of the StateFunction() is defined by the partitioning of the state space of the set of selected objects into disjoint subsets. The partitioning can be done before (or after) the Event in hand.*

*The range of the state function is a set of names of these disjoint subsets presented with a nominal variable called "state of the decision module". The nominal values are the abstractions (often - business names) of the conditions for a decision.*

For example, let's consider a decision module which can belong to an object *Aircraft*. It's state function:

*If (State Function() = "All Passengers Are On Board"), then allow Start.*

The *Aircraft*'s behaviour is coordinated with the behaviors of its *Passengers*. The selected event is *Start*. The state space has been partitioned before the *Start* into two subsets *"All Passengers Are On Board"* and *"Not All Passengers Are On Board"*.

We separate a decision module as a *module* because it can be associated (in terms of programming - reused) with different objects as a separate entity. In our example, it can be associated with an *Aircraft* or, say, a *Bus*.

We name this module a *decision* module because it forms the condition for the acceptance or refusal of an action processing an event. It is not a pre-condition because it can be derived both from the pre- and post-states of the actions in the life cycles of the set of selected objects.

A decision module cannot be classified as an object. An object owns (may change independently) its state, whereas the state of a decision module *is derived* from the states of other modules. A decision module only permits or forbids the actions specified in objects from the set of selected objects.

A decision module does not fit exactly into the definition of a crosscutting concern or an aspect [7]. It can be seen as a high-level management concern or a control concern. It can be crosscutting or not.

Finally, what we can observe about a decision module is that:

- it is recognized and can be separated at the early stages of system development such as requirements engineering;
- it is often not separated as an entity in conventional models and implementations;
- it tends to undergo frequent changes at the later stages such as maintenance and evolution.

## 3  Related Work

Modules similar to our decision modules have been also recognized in Business Rules community. These modules are called *enablers* [1,3].

"An enabler is a type of action assertion which, if true, permits or leads to the existence of the correspondent object." An enabler has varying interpretations depending on the nature of the correspondent object: it may permit (i.e. enable) the creation of a new instance; permit another action assertion; permit an action execution [3] and is often called an integrity constraint, a condition or a test.

The enablers represent only a subset of our decision modules because the decision modules

- describe assertions of a set of actions using the state space of a set of selected objects as an input;
- can both enable and disable (refuse) an action execution, the creation of a new instance and another action assertion.

In rather advanced form, such an approach to modularization can be seen in protocol models [20]. The modules called "behaviours", separated in protocol models, possess the following properties:

- use state functions that are able to read (but not change) attributes, an event pre-state of other modules [22];
- use state functions that are able to predict the post-state of other modules for the given event [22];
- often use the control flow constructions to permit events at specified values of the state function;
- are composed with different life cycle modules (objects) in such a way that the life cycle modules do not know (remain oblivious) about the "behaviours" and do not need to be changed as the "behaviours" are added or changed [19,20].

Protocol modeling makes use of an extended form of the Communicating Sequential Processes (CSP) [8] parallel composition of modules which possess internal data. The CSP parallel composition produces observationally consistent models. This means that a protocol model allows one to modify modules locally, add and delete modules so that the behaviour of unchanged modules is preserved in the behaviour of the whole system [19].

In Sect. 6, we will show that the decision modules are easily separated in protocol models as "behaviours" or, in other words, as protocol machines with derived states.

## 4    Case Study: Preparation of a Document by Several Participants

We illustrate the proposed modularization with a case study. It will be used to show how the decision rules declared in requirements can be transformed into modules of executable synchronous protocol models. It will be also used to illustrate our investigation of the applicability of Java-based techniques for implementation of decision modules.

Let us consider a system that controls a preparation of a document, e.g. a proposal, a paper or a report, by several participants. One of the participants usually plays the role of the coordinator responsible for submitting the document. There is a deadline for the document submission.

The coordinator creates the parts of the document and chooses participants. Each part is assigned to a participant. A part has its own deadline before the deadline of the document and should be submitted by the participant so that the coordinator has time to combine parts and submit the document.

If a participant misses the part deadline, the coordinator sends a reminder to the delaying participant. The coordinator can change the deadline or assign the document to another participant. Only the coordinator can cancel the preparation of the document.

## 5    Decision Modules in Requirements

In our experience of requirements engineering we have found that requirements often describe the decision modules informally.

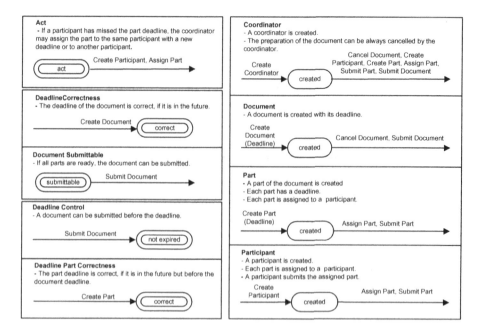

**Fig. 1.** Declarative specification

We start with an observation that almost every sentence of requirements presents a snapshot of the desired system behaviour. A snapshot is a visible abstract state captured after or before an event. Figure 1 presents all the snapshots corresponding to the case study in Sect. 4 as a declarative specification. We depict an abstract system state as a double line oval. An oval may have an ingoing or outgoing arc labeled with an action that can happen.

For example, the declaration *"A document can be submitted before the deadline"* can be presented as a decision rule or a decision module *Deadline Control*. It shows that the event *Submit Document* can only be accepted if the deadline is "not expired". In this case, the arc is ingoing.

If an event can only be accepted in the described state, then the arc is outgoing. The example is the decision module *Document Submittable: After all parts are ready, the document can be submitted.*

The state descriptions in decision modules are abstracted from the life cycle of entities of the system. An abstract state may present the state of a set of system concepts, a subset of states of the system, etc. For example, state *submittable* of the decision module *Document submittable* depends on the states of all parts of the document.

Often the decision modules give instructions or polices on what to do in a situation described as an abstract state. For example, *Act* presents a possibility to progress by creating a new participant (event *Create Participant*) who can write a part of the document (event *Assign Part*).

The elements of the life cycles of entities in the model are also present in requirements and shown in Fig. 1 as declarations. However, the states in such description are not abstract, they are the states of objects. We depict a state of an object as a single line oval. For example, we can read in requirements what an instance of the *Coordinator* can do when it is in state *"created"*. It can *Create Document, Submit Document, Create Participant, Create Part, Assign Part* and *Cancel Document*.

# 6    Decision Modules in Protocol Models

The declarative specifications are not executable. However, there is a way to present decision modules as modules of executable protocol models. We show this way of modularization after a short introduction of Protocol Modelling developed by A. McNeile [22].

## 6.1    Protocol Modeling

Protocol Modeling splits the Universe into a system and its environment. A protocol model represents the modelled system. The environment submits events to the system. The system may change its state reacting to events.

The building blocks of a protocol model [22] are protocol machines and events. They are instances of, correspondingly, *protocol machine types* and *event types*. Each protocol machine "recognises" a finite set of event types, i.e. uses the names of these event types in the specification of a protocol machine type.

In order to facilitate reuse, there are two types of protocol machines: Objects and Behaviours. Behaviours cannot be instantiated on their own but may extend functionality of Objects. In a sense, Behaviours are similar to mixins or aspects in programming languages [2,20].

A *protocol machine type* is an LTS (Labelled Transition System) extended with attributes and call-backs to enable modelling with data:

$$PM_i = (s_i^0, S_i, E_i, T_i, A_i, CB_i, ), where$$

- $s_i^0$ is the initial state;
- $S_i$ is a non-empty finite set of states;
- $E_i$ is a finite set of transition labels being the "recognized" event types $e_i$, coming from the environment. The set can be empty.
- $T_i \subseteq S_i \times E_i \times S_i$ a finite set of transitions:
  $t = (s_x, e, s_y)$, $s_x, s_y \in S_i, e \in E_i$. The set of transitions can be empty. The states are updated by transitions.
- $A_i$ is a finite set of attributes of the specified types. The standard data types such as *String, Integer, Currency, Date*, etc. plus the types of protocol machines can be used for specification of attributes. The attributes are the data containers of a protocol machine. A protocol machine Object contains at least one attribute, the Name of the Object. The set of attributes of a Behaviour protocol machine can be empty.

- $CB_i(PM_1, \ldots, PM_n, E_1, \ldots, E_m) = (PM_1, \ldots, PM_n, E_1, \ldots, E_m)$ is a call-back function. $PM_1, \ldots, PM_n$ are the protocol machines of the protocol model. $E_1, \ldots, E_m$ are the events of the protocol model. We list all protocol machines of the protocol model and the events "recognized" by $PM_i$ as the arguments of the callback function $CB_i$ because the elements of all protocol machines and all "recognized" events can be used as inputs for updating the values of the attributes, states and events of the protocol machines. These values can be updated using the callback function only as a result of a transition, i.e. as a result of event acceptance.
  If no calculation is needed for updating attributes of the protocol machine $PM_i$, the set of callback functions is empty.

  "Recognized" events are modelled from the system perspective. Each event belongs to a specified type telling the system what kind of attributes can be found in this event.
  *An event type* is a tuple $e = (A^e, CB^e)$, where

- $A^e$ is a finite not empty set of attributes of the event.
- $CB^e(PM_1, \ldots, PM_n, E_1, \ldots, E_m) = (PM_1, \ldots, PM_n, E_1, \ldots, E_m)$ is a call-back function corresponding to this event. The callback function for an event is used if the protocol model generates other events using the attributes of this event.

  Within Protocol Modelling, callback functions are the instruments for data handling. In the ModelScope tool [21] supporting the execution of protocol models, the callbacks are coded as Java classes with methods changing and/or returning the values of attributes and states of instances of protocol machines. They may also change attributes of events and generate event instances.

*CSP parallel composition.* A protocol model $(PM)$ is a CSP parallel composition of a finite number of *instances of protocol machines*. A $PM$ is also a protocol machine, the set of states of which is the Cartesian product of states of all composed protocol machines [22]:

$$PM = \|\underset{i=1}{\overset{n \in N}{PM_i}} = (s_i^0, S_i, E_i, T_i, A_i, CB_i) = (s_0, S, E, T, A, CB, ).$$

$s_0 = \bigcup_{i=1}^{n} s_i^0$ is the initial state;

$S = \prod_{i=1}^{n} S_i$ is the set of states;

$E = \bigcup_{i=1}^{n} E_i$ is the set of events;

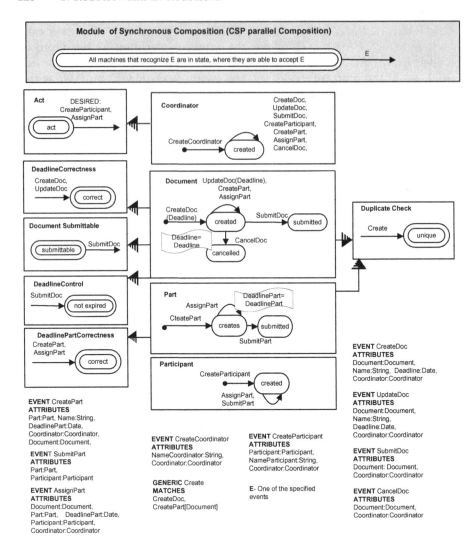

**Fig. 2.** Executable Protocol Model

$$A = \bigcup_{i=1}^{n} A_i \text{ is the set attributes of all machines;}$$

$$CB = \bigcup_{i=1}^{n} CB^i \text{ is the set of callbacks of all machines.}$$

The set of transitions $T$ of the protocol model is defined by the rules of the CSP parallel composition [8]. The rules synchronise transitions of protocol machines.

The CSP composition rules in Protocol Modelling are:

- If an event is not recognised by the protocol model, it is *ignored*.
- If an event is recognised by the protocol model and all protocol machines, recognising this event, are able to accept it, the event is *enabled*.
- If an event is recognised by the protocol model, but at least one protocol machine, recognising this event, is not able to accept it, the event is *refused*.

As the result, the composition may contain the union of transitions of composed protocol machines if the sets of the "recognised" events of protocol machines are disjoint. If the sets of the "recognised" events are not disjoint, the set of allowed transitions is defined using the Cartesian product $\prod S_i$ of states of machines, the set of events and the rules of CSP parallel composition. An algorithm of calculation of the set of transitions can be found in [26].

*Dependent Protocol Machines. Derived States.*
Transitions $T_i$ of a protocol machine $PM_i$ enable updates of only its own states; namely, those in $S_i$. On the other hand, protocol machines can read the states of other protocol machines, although cannot change them. Callback functions $CB_i$ are used to read states of specified protocol machines and update attributes and calculate derived states of protocol machines of type Behaviour.

Callback functions create dependencies between protocol machines. The dependency means that one protocol machine (usually the included protocol machine of type Behaviour) needs to read the state of other protocol machines to calculate its own state. Such calculated states are called *derived states*, which distinguishes them from the *stored states* denoted in the model [22]. A protocol machine with derived (calculated) states is called dependent.

A transition of a dependent protocol machine contains a derived state and an event, permitted in this state. The derived state can be either an input or output state of this event.

As all protocol machines are composed with he same CSP parallel composition rules, a dependent protocol machine specifies an extra "restrictions" on the acceptance of an event by other protocol machines of the protocol model. Note that these "restricted" protocol machines are not necessarily the same protocol machines, states of which have been read to derive the state of the dependent protocol machine.

The ability of protocol machines to read the state of other protocol machines is an asset for separation of decision modules. Decision modules need this to read the information of other modules and use it to specify a decision about event acceptance.

Further, there are two types of derived states possible in dependent machines, which can be used in decision modules:

(1) The pre-state of a transition which can be calculated. The pre-state is similar to guards calculated in Coloured Petri Nets (CPN) [12] and the UML state machines [23].
(2) The post-state of a transition which can also be calculated. We mentioned already that the callback functions can update the values of the attributes,

states and events only as a result of a transition, i.e. as a result of event acceptance. If a post-state refuses the event caused its calculation, the event is rolled back, i.e. the system sends a messages about the post-state value and it is returned into the state that preceded to the event acceptance. This semantics does not exist either in the UML, CPN or BPMN. An example of a decision module using a post-state will be shown in the next sub-section.

## 6.2   Protocol Model with Decision Modules in the Case Study

The protocol model of our case study is shown in Fig. 2. This protocol model can be executed in the ModelScope tool [21].

A finite set of *EVENTS* is defined for this protocol model. For example, the event type *CreateDoc* is a tuple of variables of types *Document, Coordinator, String* and *Date*. The elements *Document* and *Coordinator* are the protocol machines of types *Document* and *Coordinator* correspondingly (Listing 1).

**Listing 1.** EVENT CreateDoc

```
EVENT CreateDoc
ATTRIBUTES
      Document : Document ,
      Name : String ,
      Deadline : Date ,
      Coordinator : Coordinator
```

As we see, the event is described as a set of attributes of standard data types and the types of protocol machines *Coordinator* and *Document.*

The life cycles entities (objects) *Coordinator, Participant, Part* and *Document* are specified as protocol machines. Figure 2 shows the protocol machines graphically.

Listing 2 shows the textual specification of a protocol machine of type *Document.* Before its creation, any object is in the state @*new.* Accepting events, any object transits to states of its life cycle. For example, being in state @*new* and accepting event *CreateDoc* an object of type *Document* transits from state @*new* to state *created.*

The corresponding transition is depicted as follows: @*new\*CreateDoc= created.*

**Listing 2.** OBJECT Document

```
OBJECT Document
NAME Name
INCLUDES      DeadlineControl ,
              DocumentSubmittable ,
              DeadlineCorrectness ,
              DuplicateCheck
ATTRIBUTES
              Name : String , Deadline : Date ,
              Coordinator : Coordinator
```

```
STATES created , submitted , cancelled
TRANSITIONS @new*CreateDoc= created ,
             created*UpdateDoc=created ,
             created*CreatePart=created ,
             created*AssignPart=created ,
             created*SubmitDoc=submitted ,
             created*CancelDoc=cancelled
```

Using the protocol machines presenting the life cycles of system entities, the decision modules can be specified. In order to establish the functional relations between the states of life cycle modules (objects) and the derived states of decision modules, the decision module is described as a labelled transition system with callback functions.

For example, the *decision module DeadlineControl* in our protocol model consists of a description of the labeled transition system (Listing 3) and the corresponding java class (of the same name, Listing 4) describing functional relation between the states of the decision module and the life cycle modules.

The relation between the *DeadlineControl* and *Document* is specified with the *INCLUDE* sentence in the *Document* (Listing 2). To facilitate reuse, the *DeadlineControl* decision module can be included in any other object that have an attribute *Deadline*.

**Listing 3.** BEHAVIOUR DeadlineControl

```
BEHAVIOUR ! DeadlineControl
# Allows SubmitDoc only if
# the deadline is not expired
    STATES expired , not expired
    TRANSITIONS @any*SubmitDoc= not expired
```

The decision module *DeadlineControl* contains transition @*any* * *SubmitDoc* = *notexpired*. State @*any* literally means any possible combination of the states of the life cycle modules in the model.

The functional dependency between *DeadlineControl* and the attribute *Deadline* of the *Document* is defined in the java class *DeadlineControl* shown in Listing 4 as a callback. Behaviour *DeadlineControl* relates an instance of the *Document* with the system clock which is invisibly present in the model. The system clock gives the current date. The current date is compared with the *Deadline* of the *Document*. The derived state *"expired"* or *"not expired"* is returned to the protocol machine *DeadlineControl*.

**Listing 4.** Java Callback for BEHAVIOUR DeadlineControl

```
import java.util.Date;
public class DeadlineControl extends Behaviour{
  public String getState(){
    Date expDate = this.getDate(''Deadline'');
    Date currentDate = new Date();
```

```
    return currentDate.compareTo(expDate)>0
    ? "expired": "not_expired";
  }
}
```

The decision module *DeadlineControl* is an example of the Behaviour that calculates the post-state after proceeding of the event *SubmitDoc*. If the derived state of *DeadlineControl* after processing an event of type *SubmitDoc* has the value "expired", then the event is rolled back and the system returns into the state before processing of this event.

Figure 2 also shows the examples of the Behaviours that use the pre-state of other protocol machines for making the decision. For example, Behaviour *Document Submittable* is included into the Object *Document*. *Document Submittable* derives its state *submittable* only if all *Parts* of the *Document* are in state *submitted* (Listings 5 and 6).

**Listing 5.** BEHAVIOUR DocumentSubmittable

```
BEHAVIOUR !DocumentSubmittable
# Ensures that a document  cannot be
#submitted if it has unfinished Parts
ATTRIBUTES !Document Status: String
    STATES submittable, not submittable
    TRANSITIONS submittable*SubmitDoc=@any
```

**Listing 6.** Java Callback for BEHAVIOUR DocumentSubmittable

```java
public class DocumentSubmittable extends Behaviour {
  public String getState() {
    boolean allSubmitted =true;
    Instance[] myParts =
        this.selectByRef("Part","Document");
    if (myParts.length==0)
        {allSubmitted = false;}
    for (int i = 0; i < myParts.length; i++) {
      if ((myParts[i].getState("Part").equals("created")))
          allSubmitted = false;
      }
    return allSubmitted? "submittable": "not_submittable";
  }
  public String getDocumentStatus() {
    return this.getState("DocumentSubmittable");
    }
}
```

Figure 2 presents six decision modules: *DeadlineCorrectness, DeadlinePart-Correctness, DeadlineControl, Document Submittable, Act, Duplicate check*. The arc with the half-dashed triangle end shows the INCLUDE relation.

Several decision modules may be included into the same object. For example, four decision modules are included into object *Document*. All the decision modules processing the submitted event need to be executed to make a decision about its proceeding. Any event proceeds only if all the protocol machines recognising this event permit its proceeding.

## 6.3   Properties of Decision Modules in Protocol Models

We can name the following *properties of decision modules in Protocol Models*:

1. *Modularity:* a decision module localises the decision making rules (separates them for the purpose of reuse);
   For example, the module *DeadlineControl* can restrict the behaviour of objects *Document* and *Part* in the same way.
2. *Unidirectional Dependency*: the decision modules can read the state of other modules, but other modules do not know how the decision is made (other modules are oblivious [7]).
   For example, *DeadlineControl* reads the value of attribute *Deadline* of the object *Document* and predicts state *expired, not expired* after event *Submit-Doc*. The object *Document* remains oblivious.
3. *Mechanism to Achieve the Properties is Event-driven with CSP Parallel Composition*.
   Decision modules are incorporated into the protocol model on the basis of their ability to react to predefined events following the rules of CSP parallel composition. The CSP parallel composition of all modules in protocol model allows for local modification, adding and deleting of modules without affecting the ordering in the specified behaviour sequences of existing modules.

Executable protocol models enable separation of decision modules defined in requirements. Requirements become traceable in executable models. There are obvious advantages of modularisation of decision modules for traceability of requirements and testing and modification of models.

*Traceability.* Traceability of requirements in models is prescribed in standards and considered as a prerequisite of a proper system evolution, modifiability and long life. The developers should convince themselves and their customers that the system does what it was required to do. Modularisation of decision modules directly transforms the declarations or items of requirements into modules of the model. For example, the item "If all parts are ready, the document can be submitted" is traced in the decision module *Document Submittable*.

*Testing.* Modularisation of decision modules defines the testing strategy. Each of the decision modules specifies a finite set of tests. The set of tests is finite because the decision module partitions the data into groups. Each group results in a decision. Testing only one representative from each group is sufficient to test the decisions and the variants of behaviour resulting from this decision. For example, in order to test the decision module *Document Submittable*: "If all parts are ready, the document can be submitted" two tests should be designed:

(1) a document has been created; at least two parts have been assigned; one part has been submitted and another part has not been submitted;
(2) a document has been created; the parts have been assigned and all parts have been submitted.

*Modification.* In our model we have not separated the decision module *Cancel Document*. However, we can easily modularize cancellation of a document and compose it with the model. A new decision module will define that *"If a document is in a state created, it can be canceled or submitted"*.

Systematic separation of decision modules from requirements to models and implementation promises advantages for traceability of requirements, testing and modification of the implementation. In the next section we investigate if the decision modules with the same properties as in protocol models can be implemented using such a mainstream programming language as Java.

## 7   Decision Modules in Java

The implementation of decision modules using mainstream programming languages is the question that needs investigation. To the best of our knowledge, there are no systematic implementation approaches for separation of enablers.

The research question of this paper is the following:
*Is it possible to implement the decision modules using mainstream object-oriented language techniques in such a way that the implementation of decision modules would have the same properties as the decision modules in executable protocol models, namely:*
- *modularity;*
- *unidirectional dependency;*
- *event-based composition?*

For our experiments with the implementation of decision modules we have chosen Java as one of the mainstream object-oriented programming languages.

First, we investigated if decision modules can be implemented within common Java paradigm, that is, without using any frameworks and special libraries. We consider this rather important because relying upon specialised libraries and frameworks usually makes the implementation less generic with respect to, for example, underlying architecture. It can also make the solution platform- and vendor-specific violating a well known Java principle "write once, run everywhere".

Further, we also investigate the expressivity of Enterprise Java Beans (EJB3) and aspect-oriented Java (AspectJ) [15,27] for implementation of enables and decision modules.

## 7.1   Using Object Composition

It seems that a simple way to implement decision modules is to use object composition where they are included in life cycle modules as object fields. In the Listing 7 both OBJECT *Document* and BEHAVIOUR *DeadlineControl* are shown as Java classes, the former includes the latter as an instance variable. As we said in Subsect. 6.1, the difference between life cycle modules(objects) and behaviours in Protocol Modelling is that behaviours cannot be instantiated on their own but rather extend functionality of objects. In the implementations in this paper, we do not implement this restriction. That's why there is no need in a separate class Object and both classes extend the same parent class Behaviour.

Listing 7. Implementation using Object Composition

```java
class Document extends Behaviour{
    private String name;
    private Date deadLine;
/* 'INCLUDES' in the model is implemented
as object composition */
    private DeadlineControl deadlineControl;
    public Document(String name, Date deadLine){
        this.name = name;
        this.deadLine = deadLine;
        this.state = "created";
/*if deadline changes DeadlineControl
has to be somehow notified */
        this.deadlineControl =
          new DeadlineControl(deadLine);
    }
/* This method has to check itself the state
of DeadlineControl */
    public void submitDoc(){
        if(deadlineControl.getState().
        compareTo("not_expired") == 0) {
            this.setState("submitted");
        } else {
            this.setState("cancelled");
        }
    }
}

public class DeadlineControl extends Behaviour {

/* Date needs to be passed to DeadlineControl */
    private Date deadline;
    DeadlineControl(Date deadLine) {
        this.deadline = deadLine;
```

```
    }
    @Override
    public String getState () {
        Date currentDate = new Date ();
        return
          currentDate.compareTo ( deadline ) > 0
                        ? "expired" : "not_expired";
    }
}
```

Such an implementation is quite traditional and completely within the scope of plain Java. However, its limitations are obvious:

- The communication of objects is not event-driven.
- The dependency of modules is bi-directional. The life cycle module *Document* is not oblivious about the functionality of the decision module *DeadlineControl* because it has to
  - specify *DeadlineControl* as its object field and
  - explicitly invoke the *deadlineControl.getState()* method.
  - even the state of the decision module *DeadlineControl* "not expired" is used in the code of the life cycle module *Document*.
- The implementation of the decision module is also dependent, because it has to know the exact name, the type, and the value of a constrained attribute (e.g. *Date deadline*.)

Consequently, changing (for example, changing the module name or the state name "not expired") or adding new functionality within decision modules would require refactoring and subsequent regression testing of all affected life cycle modules. The limitations above make such decision modules not generic enough to be used to implement shared behaviours among different life cycle objects.

### 7.2   Using Publisher-Subscriber Design Pattern and Java Reflection

Further generalization can be done using Java reflection and the publisher-subscriber design pattern. Java reflection makes it possible to retrieve the name of a field of a known type to the decision module. Using publisher-subscriber design pattern, we can implement event-driven mechanism, which is in the core of the Protocol Modeling approach.

Here we implemented the generic functionality of the behaviour protocol machines (Sect. 6) in the parent class *Behaviour*. In particular, *Behaviour* implements the reflection on all allowed generic data types. The *Behaviour* class can be put in a separate Java package among other application independent elements of Protocol Modeling such as *Object*, *State*, *Attribute*, or *Event*. This package - we will further refer to it as a *"behaviour engine"* - should also include generic Protocol Modelling mechanisms such as object instantiation and the CSP composition mechanism. We will introduce the latter in the following subsections.

Listing 8 shows the *Document* class, which now implements interface *SubmitDocEventListener* within the publisher-subscriber design pattern.

*DeadlineControl* has now a new attribute *deadlineAttribute*, which is used to invoke the name of the checked attribute *deadline* of the class *Document* via Java reflection inside the *getDate()* method. This method is defined in the parent class *Behaviour*.

**Listing 8.** Implementation using publisher-subscriber design pattern and Java Reflection

```
class Behaviour {
  /*
  . . .
  The rest of BEHAVIOUR functionality
  . . .
  */
      public Date getDate(String dateFieldName){
      //Reflection to get access to the value
      //of dateFieldName of type Date
          Field field;
          field =
            this.getClass().
              getDeclaredField(dateFieldName);
          field.setAccessible(true);
          return (Date) field.get(this);
      }
}


public class Document extends Behaviour
      implements SubmitDocEventListener {

      private String name;
      private Date deadLine;
  /*    'INCLUDES' in the model is implemented
  as object composition */
      private DeadlineControl deadlineControl;

      public Document(String name, Date deadLine){
          this.name = name;
          this.deadLine = deadLine;
          setState(State.NEW);
          //passes the deadline attribute
          this.deadlineControl =
            new DeadlineControl(''deadLine'');
      }
```

```
/* Implementation of listener method
from SubmitDocEventListener interface */
    @Override
    public void submitDocEventReceived (){
        if (deadlineControl.getState(this) ==
            DocManState.NOT_EXPIRED) {
            this.setState(DocManState.SUBMITTED);
        }
    }

}
public class DeadlineControl extends Behaviour{
    private String deadlineAttribute;

    DeadlineControl(String deadline) {
        this.deadlineAttribute = deadline;
    }

        public DocManState getState(Behaviour inst){
        Date expDate =
            inst.getDate(this.deadlineAttribute);
        Date currentDate = new Date();
        return
            currentDate.compareTo(expDate) > 0
            ? DocManState.EXPIRED : DocManState.NOT_EXPIRED;
    }
}
```

In the enhanced code above we also make use of the class *DocManState*, which specialises the application dependent functionality of the behaviour engine's generic class *State* and contains the enumeration of all possible states of the objects in the *Document Manager* model.

The publisher-subscriber design pattern implements the Protocol Modelling event-based communication of modules. Java reflection allows reducing the dependency of the decision module on a particular life cycle module.

Still, OBJECT *Document* has to be aware of the functionality of the BEHAVIOUR *DeadlineControl* as it has to invoke it inside the event handler *submitDocEventReceived()*. The dependency of modules is bi-directional.

### 7.3    Using Interceptors Within Enterprise Java Beans Framework

A decision module can be seen as a managerial concern or a control concern. In mainstream languages, concerns are often implemented using the aspect mechanism.

We intend to investigate if the aspect mechanisms in Java can support implementation of decision modules that have only unidirectional dependency with life cycle modules, that is, the decision modules can read the state of the life cycle modules and permit or forbid proceeding of events while the life cycles are oblivious to decision modules.

The standard Java currently has only one aspect mechanism implemented in the Java Enterprise Edition (Java EE [6]), which supports Enterprise Java Beans 3 (EJB3) specification. EJB3 supports special objects called interceptors, which have the "around invoke" aspect semantics. Interceptors are invoked by the Java EE container run by an application server. Each EJB may have a set of "business methods" which can be surrounded by additional functionally provided by a decision module via container. The decision module is implemented as an interceptor. The container is instructed by an EJB3 annotation *@Interceptors* to call an interceptor before the invocation of a business method of a bean.

In the Listing 9, the life cycle module is implemented as class *Document*. It is a "stateless" bean [6], which the corresponding annotation *@Stateless* declares. The only thing the code developer has to do with the life cycle module is to choose the business method (or methods) that should be intercepted and annotate this business method with the *@Interceptors(DeadlineControlInterceptor.class)* annotation. In our case, this is the *SubmitDoc()* method. This annotation informs the application server that before submitting the document the corresponding deadline control interceptor has to be invoked.

**Listing 9.** Implementation of OBJECT type Document as a stateless bean using EJB3 specification

```
@Stateless
public class Document implements DocumentRemote {

    private String name;
    private static Date deadLine;
    private String state;

    public Document() {
        this.state = "@new";
        /*..*/
    }

    @Interceptors(DeadlineControlInterceptor.class)
    @Override
    public void submitDoc() {
        this.state = DocManState.SUBMITTED;
    }
}
```

Interceptor *DeadlineControlInterceptor* (Listing 10) is a Java class. It has one special method annotated as *@AroundInvoke*. Via its only parameter *InvocationContext*, it has access to the life cycle module's instance. The Java reflection mechanism provides access to the *deadLine* attribute of the *Document* object.

**Listing 10.** Implementation of DeadlineControl as an interceptor using EJB3 specification

```
class  DeadlineControlInterceptor  {

    @AroundInvoke
    public  Object  getState(InvocationContext  ic)
    throws  Exception  {
        Date  currentDate  =  new  Date();
/*  Using  InvocationContext  to  get  the  object
    and  reflection  to  get  the  value  of  its
   "deadLine"  attribute  */
        Field  fld  =  ic.getMethod().
        getDeclaringClass().
            getDeclaredField("deadLine");
        fld.setAccessible(true);
        Date  dt  =  new  Date();
        Date  expDate  =  (Date)  fld.get(dt);
        if  (currentDate.compareTo(expDate)  >  0)  {
            return  null;  //Method  submitDoc()  is  not  called
        }  else  {
            return  ic.proceed();
        }
    }
}
```

Using *InvacationContext*, the decision module *DeadlineControlInterceptor* obtains the name of the attribute *"deadLine"* to read its value from the life cycle module. The value of the *"deadLine"* is assigned to the *expDate (expiration Date)* and compared with the current date.

The implementation above is generic enough as it allows using the same decision module among multiple life cycle modules. The only restriction remains that the name of the constrained attribute "deadLine" has to be the same among all of them. The unidirectional dependency is achieved using the interceptor mechanism supported by the application server. The event-based communication and composition is also used (although not shown in the listings above).

### 7.4 Using Enterprise Java Beans Framework and Decorator Design Pattern

One may argue that using reflection is not safe and should be avoided whenever it's possible. In some cases, life cycle modules to be extended by decision modules may have the same external behaviour, e.g. *Document* and *Part* in our running case study. In such a case, decision modules may be implemented as wrappers to life cycle modules using the Decorator design pattern. In the EJB3 specification this pattern is supported as well. Decorators implement a mechanism that is close to interceptors. They add functionality to the decorated classes. However, instead of implementing cross-cutting concerns useful for different class types, they extend the behaviour of a class implementing a certain interface.

In the following Listing 11 the deadline control functionality is implemented as a decorator class *DocumentDeadlineControlDecorator*.

**Listing 11.** Implementation of DeadlineControl using Delegation within EJB3 specification

```
@Decorator
public abstract class
    DocumentDeadlineControlDecorator
        implements DocumentRemote {

    @Inject
    @Delegate
    DocumentRemote doc;

    @Override
    public void submitDoc() {
        Date currentDate = new Date();
            if(currentDate.
                compareTo(doc.getDeadLine()) >0){
                System.err.println("Expired");
            } else {
                doc.submitDoc();
            }
    }
}
```

The code shows the *Document* or *Part* class injected via their common interface *DocumentRemote*. The *@Inject* annotation uses the dependency injection mechanism [6] to give the decorator access to the decorated class. The *@Delegate* annotation gives the container access to all exposed methods of all the classes implementing the *DocumentRemote* interface. In our example, the call of the *submitDoc()* method of *Document* happens only if the deadline is not expired. As one can see, the techniques based on the dependency injection mechanism provide the implementation means to produce the decision modules with all the desired properties: modularity, unidirectional dependency with other modules, event-based communication and composition of modules.

The disadvantage of the decision modules' implementation approach using EJB3 is obvious: it's too heavy. The overhead of running the application server just for the sake of support of decision modules is not sufficiently justified. However, if the system is already implemented as an enterprise application, this may be a viable solution. EJB3 is supported by a large variety of certified application servers [25], both open source and proprietary. In order to completely avoid a vendor lock the EJB3 platform may be substituted by a platform independent solution, for example, the Spring framework [27]. It has an additional benefit, as it supports the AspectJ [5] specification, which implements the aspect paradigm much more thoroughly than EJB3 does. We didn't experiment with Spring, but a code snippet like the one below can be already envisioned (Listing 12).

**Listing 12.** Implementation of DeadlineControl as an aspect using Spring framework specification

```
@Aspect
public class DeadlineControlAspect {
/* ... */
    @Around(''execution(* documentmanager.submitDoc(..))'')
    public void DeadlineControl(JoinPoint joinPoint){

        /* add decision module functionality here */

    }
}
```

Still, Spring is an additional layer on top of an application server. In the following section we show how AspectJ as a special library for plain Java can be used to implement decision modules.

### 7.5   Using AspectJ

The idea to implement business rules as aspects is not new. The authors of [13,16,17] point out that aspects allow the developers to separate the business logic from the application's core functionality encapsulating in aspects both crosscutting features as well as their "connectors" [17] to business objects. This makes it possible to "completely remove the source code pertaining to the business rules" [13] from the business objects. In our terminology this is called unidirectional dependency or obliviousness. In this subsection we show how the entire set of Protocol Modelling properties may be implemented using aspect technology for the plain Java.

We implemented our running example using an AspectJ plugin for Eclipse [5]. In the implementation, we continued to separate the generic Protocol Modelling behaviour from the application (*Document Manager*) specific functionality.

Apart from the *Behaviour* class, already implemented earlier, we added to the generic implementation ("behaviour engine") two public interfaces *LifecycleModule* and *DecisionModule*.

The interface *LifecycleModule* contains the list of its decision modules and the declarations of methods linking a life cycle module to its decision modules. This is the implementation of the protocol model INCLUDES declaration (Listing 2).

The interface *DecisionModule* declares the *decide()* method, which, being implemented, have to return *true*, if the decision module is in the right state allowing proceeding the event specified for this decision module or *false* otherwise.

Further, we implemented the protocol model generic behaviour as an abstract aspect *BehaviourProtocol* (Listing 13).

**Listing 13.** Implementation of the Protocol Modeling behaviour as an abstract aspect using AspectJ

```
public abstract aspect BehaviourProtocol {
  public abstract pointcut stateChanges(LifecycleModule lc);

  void around(LifecycleModule lc): stateChanges(lc) {
    for (int i = 0; i<lc.getDecisionModules().size(); i++){
      if (!((DecisionModule) lc.getDecisionModules()
          .elementAt(i)).decide(lc)){
        System.out.println("NO_GO!");
        return;
      }
    }
    proceed(lc);
  }
/* ... */
}
```

The most important part of our "engine" is the AspectJ advice *state-Changes()* with "around invoke" semantics. It iterates through all the life cycle module's (LC) decision modules (DM) using their *decide()* methods. If the state of each decision module permits to proceed, the AspectJ's *proceed()* method is invoked, which allows the corresponding LC module's method to run. As one can see in Listing 13, if several DM's are used for a single LC, the AND semantics is implemented with respect to the DM invocation: each of them has to be in the right state that permits proceeding. If necessary, any other semantics of logical composition of aspects (e.q., OR, XOR) can be realized generically at the implementation level.

Listing 14 shows the application specific part of the AspectJ implementation. There is an aspect implementing the *BehaviourProtocol* abstract aspect. It declares the *Document* class as a LC and the *DeadlineControl* class as its DM and also links them to the aspect. Next, the *DeadlineControl*'s *decide()* method is implemented by the aspect. Finally, the pointcut is created, which links the advice *stateChanges* to the *Document*'s method *submitDocEventAJ()*.

**Listing 14.** Implementation of the application specific behaviour using AspectJ

```
public aspect BehaviourProtocolDocManImpl
                        extends BehaviourProtocol {
/* Document as a life cycle module */
  declare parents: Document
                        implements LifecycleModule;
  public Object Document.getData() { return this; }
/* Its decision module */
  declare parents: DeadlineControl
                        implements DecisionModule;
/* GO-No GO method for the decision module */
```

```
public boolean DeadlineControl.decide(LifecycleModule lc)
{
    System.out.println("DeadlineControl_Works!");
/* Here the DM gets the information about types of the LC
   fields to check and their correct states for GO */
    if (getState((Behaviour) lc.getData()) ==
                                DocManState.NOT_EXPIRED ){
        return true;
    } else{
        return false;
    }
}
/* stateChanges is invoked for each target being a life
   cycle module with the signature of the method aspect
   is weaved to */
    public pointcut stateChanges(LifecycleModule lc):
        target(lc) &&  call(public void submitDocEventAJ())
}
```

Listing 15 shows the AspectJ implementation of the *Document* class. As one can see, this is a "purely oblivious" implementation without any knowledge about the decision module. The decision module can be implemented the same way as shown in Listing 8. To obtain its current state, it still needs Java reflection and the knowledge about the LC's field type. However, as we pointed out before (Subsect. 7.2), it is possible to implement any type-related functionality, which uses reflection, as a member method of the generic class *Behaviour*.

**Listing 15.** Document class in the AspectJ implementation

```
public class Document extends Behaviuor
    private String name;
    private Date deadLine;
    public Document(String name, Date deadLine) {
        this.name = name;
        this.deadLine = deadLine;
        setState(State.NEW);
    }
    public void submitDocEventAJ() {
        this.setState(DocManState.SUBMITTED);
    }
/* ... */
    }
}
```

To support modularity, the AspectJ implementation clearly separates the core and business rule logics between LC and DM implementation classes. The former are completely oblivious to the latter. The even-driven mechanism can be easily implemented using the publisher-subscriber pattern as we have shown before in Subsect. 7.2. Moreover, the generic Protocol Modelling behaviour can be further separated from the application specific one. This way, the usability of the approach can be facilitated.

### 7.6   Using Mixins

Another promising approach would be to program with mixins [18]. When a class implements a mixin, it implements an interface extended with this mixin and, this way, implements mixin's attributes and methods. This description is very close to the functionality of *BEHAVIOUR* in protocol models. Unfortunately, direct realisation of mixins in mainstream languages is largely absent, at least without making use of special or not well known libraries. Despite some anecdotal claims, the support of mixins in Java is hardly expected in foreseeable future as well. The newly released Java 8 SE specification [11] does not support them either.

A partial solution could be to use newly introduces in Java 8 SE [11] so called "virtual extension methods", which simply allow one to add default method implementations to the interface not changing the implementation classes. Whether or not such a feature could be sufficient enough for decision module implementations needs further experiments. In our future study we intend to investigate as to how some known ad-hoc approaches [14] can be used to program decision modules with mixins.

### 7.7   Properties of Decision Modules in Java Implementations

Table 1 summarises the implementation examples above with respect to their adherence to the properties of decision modules in Protocol Modelling as they described in Subsect. 6.3. The table shows that the aspect-oriented implementation techniques provide full support for the modularization with decision modules.

## 8   Discussion

### 8.1   Decision Abstractions in Behaviour Modelling Practice

Decision modules are the abstractions of the business system modelling domain.

The practice shows that the most changeable parts of functionality of information and case management systems are the parts that present the rules of handling the cases and information. The rules of handling insurance claims change every year. The rules of proposal selection for funding and crediting are constantly modified following the changes in the economic situation. The rules of dealing with private health information in patient files, the rules of using the information on the web, all undergo changes. Localization of such rules in separate modules and the ability to modify those modules without changes in other modules are the desired requirements supporting changeability of systems during their evolution. Complex automated control systems may experience less

**Table 1.** Protocol Modelling decision modules properties in different Java implementations

| Technique | Modularity | Unidirectional dependency | Mechanism: Event-Driven (CSP\|\|) |
|---|---|---|---|
| Object Composition | yes | no | no |
| Publ.-Subscr.& Java Reflection | yes | partially, state reading:yes obliviousness:no | yes |
| EJB 3 with Interceptors | yes | yes | yes |
| EJB 3 with Delegation | yes | yes, for a given interface | yes |
| Aspects with AspectJ | yes | yes | yes |

changes but they still need to overcome modernization. The localization of decision points in such a way that their changes does not change the rest of the system can simplify regression testing of system modifications.

The need of localising decisions seems being realised in the draft version of the new Case Management Model and Notation (CMMN) [24] standard developed by OMG. The standard includes a decision module called *Sentry*. "Sentry watches out for important situations to occur (or events), which influence the further proceedings of a Case. . . A Sentry is a combination of an event and/or condition. When the event occurs, a condition might be applied to evaluate whether the event has effect or not" [24](p. 23).

Thus, on the one hand, the need of decision points as separate entities has been recognised by the OMG community. On the other hand, the Protocol Modelling semantics forms a solid basis for building executable models with decision modules. There is also the ModelScope tool [21] that supports the execution of protocol models. This is a good starting point. In this paper we have shown the possibilities of implementation of decision models with the same properties as in protocol models.

However, there are barriers to widespread adoption of the new protocol modelling style.

– *Unawareness.* The first barrier is unawareness of the modelling community about this style of modelling. The CMMN standard is young and still under development. The description of the standard does not exactly follow the protocol modelling semantics. The mutual adaptation of the Protocol Modelling and the CMMN standard would contribute to the awareness about decision modules.

- *A Small Number of Success Stories.* For the moment, success stories have been collected at the official web page of the company called Metamaxim [21]. A systematic application was fulfilled for the use case of basic insurance for Oracle Nederland [28]. In order to convince businesses to use the new modelling style, more success stories have to be collected and distributed to the modelling community and businesses.
- *Legacy Models.* There are many legacy models in the key business areas like banking and government services. These models are built using the traditional process modelling style. To adopt a new modelling style, companies need a very good motivation for new investments in those models. Modelling does not give direct return on investments. Better understanding and reasoning are not tangible enough. The advantages of the new modelling style need further valorisation.

## 8.2   Decision Modules in Implementations. The Way to Go?

The bottleneck in system development is often the implementation of changes. For example, the maintenance teams of insurance applications experience stress every year as the new rules of claim handling are accepted by the governments, say, in November-December. The changes often need to be implemented and work perfectly from the first day of January. Most of the time, the modifications concern decision rules. If the implementation follows the new modelling style and supports local modifications which guarantee that the not-modified parts preserve their behaviour, the time for implementation and testing activities will be shortened. This evidence will be the best argument in favour of the new modelling and implementation style. We see the best way to obtain such an evidence in refactoring an existing application in some traditional case management domain. To do so, we need a proper tool support for different stages of the software development process.

- *Refactoring of Conventional Process Models.* The first group of tools should be able to refactor or transform the conventional process models into protocol models with separated decision models. These tools should help to overcome the barrier of legacy systems and also increase the awareness in the new style of modelling and the properties of models with separated decision modules.
- *An Open Source Execution Tool for CMMN Models with Protocol Modelling Semantics.* The most convincing way of promoting the new approach is to let the user to play with it. Even more importantly, executable Protocol Modelling would allow the developers to get insights into the model at early stages of the development and avoid more costly mistakes at the later stages.
- *Implementation libraries and plugins.* The Protocol Modelling implementation style has to be accompanied by open source libraries which should implement its generic functionality. In our experiments with Java and AspectJ we have found that this generic part can be factored out from the application specific

behaviour into a separate package. Further, using the plugin mechanism, a "behaviuor engine" package and, thus, the decision module-based approach can be made a part of the development environments such as Eclipse or Net-Beans.

In our future work we intend to follow the directions indicated in the above list.

## 9    Conclusion

In this paper we have defined decision modules and investigated the possibilities of Java implementation of decision modules identified in requirements and modularized in protocol models.

Decision modules separate a specification of the state of a non-empty set of system objects in the form of a calculated state allowing or forbidding a set of system actions. The calculated states serve as conditions for making decisions about the possible system actions. Separation of such modules facilitates requirements traceability, test generation and modification of models and implementations.

We have shown a possible way to separate decision models in declarative models, executable protocol models and Java programs.

To answer our research question, we conclude that it is indeed possible to implement functionality of decision modules using such mainstream object-oriented language techniques as EJB3 and AspectJ so that such implementations would have the same properties as the decision modules in executable protocol models. These techniques support all the decision modules' properties and provide the means to make generic implementations. The usability of such a solution depends on the development of necessary libraries and plugins. In this paper we have collected the experience for creating a "behaviour composition engine" for the implementation of applications with life-cycle and decision modules.

## References

1. von Halle, B.: Business Rules Applied. Wiley, New York (2001)
2. Bracha, G., Cook, W.: Mixin-based inheritance. In: OOPSLA/ECOOP 1990 Proceedings of the European conference on object-oriented programming on Object-oriented programming systems, languages, and applications, pp. 303–311 (1990)
3. Business Rules Group. Defining Business Rules. What Are They Really? (2000). http://www.businessrulesgroup.org/first_paper/br01c0.htm
4. Date, C.J.: What not How: The Business Rules Approach to Application Development. Addison-Wesley, Boston (2000)
5. Eclipse. AspectJ project. http://projects.eclipse.org/projects/tools.aspectj
6. EJB 3.2 Expert Group. JSR-318 Enterprise JavaBeans, Version 3.2 (2013)
7. Filman, R., Elrad, T., Clarke, S., Akşit, M.: Aspect-Oriented Software Development. Addison-Wesley, Boston (2004)
8. Hoare, C.: Communicating Sequential Processes. Prentice-Hall International (1985)
9. IDC. IDC survey (2007). http://ceiton.com/CMS/EN/workflow/introduction.html/

10. Taylor, J., Raden, N.: Smart (Enough) Systems. Prentice Hall, Upper Saddle River, NJ, USA (2007)
11. JSR-000337 Java SE 8 Release (2014)
12. Jensen, K.: Coloured Petri Nets. Springer, Heidelberg (1997)
13. Kellens, A., Schutter, K.D., D'Hondt, T., Jonckers, V., Doggen, H.: Experiences in modularizing business rules into aspects. In: ICSM 2008, pp. 448–451 (2008)
14. Kerflyn's Blog. Java 8: Now You Have Mixins?. http://kerflyn.wordpress.com/2012/07/09/java-8-now-you-have-mixins/
15. Kiczales, G., Lamping, J., Mendhekar, A., Maeda, C., Lopes, C., Loingtier, J.-M., Irwin, J.: Aspect-oriented programming. In: Proceedings of the European Conference on Object-Oriented Programming, vol. 1241, pp. 220–242 (1997)
16. Cibrán, M.A., D'Hondt, M.: Composable and reusable business rules using AspectJ. In: Workshop on Software engineering Properties of Languages for Aspect Technologies (SPLAT) at the International Conference on AOSD. Boston, USA (2003)
17. Cibrán, M.A., D'Hondt, M., Jonckers, V.: Aspect-oriented programming for connecting business rules. In: 6th Proceedings of International Conference on Business nforamtioon Systems, Colorado Springs, USA (2003)
18. Flatt, M., Adsul, B., Felleisen, M.: A programmer's reduction semantics for classes and mixins. In: Alves-Foss, J. (ed.) Formal Syntax and Semantics of Java. LNCS, vol. 1523, pp. 241–269. Springer, Heidelberg (1999)
19. McNeile, A., Roubtsova, E.: CSP parallel composition of aspect models. In: AOM 2008, pp. 13–18 (2008)
20. McNeile, A., Roubtsova, E.: Aspect-oriented development using protocol modeling. In: Katz, S., Mezini, M., Kienzle, J. (eds.) Transactions on Aspect-Oriented Software Development VII. LNCS, vol. 6210, pp. 115–150. Springer, Heidelberg (2010)
21. McNeile, A., Simons, N.: http://www.metamaxim.com/
22. McNeile, A., Simons, N.: Protocol modelling: a modelling approach that supports reusable behavioural abstractions. Softw. Syst. Modeling 5(1), 91–107 (2006)
23. OMG. Unified Modeling Language: Superstructure version 2.1.1 formal/2007-02-03 (2003)
24. OMG. Case Management Model and Notation. Version 1.0, formal/2014-05-05 (2014)
25. Oracle. JavaEE Compatibility. http://www.oracle.com/technetwork/java/javaee/overview/compatibility-jsp-136984.html
26. Roubtsova, E., Roubtsov, S.: A test generator for model-based testing. In: Proceedings of the Fourth International Symposium on Business Modeling and Software Design, BMSD 2014, 24–26 June, 2014. Luxembourg (2014)
27. Spring. Spring Framework. http://projects.spring.io/spring-framework/
28. Verheul, J., Roubtsova, E.: An executable and changeable reference model for the health insurance industry. In: The 3rd International Workshop on Behavioural Modelling - Foundations and Application, BM-FA 2011, Birmingham, UK, pp. 33–40. ACM DL (2011)

# Concern-Oriented Behaviour Modelling with Sequence Diagrams and Protocol Models

Wisam Al Abed, Matthias Schöttle$^{(\boxtimes)}$, Abir Ayed, and Jörg Kienzle

School of Computer Science, McGill University, Montreal, QC H3A 0E9, Canada
{wisam.alabed,matthias.schoettle,abir.ayed}@mail.mcgill.ca,
joerg.kienzle@mcgill.ca

**Abstract.** Concern-Oriented REuse (CORE) is a multi-view modelling approach that builds on the disciplines of model-driven engineering, software product lines and aspect-orientation to define broad units of reuse, so called concerns. Concerns specify the essence of a design solution and its different variations, if any, using multiple structural and behavioural views, and expose the encapsulated functionality through a three-part interface: a *variation*, a *customization* and a *usage* interface. Concerns can reuse other concerns, and model composition techniques are used to create complex models in which these concerns are intertwined. In such a context, specifying the composition of the models is a non-trivial task, in particular when it comes to specifying the composition of behavioural models. This is the case for CORE message views, which define behaviour using sequence diagrams. In this paper we describe how we added an additional behavioural view to CORE – the *state view* – that specifies the allowed invocation protocol of class instances. We discuss why Protocol Modelling, a compositional modelling approach based on state diagrams, is an appropriate notation to specify such a state view, and show how we added support for protocol modelling to the CORE metamodel. Finally, we demonstrate how to model using the new state views by means of an example, and explain how state views can be exploited to model-check the correctness of behavioural compositions.

## 1 Introduction

*Model-Driven Engineering* (MDE) [21] is a unified conceptual framework in which software development is seen as a process of *model production, refinement* and *integration*. Models are built representing different views of a software system using different *formalisms*, i.e., modelling languages. The formalism is chosen in such a way that the model concisely expresses the properties of the system that are important at the current level of abstraction. During development, high-level specification models are refined or combined with other models to include more solution details, such as the chosen architecture, data structures, algorithms, and finally even platform and environment-specific execution properties. The manipulation of models is achieved by means of *model transformations*. Model refinement and integration continues until a model (or code) is produced that can be executed.

© Springer International Publishing Switzerland 2015
E. Roubtsova et al. (Eds.): BM-FA 2009-2014, LNCS 6368, pp. 250–278, 2015.
DOI: 10.1007/978-3-319-21912-7_10

MDE, while successful in many areas, still faces important challenges in practise. One main challenge is *model reuse* [25]: typically, models for a system under development are created from scratch, rather than reusing already existing models. This makes modelling more cumbersome than coding, since most modern programming languages offer extensive libraries that facilitate code reuse. Furthermore, models of complex applications tend to grow in size, to a point where even individual views are not readily understood or analyzable anymore. This is particularly true for behavioural models that are executable or used as source models for code generation, since they need to specify the behaviour in great detail.

Concern-Oriented REuse (CORE) is a multi-view modelling approach aimed at addressing the reuse and scalability issues of model-driven engineering. CORE extends MDE with best practices from research in both software product lines and aspect-orientation to define broad units of reuse, so-called *concerns*. These concerns specify the essence of a design solution and its different potential variations using multiple structural and behavioural views. The modelling notations used within a concern offer aspect-oriented features that make it possible to separate and modularize crosscutting properties and functionality. Currently, CORE incorporates feature models, goal models, class diagrams, sequence diagrams, and – thanks to the research described in this paper – protocol state machines, all with aspect-oriented extensions.

Concerns can easily reuse other concerns thanks to their three-part interface (a *variation*, a *customization* and a *usage* interface), thus creating concern hierarchies with complex dependencies. Syntactic or semantic model composition techniques [20] are used to flatten concern hierarchies and create complex models in which the concerns are intertwined that can then be executed or from which code is generated.

Specifying this composition is a non-trivial task, in particular when it comes to specifying the composition of behaviour. Structural composition of class diagrams in CORE boils down to merging of model elements. For two classes, for instance, this yields a new class that has the properties from both of the merged classes. Experience shows that the symmetric merge operation is conceptually easy to master by modellers.

Behavioural composition of sequence diagrams in CORE is asymmetric in nature. One sequence diagram can invoke an operation that is defined by another sequence diagram, which means that the weaver has to insert the behaviour of the called operation into the sequence diagram that made the call. Furthermore, aspect message views can modify the behaviour of a sequence diagram by adding additional behaviour before and/or after the already existing sequence of interactions. Understanding the resulting behaviour becomes tricky, in particular if the different behavioural specifications are scattered in multiple models. Also, as for all asymmetric approaches, the order of composition matters in the case where several aspect models want to add behaviour at the same place.

The complexity of understanding aspect dependencies and interactions, unwanted or wanted, has been a subject of study for many years now [18], and recognized as a major problem in aspect-oriented software development. This paper presents how we integrated protocol modelling (PM) [15] into CORE to allow the modeller to specify operation invocation protocols for class instances. We present some important properties that make PM an adequate notation for expressing state views in CORE design models, and show how we integrated a restricted form of PM into the CORE metamodel. We then discuss how this restricted PM can be used by a modeller to specify state views, and how it can be exploited by our TouchCORE tool [1,2] to perform consistency checking of behavioural specifications that cross model boundaries.

The remainder of the paper is structured as follows. Section 2 reviews some of the most important concepts of CORE. Section 3 enumerates the requirements that a modelling notation needs to fulfill in order to be useful in the context of CORE. Section 4 shows how we introduced a restricted form of PM into the CORE metamodel. Section 5 discusses how we envision modellers to use our new state views within CORE by means of the AspectOPTIMA [10] case study. Section 6 elaborates how the PM approach satisfies our requirements. Section 7 summarizes related work, and the last section draws some conclusions.

## 2    Background on CORE

In contrast to model-driven engineering's focus on models, the main unit of modularization, abstraction, construction, and reasoning in concern-driven software development (CCD) is the *concern*.

A concern is any domain of interest to a software engineer. It can (but does not have to) be a crosscutting concern as advocated by aspect-oriented software development. A concern is a unit of modularization that encapsulates a *set of models* describing all properties of that concern required to sufficiently understand and use the concern. Typically, the models within a concern span multiple phases of software development and levels of abstraction. The models are built using the most appropriate modelling formalisms to express the properties of the concern that are relevant at each level of abstraction. Consequently, a concern is typically described by many modelling notations, which may be object-oriented in nature, but typically also need to offer other language mechanisms (e.g., aspect-oriented features) in order to properly handle the crosscutting nature of certain properties encapsulated within a concern. Finally, a concern also encapsulates all relevant variations/choices that are available/encapsulated within a concern, together with guidance on how to choose among those variations.

The key concept of concern-orientation promoting modularity is the *three-part interface* [3] that every concern must provide:

- The *Variation Interface* describes the available variations of the concern and the impact of different variants on high-level goals, qualities, and non-functional requirements. The variations of a concern are represented with a *feature model* [7] (described in more detail in Subsect. 2.1) that specifies the individual features a concern offers, as well as their dependencies. The impact of choosing a feature on soft-goals and system qualities is specified with goal models [6].

– The *Customization Interface* describes how a chosen variant can be adapted to the needs of a specific application. Each variant of a concern is described as generally as possible to maximize reusability. Therefore, some elements in the concern are only *partially* specified and need to be related or complemented with concrete modelling elements of the application that intends to reuse the concern. The customization interface is hence used when a specific variant of a reusable concern is *composed* with the application.

– The *Usage Interface* describes how the application can finally access the structure and behaviour provided by the concern.

## 2.1   Designing a Concern

Building a concern is a non-trivial, time consuming task, typically done by or in consultation with a domain expert; it requires a deep understanding of the nature of the concern to be able to identify and specify all *features* of a concern. In CORE, this is done with feature models (see Subsect. 2.1.1). Once identified, each feature of a concern has to be realized, i.e., the structure and behaviour of the functionality it encapsulates needs to be specified. In CORE, this is done with Reusable Aspect Models (RAM) [9,12], an aspect-oriented multi-view modelling notation based on UML class and sequence diagrams (see Subsect. 2.1.2).

### 2.1.1   Feature Model

The features of a concern include all prominent or distinctive user-visible aspects, qualities and characteristics related to the concern. Once identified, the concern designer summarizes all relevant variations of the functionality pertaining to a concern, as well as all extensions of the functionality, with a *feature model* [7]. Feature models specify the relationships and dependencies that exist between features effectively and express them visually as a tree with different parent-child relationships (*mandatory, optional, xor* and *or*) and cross-feature dependencies (*requires* and *excludes*) that are not limited to just parent-child relationships.

Figure 1 shows the feature model of a low-level software design concern called *Association*. It occurs very frequently in object-oriented designs that an object of class A needs to be associated with other objects of class B. Implementing associations with multiplicity 0..1 or 1 is easy, since it simply requires the class A to store a reference to an instance of class B. Implementing an association where the upper bound of the multiplicity is greater than 1, e.g., 0..*, can be done in many ways, and it is the job of a designer to determine the most appropriate way. Typically, the design has to introduce an intermediate collection data structure that stores the instances of B and refer to it from within class A. Operations need to be provided that add and remove instances of B from the collection contained in the object of class A.

What kind of collection to use depends on the functional requirements of the association. For example, an {ordered} association has to be designed with

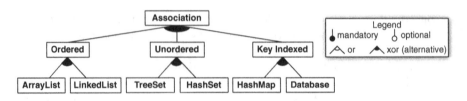

**Fig. 1.** *Association* concern feature model

a collection that orders the elements it contains, e.g., a queue (FIFO), a stack (LIFO), or a priority queue (sorted using some criteria). A qualified association has to be designed with some sort of dictionary or map that allows the retrieval of objects by means of a key. Furthermore, an abstract data structure may have many different internal implementations. For example, a queue can be structured internally as an array or a linked list, the choice of which affects the algorithms for insertion, deletion, and iteration. This ultimately impacts the non-functional properties of the application, e.g., memory usage and performance, which are expressed by means of the impact model (see Subsect. 2.1.5).

### 2.1.2    Realizing Features

A concern can encapsulate complex functionality; however, this complexity is decomposed into several features that each modularize a coherent part of that functionality. The root feature of a concern, for instance, encapsulates structural and behavioural properties that are always present. Optional features modularize structure and behaviour that is only relevant when that particular feature of the concern is chosen.

In CORE, a feature is realized by a structural view (class diagram) and one or more message views (sequence diagrams). The class and sequence diagram notation used are extended with aspect-oriented features as described in the Reusable Aspect Models (RAM) approach [9,12]. This makes it possible for the realization models of one feature to augment the structure and behaviour of the realization models of their ancestor features.

Concretely, if feature $A$ is the parent of feature $B$, then the model *BReal* that realizes feature $B$ extends the model *AReal* that realizes the feature $A$. Because $B$ is a sub-feature of $A$, the concern designer's intent is to add additional structural and/or behavioural model elements to *AReal* that provide *additional, alternative* or *complementary* properties to what already exists in *AReal*. By default, *BReal* has full visibility of all elements visible in *AReal*. As a result, *BReal* can use the structure and behaviour provided by *AReal* when needed. Furthermore, any model elements used in *BReal* that have the same name as an existing model element in *AReal* are considered to be the same, i.e., their properties are going to be merged by the TouchCORE tool using the weaving algorithms defined in [9] to produce a "woven" model that realizes both features. This allows *BReal* to augment the *customization* and *usage interface* of *AReal* with additional structure and behaviour.

### 2.1.3   Structural View – Class Diagrams

To realize a feature, the concern designer specifies in the structural view the classes relevant to the feature, together with their attributes and operations, as well as any associations among classes. The notation used is UML class diagrams, with the additional possibility of marking classes, attributes and operations as *partial* by prefixing their name with a vertical bar: '|'. Partial model elements are included in the concern's customization interface, and designate model elements that are *general* from the point of view of the current concern, which means that they must be mapped to application-specific model elements before the concern can be used.

Because a concern is split into features, the structural view of a feature is of reasonable size (typically containing 1–6 classes with 1–10 public operations each). As a result, the complexity of a concern is split into several models that usually fit into the limited active *working memory* of a human [16]. This makes the elaboration, understanding and evolution of the models involved in the realization of the feature easy and less error prone [24] than if the entire concern model had to be specified in one model.

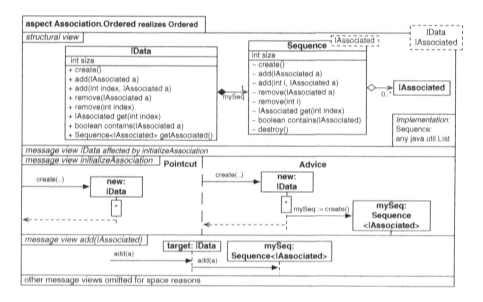

**Fig. 2.** CORE-RAM model realizing *Ordered* of the *Association* concern

The top part of Fig. 2 shows the structural view of a CORE-RAM model that realizes the *Ordered* feature of the *Association* concern shown in Fig. 1. The structural view describes the structural design of an ordered association between two classes with a multiplicity of 0..*. The structural view defines a partial class |Data, which uses a Sequence to link an instance of |Data to many instances of the partial class |Associated in an ordered way. The class Sequence refers to a Java implementation of java.util.List.[1]

|Data and |Associated are partial classes, i.e., incomplete classes (highlighted by a vertical bar '|') that must be mapped to another class whenever this feature is used within another concern. These classes are partial since at this point it is not yet known what actual application classes will need to be associated with each other. All partial classes (and operations) are part of the customization interface of a CORE model: any model that wants to use the *Ordered* feature of the *Association* concern must map |Data and |Associated to two of its own classes.

In CORE, there are four types of visibility modifiers for operations: public (+), protected (#), private (-) and concern-private (~). All public operations are part of the usage interface of a CORE model, i.e., they are the operations that another model can invoke to trigger the behaviour realized by the feature. Protected operations can only be invoked from within the same class or subclass, private operations can only be invoked from within the same class, and concern-private operations can be called only by classes included in the same concern.

### 2.1.4   Message View – Sequence Diagrams

Message views describe the behaviour of the feature being modelled. There is one message view for each public operation defined by a class in the structural view. Each message view describes the sequencing of message interchanges that occur between instances of classes of the concern when providing the functionality offered by the public operation.

In the *Association<Ordered>* model, the class |Data has eight public operations. All these operations involve interactions with an instance of the class Sequence. For space reasons, Fig. 2 only shows the message view for the constructor of |Data (create) and one of the add operations. The add operation illustrates how the call is forwarded to the Sequence class. Because the behaviour of the constructor of |Data is not known yet, it is advised using an *aspect message view* to initialize the Sequence class. The advice of initializeAssociation describes that after the behaviour of the specific constructor, the Sequence is created and assigned to mySeq.

### 2.1.5   Impact Model

After realizing all the features of a concern, the concern designer has to specify the impact that the realization of each feature has on soft goals and system qualities. In CORE, this is done with impact models, which are based on goal modelling as defined by GRL [6]. For instance, the choice of *ArrayList* might provide better access performance than *LinkedList*. However, *ArrayList* uses more memory than *LinkedList*. Further details on how to define impact models are provided in [3].

---

[1] TouchCORE, the CORE tool, allows the reuse of existing classes provided by the programming language or frameworks being used.

## 2.2   Reusing Concerns

Once a concern has been designed, the expert knowledge and solutions encapsulated within can be reused whenever possible. While designing a concern is challenging, time consuming and requires in-depth domain expertise, reusing an existing concern is simple, and involves three steps:

1. A *concern user* must first *select the feature(s)* with the best impact on relevant soft-goals and system qualities from the variation interface of the concern based on the provided impact analysis. Based on this configuration, the TouchCORE tool then merges the models that realize the selected features to yield a new model of the concern corresponding to the desired configuration.
2. Next, the *concern user* has to adapt the generated concern realization model to the application context by mapping all customization interface elements, i.e., the model elements designated by a '|' prefix, to application-specific model elements.
3. Finally, the *concern user* can use the functionality provided by the selected concern feature's usage interface within his own application models. This typically consists of instantiating classes provided by the concern, and invoking their public operations from within the application-specific message views.

# 3   Requirements for Concern-Oriented Specification of Invocation Protocols

Specifying complex behaviour of a concern by composing several partial behaviours described in multiple message views is a non-trivial and error-prone task. Aspect message views can augment behaviour defined in other message views to include additional control flow directives and operation invocations. Furthermore, if several aspect message views are applied to the same base behaviour, the order in which the message views are applied usually changes the resulting behaviour.

In order to help the concern designer in defining correct behavioural specifications that extend the behaviour of parent realization models and to help the concern user to correctly invoke functionality provided by reused concerns, we decided to introduce an additional behavioural view into CORE-RAM that allows the concern designer to specify operation invocation protocols for the classes encapsulated within a concern. Using those protocol models, model checkers can verify that the behavioural specifications expressed in the sequence diagrams within a concern as well as the behavioural specifications obtained by composing models of reused concerns with the application model are valid, i.e., they do not violate any of the protocols defined for any of the features as well as for the application. This makes it possible to detect unwanted and incorrect behaviour resulting from feature and concern interactions and erroneous composition specifications.

In Subsect. 3.1 we list the requirements that a modelling notation needs to fulfill in order to be useful in the context of concern-oriented modelling. Then, in

Subsect. 3.2 we briefly present the *Protocol Modelling* approach (PM), and show how we adapted it to fit our needs. Finally, in Subsect. 3.3 we highlight the key differences between protocol machines and state views.

### 3.1  Requirements for the Protocol Specification Notation

Based on experience gained from creating several software design concerns with CORE-RAM, the notation for expressing protocols must have the following properties:

1. **Expressiveness:** In CORE-RAM, the structural view presents the classes together with the operations they offer, and the message views present the interaction between objects when one of the public operations is invoked. This does not convey complete information on the order in which operations can be invoked on object instances. The notation we are looking for should support the specification of such invocation protocols, i.e., it has to be possible to state when an operation is allowed to be executed, and when it is forbidden.
2. **Conciseness:** The notation should be capable of specifying invocation protocols of class instances in a straightforward and concise way. This requirement is important to reduce accidental complexity [26].
3. **Diversity:** The notation should not be similar to sequence diagrams. This will force the modeller who is specifying the protocols to look at the design concern from a different point of view from how they specified the behaviour of the operations with sequence diagrams.
4. **Modularity:** To be useful in the context of concern-orientation, the modelling notation needs to be able to modularize the protocol of classes that belong to a feature of the concern. It should be possible to specify the protocols for the classes within a feature in isolation from the protocols of other classes of the concern.
5. **Composition:** Since a modeller can elaborate a complex design concern by composing multiple CORE-RAM feature realization models, the modelling notation for specifying protocols must support composition. Whether a child feature extends properties of parent features, or whether concerns reuse other concerns and therefore customize the realization model of the reused concern to their specific application, the protocols for object instances can change.

   To illustrate the kind of protocol compositions that the notation must support, imagine the following example: Feature $A$ is the parent of feature $B$ in concern $R$. The concern designer of $R$ creates the realization model *BReal* that realizes feature $B$ and extends the model *AReal* that realizes the feature $A$. The concern user of $R$ selects $A$, and therefore customizes the model *AReal* by mapping its customization interface to model elements in the application-specific model *App* that he is building.

   The composition operator(s) of the protocol notation must support:
   (a) **Adding New Operations:** Both the concern user (in *App*) and the concern designer (in *BReal*) might define new operations, which need to be integrated by composition with the protocol of the classes in *AReal*.

In case of customization, the *public protocol* of classes in *A Real* need to be integrated with the protocol of classes in *App*. In the case of model extension, the *complete protocol* of *A Real* needs to be integrated with the complete protocol of *BReal*.

(b) **Adding Constraints:** Both the concern user and the concern designer might need to define additional constraints on the protocol of *A Real*. It should therefore be possible to restrict the public or the complete protocol of *A Real*, respectively, by forbidding the execution of an operation in certain cases.

(c) **Coupling Protocols:** A CORE-RAM model can depend on multiple other models. For example, *BReal* can both extend *A Real* and also reuse another concern *C*. In that case, it should be possible for the concern designer of *BReal* to specify a coupling between the protocols of *A Real* and *C* in the case where classes from *A Real* and *C* are mapped to the same class in *BReal*.

6. **Verification:** The protocol modelling notation should be appropriate for:

(a) **Verifying Internal Consistency** of CORE-RAM Models: It should be possible to verify that a *concern designer* is specifying the behaviour provided by the CORE-RAM model that realizes a feature in a consistent way, i.e., that there are no contradictions between the specified object invocation protocols and the interactions between objects specified in the message views.

(b) **Verifying Usage Consistency** for concern reuses: It should be possible to verify that a *concern user* is calling the public operations provided by the customized CORE-RAM model of a reused concern in the right order. In other words, the notation should support the definition of a *public protocol*.

(c) **Verifying Increment Consistency** for CORE-RAM models that extend parent realization models: It should be possible to verify that a *concern designer* that extends a CORE-RAM model realizing a parent feature is calling the operations provided by the parent in the right order. In other words, the notation should support the definition of a complete protocol that includes *public*, *concern-private* and *private* operations.

(d) **Verifying Composition Consistency** for woven CORE-RAM models: To verify that the concern designer or concern user have specified the behavioural compositions correctly, it should be possible to verify that all scenarios specified within woven message views are acceptable according to the combined protocol specifications of each model.

## 3.2   Specifying Protocols in a Concern-Oriented Way

Historically, protocols have been defined using state-based notations such as finite automata. State diagrams in general are also significantly different from sequence diagrams, which satisfies requirement 3. We therefore investigated several state-based aspect-oriented approaches, including HiLa [27] and the framework designed by Elrad et al. [4] (details on these approaches and their limitations for expressing protocols are given in Sect. 7). We ended up using the *Protocol Modelling* notation (PM) [15], which was specifically designed for modelling protocols and comes with a formally defined composition operator. In CORE-RAM, protocol models that specify invocation protocols are elaborated within separate *state views* (SV), one for each class that is present in the structural view.

The PM approach is based on the concept of a "Protocol Machine", a reusable behavioural component of the model that can either ignore, accept or refuse events that are presented to it. By associating a protocol machine with each class in a CORE-RAM model, we can therefore specify invocation protocols for all instances. This satisfies requirement 1. The PM approach is modular: a protocol model of a system is composed of a set of protocol machines and each machine describes a partial behaviour. This satisfies requirement 4. PM supports a highly compositional style of modelling; the partial behaviours are composed together to create the behaviour of the full system using a parallel composition operator (P || Q) as defined by Hoare in the Communicating Sequential Processes (CSP) approach [5]. CSP || composition has the advantage of being a well-defined and understood concept, and it enables the modeller to perform local reasoning on models. Furthermore, it gives the modeller the ability to deduce the properties of the whole system from the knowledge of the behaviour of the composed protocols [13].

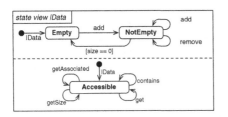

(a) Orthogonal State Machines          (b) Single State Machine

**Fig. 3.** State view for the |Data class in *Ordered*

Figure 3a shows how we used PM to describe the protocol of the |Data class of the *Association<Ordered>* CORE-RAM model shown in Fig. 2. The state view of |Data has two state machines. The first one is describing the fact that calling an **add** operation changes the state of a |Data object from *Empty* to *NotEmpty,* and that **remove** operations should only be called after at least one **add** was invoked. Also, when removing the last |Associated object from the sequence of objects, the state of the |Data instance changes back to *Empty.* The second state machine describes the protocol for the getter and query operations. Since they do not alter the state of the object when called, there are no restrictions specified on their protocol. This is a great example on how PM supports conciseness (requirement 2). Each state machine is simple: it only focuses on operation invocations and how they alter the object's logical state. To obtain the complete protocol for |Data instances, the modeller can apply the CSP operator mentally on the two state machines, which yields the composed state machine shown in Fig. 3b. Notice that the state view with two state machines, even for a simple class such as |Data, is easier to understand than the more cumbersome composed state view.

### 3.3    Differences Between PM and State Views

PM is a powerful technique that was designed for a slightly different purpose. While our requirements are clearly focussed on documentation and verification, the goals of PM include system interaction modelling, protocol execution simulation, test and code generation. For that reason, we decided to adapt the main ideas of PM within CORE-RAM, but to omit some of the advanced features that we do not currently have a need for. In summary, the differences between the original PM approach and how we are currently using it in CORE-RAM are:

- While PM models specify any general event interchange, we only focus on modelling operation invocations.
- PM focusses on modelling interactions with a system, and therefore presents all the state machines of a system together. Consequently, all events are global (to the system being modelled), so they need to have unique names. To obtain the complete interaction protocol of the system, all state machines are composed with each other. In the case of a CORE-RAM model, only state machines that are contained in the same state view are related to each other (and logically composed with each other). Additional state view relationships are created when classes from different aspects are mapped together, which results in a logical composition of all the state machines that the respective views contain. Because of that, the events in CORE-RAM are not global to the whole system; they only need to be unique within all state views that are describing protocols of the same class. For example, the state view of |Data in Fig. 3 is composed of two state machines separated by a dashed line. These state machines are related to each other since they are in the same state view and CSP composition is logically applied to them. Conversely, the state machines of the state view |Data and those of Sequence (not shown in this paper) are independent, since they describe the behaviour of objects that are instances of different classes.
- PM introduces a new type of state – the *derived state* – which replaces transition guards. The main advantage of derived states is that they can be reused by different state machines, unlike guards, which are attached to transitions. Also, derived states offer the possibility to disallow events that could lead the system into an undesired state. For example, a derived state could be used to specify that a withdraw event should not be accepted on a bank account object if it would lead to a negative balance. So far, we did not need such expressive power in our case studies with CORE-RAM.
- Event abstraction in PM is realized by using special events called *generic events*. This kind of event is used to abstract away the difference between

events that have the same effect to enable reuse of existing protocol machines in different contexts [14]. In the case of CORE-RAM, a similar kind of protocol reuse is achieved when renaming an operation in an instantiation directive.

## 4  Integrating PM into CORE-RAM

This section describes how we integrated our customized version of PM into CORE by extending the CORE-RAM metamodel.

The structural view and message view in CORE-RAM are based on *class diagrams* and *sequence diagrams* as defined by the *Unified Modelling Language (UML)* [17]. The metamodel for these two CORE-RAM views is, however, considerably simplified compared to the UML metamodel, for instance, [22] describes how this was achieved for message views. Following the same idea, we studied the metamodel for PM and looked at the UML metamodel for state diagrams and how it is integrated with UML class and sequence diagrams. Based on the integration strategy outlined in [23], we then defined a simplified metamodel for CORE-RAM state views as presented in the following subsections.

### 4.1  Current Metamodel of CORE

Before discussing the state view metamodel, an overview of the current metamodel of CORE-RAM is presented so that the reader can understand what existing model elements the state view metamodel can reuse/reference.

**Overview.** The unit of modelling in CORE is a *concern*. *COREConcerns* contain at least two *COREModels*, a feature model and an impact model. The feature and impact model part of the CORE metamodel, however, is not shown here for space reasons. For this paper, the most important model is the *RAMAspect*, which contains all other model elements that realize a feature directly or indirectly (see Fig. 4). An aspect is a *CORENamedElement* that has beside its *StructuralView* and the *AbstractMessageViews* many *Instantiations*. An *Instantiation* describes a dependency on some other aspect (which can either be a customization, if the instantiation is part of a *COREModelReuse*, or an extension, if the aspect extends an aspect that realizes a parent feature). The instantiation contains *COREMappings*, that describe which element from the external aspect is mapped to an element in the current aspect. *ClassifierMapping* and *OperationMapping* describe mappings for classes and operations, respectively.

**Structural View.** The *StructuralView* represents the class diagram and its basic structure, and its metamodel is shown in Fig. 5. This view contains a list of *Classifier* and *Association*. *Classifier* is a *Type*, i.e., an abstract class that has a name and contains a list of operations. An *Operation* has a name, a return type, may have one or more parameters, and is described by four properties: *abstract*,

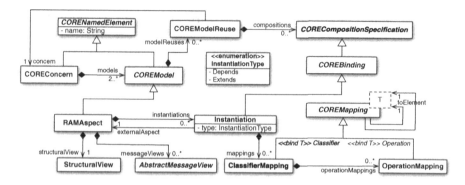

**Fig. 4.** Overview of the CORE-RAM metamodel

*partial, static* and *visibility*. A *Parameter* has a type and a name. *Class* inherits from *Classifier*, has a list of attributes, and is described by two properties: *abstract* and *partial*. *Classifier, Operation* and *Parameter* are all *MappableElements*, meaning that they can be mapped when customizing or extending another aspect.

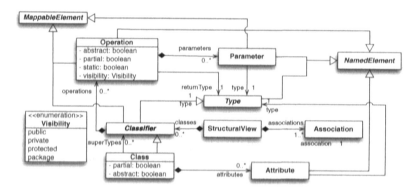

**Fig. 5.** Structural view metamodel

**Message View.** The *MessageView* represents the sequence diagram and an excerpt of its general structure is shown in Fig. 6. The sequence diagrams used in CORE-RAM, unlike UML sequence diagrams, describe only interchanges of messages in the form of operation calls. A *RAMAspect* can contain more than one *MessageView*. The latter is specified for a specific *Operation* (coming from the structural view) and contains the specification of the operation's behaviour. However this is not mandatory, because partial operations don't specify behaviour. *Interaction* describes the actual behaviour in the form of operation invocations. For this purpose it contains, besides other entities, at least one *Message*.

One of the properties of a *Message* is its return value, and this information is represented in the form of a *ValueSpecification*. The latter was inspired from the UML *ValueSpecification* which is "an abstract metaclass used to identify a value or values in a model. It may reference an instance or it may be an expression denoting an instance or instances when evaluated" [17].

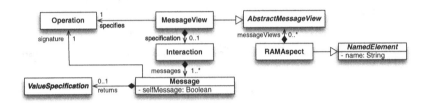

**Fig. 6.** Simplified metamodel of message view

## 4.2   State View Metamodel Based on PM

The CORE-RAM state view metamodel presented in Fig. 7 supports the simplified PM approach as described in Sect. 3. Three entities from the existing CORE-RAM metamodel were reused in the state view metamodel: *Classifier* and *Operation* from the structural view metamodel, and *ValueSpecification* from the message view metamodel.

A *RAMAspect* can now have several *StateViews*, one *StateView* for each *Classifier* in the *StructuralView*. Because state views are mainly used for documentation and verification purpose, we do not make them mandatory. Hence, an aspect can have zero *StateViews* (which also makes the new metamodel backward compatible with the old one). Besides, partial classes sometimes do not have operations, thus a protocol cannot be defined for them. A *StateView* knows for which *Classifier* it specifies a protocol for, and it contains a set of *StateMachines*. A StateMachine has at least one state, exactly one start state and at least one transition.

A *StateMachine* is the entity that defines the reusable protocol component of the model, which can be composed with other *StateMachines* using the CSP ‖ operator. This entity is composed of a set of states, one of which is the start state, and a set of transitions.

A *State* represents a logical state of the object for which we are defining the protocol. A *State* has a name, a set of outgoing *Transitions*, i.e., allowed operation calls from this state, and a set of incoming *Transitions*, i.e., operation calls that led the object to be in this *State*.

A *Transition* connects two states: *startState* designates the state in which the object must be to accept an operation call, and *endState* is the new state of the object after the call has been made. *endState* and *startSate* can refer to the same state, since some operation calls, e.g. getters, do not alter the state of the object. Since in RAM we are only interested in operation call events, a *Transition* has a signature of type *Operation,* i.e., it stands for calls to that operation only. Moreover, a *Transition* has at most one guard, which is a condition that has to evaluate to `true` for the protocol to accept a call to the transition's operation. *Guard* is of type *ValueSpecification,* a component that was borrowed from the *MessageView* metamodel, which in turn was inspired from the UML metamodel.

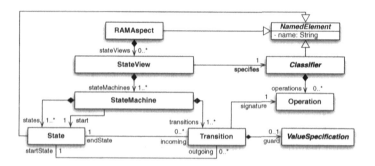

**Fig. 7.** State view metamodel

# 5    AspectOptima

AspectOPTIMA [10, 11] is an aspect-oriented framework providing customizable transaction support to applications. The current *AspectJ* implementation of AspectOPTIMA consists of 42 aspects that modularize and implement critical transaction system features in a reusable way. The aspects can be combined in different ways to create different implementations of transaction models, concurrency control and recovery strategies.

To demonstrate the effectiveness of the new state views, we elaborated a concern-oriented design of parts of the AspectOPTIMA framework. So far, we modelled 5 essential features of the *Transaction* concern: *ExecutionContext,* the root feature, and the optional features *Tracing, OutcomeAware, Checkpointing* and *Recovering.* The feature model is shown on the left side of Fig. 8. Each of the features has been realized in one CORE-RAM model. The dependencies between the realization models are depicted on the right side of Fig. 8. They all directly or indirectly extend the base feature realization model *ExecutionContext.* Also, some of them reuse other concerns, such as *Traceable, Checkpointable,* and *Association.* Indirectly, the *Copyable* and *AccessClassification* concerns are also reused.

For space reasons we can not present the complete CORE-RAM models in this paper. The interested reader can download the complete models together with our tool from [1].

The base feature is called *ExecutionContext,* and its realization model is shown in Fig. 9. The main idea of *ExecutionContext* is that it allows instances of

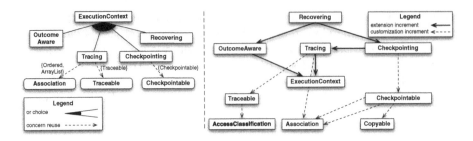

**Fig. 8.** Feature model (left) and CORE-RAM realization models with dependencies (right) of AspectOPTIMA

the class |Participant to enter what is called a Context – an abstraction of an area of computation. When inside, the participant is associated with the context until it leaves the context again. The |Participant class provides operations for entering and leaving, and querying the current context.

An execution context on its own is not very useful. This is why the sub-features of *ExecutionContext* are related to it with an *or* dependency. At least

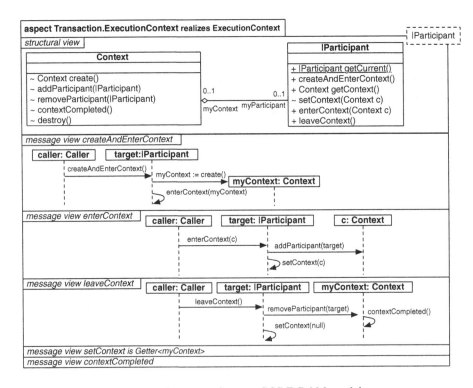

**Fig. 9.** *ExecutionContext* CORE-RAM model

one of the features must be chosen for an execution context to be of use. *Tracing* is one of those sub-features, and its structural view is presented in Fig. 10.

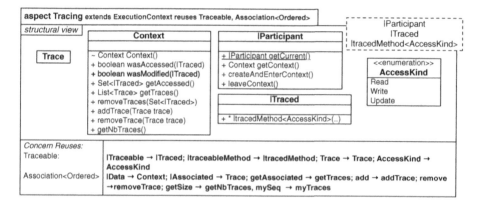

**Fig. 10.** Structural view of the *Tracing* CORE-RAM realization model

*Tracing* depends on several other models to implement its behaviour. First, it is an extension of the *ExecutionContext* model, which already defines the classes `Context` and `|Participant` together with the behaviour that allows a participant to enter and leave a context. *Tracing* adds additional behaviour that ensures that while inside a context, all operation invocations on instances of the class `|Traced` are recorded with the context. Such a feature can be useful for debugging or logging purposes. To achieve the desired behaviour, *Tracing* reuses the *Traceable* concern to provide the behaviour of creating a trace for a method invocation, and also *Association<Ordered>* (see Fig. 2) to associate an ordered list of traces with the context.

In Subsect. 3.1 we listed several consistency verifications that we would like to be able to conduct using our new state views. The following subsections illustrate some of them.

### 5.1  State Views for Public Operations

One requirement was *verifying usage consistency, meaning* that it should be possible to use the state view to ensure that a model user specifies behaviour in the sequence diagrams that call the operations of the customized aspect in the right order. Since a model user can only call public operations of the model it is customizing, it is in this case enough to define a state view that only specifies the protocol for the public operations.

For instance, *Tracing* customizes the *Association<Ordered>* model to enable a `Context` instance to store a list of `Traces`. In this case the *concern designer* of *Tracing*, which is the *concern user* of *Association* needs to understand the public behaviour of the `|Data` class to be able to use it correctly. All invocations of the operations on the `|Data` class must respect the public protocol as specified in Fig. 3. For example, Fig. 11 shows the message view of the operation `removeTraces`. This operation, given a set of `Traced` objects, removes all the traces that belong to these objects from the context. The operations used by this message view, `getTraces` and `removeTrace`, are added to the `Context` class because the reuse instantiation directive maps `|Data` to `Context`, `getAssociation` to `getTraces` and `remove` to `removeTrace` (see reuse compartment in Fig. 10). Since there is no restriction for calling `getAssociated` before `remove` according to the public state view of *Association<Ordered>* (Fig. 3), the message view of `removeTraces` is using the operations of `|Data` class correctly. The CORE modelling tool should detect protocol violations and signal them to the concern users.

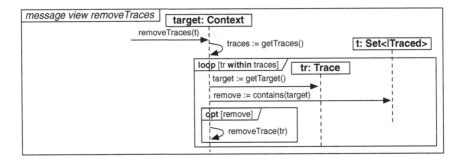

**Fig. 11.** *removeTraces* message view

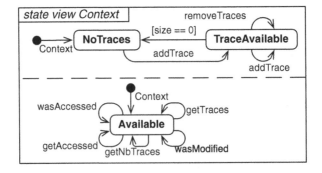

**Fig. 12.** Public SV *Tracing.Context*

Applying the same idea to the next level, the *concern designer* should specify a public state view for *Tracing* that documents the correct use of the concern to the *concern users* and allows the modelling tool to verify its correct use. To model the public state view of the class `Context`, a *model designer* needs to consider the public operations of this class and determine for each operation the possible constraints for calling it. In our case, the major constraint for `Context` is that the operation `removeTraces` can not be called unless a trace was added previously through `addTrace`. Figure 12 describes a public state view for `Context` that expresses this constraint.

## 5.2    Internal State Views

To be able to do a similar verification for model increments, a more elaborate "internal" state view needs to be defined that describes the invocation protocol detailing not only the public, but also the internal operation invocations that are acceptable during the life time of an object. This internal state view should describe how non-public operation invocations relate to public ones and to each other. This makes it possible to *verify increment consistency and composition consistency.*

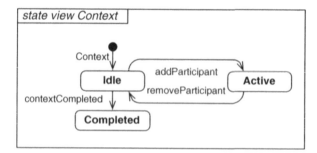

**Fig. 13.** Internal SV *EC.Context*

For example, Fig. 13 shows the state view of the class `Context` of the *Execution-Context* realization model (see structural view in Fig. 9). It states a participant can be added to a context and removed again multiple times in a row, if desired. However, once `contextCompleted` is invoked, no more operation calls are allowed on a context instance. The `Context` state view is an internal state view, since this class does not have any public operations. Because *Tracing* extends *ExecutionContext*, the `Context` class in *Tracing* is mapped to the `Context` class in *ExecutionContext*. The *model designer* of *Tracing* should hence specify any protocol restrictions that should be defined between the operations added to `Context` by *Tracing* and the operations that come from *ExecutionContext*.

One constraint that a `Context` object in *Tracing* must not violate is the fact that the operation `addTrace` should only be called when a participant entered the context, i.e., when the context is in the state *Active* after `addParticipant` is called. Figure 14 shows the state machine that expresses such a behavioural constraint.

Composing the public and the internal state views using CSP composition results in the state view shown in Fig. 15. The composed view can subsequently

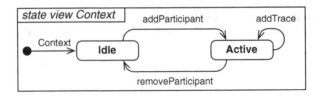

**Fig. 14.** Internal SV of *Tracing.Context*

be used to verify the consistency of message views that were specified in models that reuse or extend *Tracing*.[2] .

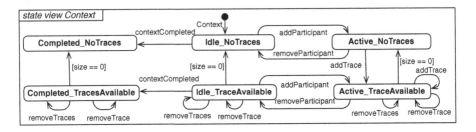

**Fig. 15.** Composed SV of *Context* with features *ExecutionContext* and *Tracing*

## 6   Discussion

This subsection discusses how our new state views satisfy the requirements we detailed in Subsect. 3.1.

**Expressiveness and Diversity:** The structural view in a CORE-RAM model specifies the classes that a feature defines and *what* functionalities they offer. The message views show *how* instances of these classes interact with each other and with objects of other concerns to achieve this functionality. They also show for these scenarios *in what sequence* the operations of an object are called. For example, the *removeTraces* message view (Fig. 11) presents an overview of the interactions between Context, Trace and Set<|Traced> objects when the removeTraces(Set<|Traced>) operation is called, and shows the scenario where getTraces is called before removeTrace(Trace). From a *diversity* perspective, the state views of *Context* (Figs. 12 and 14) complement the message views by giving information about *how* individual objects are to be used, i.e., the

---

[2] For simplicity and readability reasons, the state machine with the getters and query operations from *Association<Ordered>* were not added to Fig. 15. To create the actual woven model it suffices to add to each of the depicted states all self-transitions of the state *Available* from the state view in *Association<Ordered>*.

order in which an object's operations should be called, *from a state perspective.* For example, the fact that `addTrace` should be called after `addParticipant` is invoked is clearly expressed as a constraint in the *Context* state view in Fig. 14. We have so far not encountered a situation in which it was not possible to express a protocol using our new state views.

**Conciseness:** Measuring conciseness of a modelling notation objectively is difficult [19], and we therefore discuss conciseness of the protocol modelling notation only informally. The protocol of the objects can be concisely described using public and private state views. Woven state views that combine the protocol of several models can be generated on demand. To further increase conciseness, we made it optional to specify a protocol for operations that have no effect on the conceptual state of an object. In other words, if no transition is defined for an operation we assume that there is no restriction on its use. Finally, we added generic events to increase conciseness of state views, which can be used to group operations when operations affect the state of an object in the same way. For example, the getters and query operations in *Context* can be replaced by one event that can be called *getters_queries* as follows: *getters_queries =* {*wasAccessed OR getAccessed OR getTraces OR wasModified OR getNbTraces*}. As a result, only one transition needs to be shown in the state view, where otherwise five transitions with the same source and target states would have to be shown.

**Modularity:** CSP ∥ composition allows the concern designer to specify the state views *for each feature within a concern independently*, and compose them together to form the complete description of the protocol of a class. Likewise, protocols of classes within a concern are modelled independently, and *the concern user can specify how to combine the protocols of the concern classes with his application classes* when customizing the model during the reuse process. For example, the *Tracing* feature was modelled separately of the *Association* concern, i.e., the protocols for `Context` and ∣`Data` are specified separately, and combined by the concern user by mapping ∣`Data` to `Context`. Modularity can even be exploited within a CORE-RAM model, since *the concern designer can specify the protocol of a class using multiple state machines* if he judges that using one state machine will be too complicated or cumbersome. For example, the getters and query operations of the class `Context` in *Tracing* were modelled in a separate state machine in the public state view to increase readability (see Fig. 12).

**Composition:** The CSP ∥ composition operator offers a straightforward way to support adding of new operations, adding of constraints and coupling of protocols.

- **Adding new operations:** This kind of transformation is easily expressed by adding a new state machine that integrates the new operation into the existing protocol. For example, *Tracing*.`Context` is using the operations of *Association*<*Ordered*>. ∣`Data` to manage the list of `Traces`, and additionally defines a new operation `removeTraces`. This operation affects the conceptual state of

|Data, and therefore needs to be integrated in the protocol defined for |Data. For this reason, a state machine was defined (Fig. 12) to clarify the relationship between the behaviour of |Data and the new added operation. Other operations were added, i.e., wasAccessed, wasModified and getAccessed, but since they do not affect the state of a |Data object they were added to the queries state machine. Notice that Context of *Tracing* is extending the behaviour of Context coming from *ExecutionContext* by adding all the operations coming from |Data and all the newly defined operations. To determine the complete protocol of the new, composed Context object, the state views of the three classes, i.e., *ExecutionContext*.Context, *Tracing*.Context and *Association<Ordered>*. |Data are composed.

- **Adding constraints:** CSP || composition works by synchronizing state machines on events that are common in the alphabets of these entities. Regulation of the behaviour of an object by restricting operations is possible due to the ability of a composed state machine (M1 || M2) to refuse an event if M1 or M2 can not process this event in the current state. For instance, the feature *Recovering*, whose structural view is not shown here for space reasons, needs to change the protocol of Context defined in *ExecutionContext*. In EC.Context, a participant can enter a context, leave it, enter it again, and so on, as shown in Fig. 13. In a recovering context, once a participant is added, it has to set the outcome of the context before leaving. Furthermore, once this is done, no participants can be added anymore. Figure 16 shows the protocol defined by *Recovering*, which is composed with the state views of *ExecutionContext*,

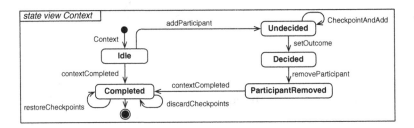

**Fig. 16.** Adding constraints example

*OutcomeAware*, *Checkpointing* and *Tracing*. Once the Context is created and addParticipant, setOutcome and removeParticipant operations are invoked, the context object will be in the state *Idle* in the machine of Fig. 13, and *ParticipantRemoved* in the machine of Fig. 16. According to the rules of PM, it is not allowed for addParticipant to be called again on the object. The machine in *ExecutionContext* allows processing addParticipant, *but* the machine of *Recovering* has the operation in its events but it does not allow processing from the state *ParticipantRemoved*. As a result, addParticipant is rejected by the composition. Only contextCompleted is allowed by the composed protocol.

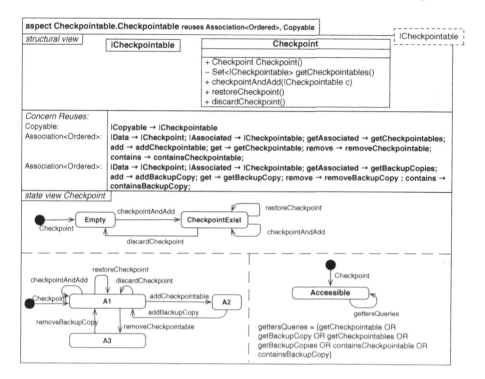

**Fig. 17.** CORE-RAM model of *Checkpointable*

- **Coupling Protocols:** Orchestrating the behaviour of the concerns that a model is extending and depending on is done simply by specifying the common behaviour in a separate state machine. For example, in *Tracing*, the class Context is mapped on the one hand to the class Context in *ExecutionContext* and on the other hand to the class |Data of *Association<Ordered>*. The behaviour of the object |Data is restricted by the behaviour of the object Context of the *ExecutionContext* concern as follows: adding traces should be done only when the Context is active, meaning the operation addTrace (coming from add in *Association<Ordered>*) should only be invoked after the invocation of addParticipant and before that of removeParticipant. The internal state view of Context shown in Fig. 14 presents the state machine needed to specify such an orchestration.

Sometimes orchestrating the behaviour of multiple objects can be tricky. Figure 17 shows the design of a concern called *Checkpointable*. This concern can be used to add fault tolerance to a software application: it provides the functionality to create snapshots of the state of objects and restore the states in case of a failure. The class |Checkpointable represents the object that contains the state that needs to be recoverable and Checkpoint is the class responsible for handling the process. The Checkpoint needs to keep two lists of objects: the first contains references to the original "checkpointed" objects and the second contains the copies of the original objects at a specific moment of their life cycle. Whenever an object is "checkpointed", it is added to the first list and its copy is added to the second list. Therefore, *Checkpointable* needs the functionality offered by *Association<Ordered>* to manage these lists *twice*, and the protocols of the two lists need to be synchronized.

Figure 17 shows the state view of `Checkpoint`. Adding a backup copy should always follow adding a checkpointable, and the same goes for removing. The behaviour of the two |Data objects needs to be orchestrated, and this is described by the bottom left state machine. The operation `checkpointAndAdd` is the public operation responsible for creating the copy and adding both the object and its copy to the lists. Calling this operation includes calling `addCheckpointable` and `addBackupCopy`,[3] which means that, according to the state view of |Data, `removeCheckpointable` and `removeBackupCopy` can be called at this point.

**Verification:** Section 5 discussed in detail how the CORE state views can be used to verify internal consistency, usage consistency, increment consistency and composition consistency.

# 7    Related Work

State transition modelling is an effective concept to capture software systems behaviour and protocols. In this section we describe some approaches that applied aspect-oriented modelling techniques in the context of state transition modelling.

The UML Superstructure document [17] describes several concepts for designing object-oriented systems. This modelling language provides different views to capture the static and dynamic behaviour of a software system. UML class diagrams represent the artifact used to model and describe the structural view of objects. This view is complemented by a state transition modelling artifact inspired from David Harel's statecharts. The document defines a *State Machine Package* where two kinds of state machines are described: *Behaviour State Machines* and *Protocol State Machines*.

Behaviour State Machines are used to specify discrete behaviour of a part of a designed system through finite state transitions. It can be attached to a "behavioured classifier" which is called its context. The latter defines which attributes and operations are defined for this state machine. State machines can have orthogonal regions.

Protocol State Machine is a specialization of Behaviour State Machine. It expresses the usage protocol or lifecycle of a classifier. It specifies the allowed call sequences on the classifier's operations.

In UML, a state machine can be extended, i.e., regions, vertices and transitions can be added and redefined. A simple state can be redefined to a composite state and a composite state can be extended by extending its regions or adding

---

[3] `addCheckpointable` and `addBackupCopy` are the same operation `add` of class |Data as it is shown in the instantiation compartment of the Fig. 17.

new ones. State machine extension was introduced following the example of class specialization. Unlike CORE-RAM, where the general and the specialized state machines can be composed together, the relationship between states that extend other states in UML is not clear. There is no explicit composition defined between state machines belonging to different classifiers, neither is event abstraction or event reinterpretation. Moreover, there is no tool, to our knowledge, that supports state machine inheritance.

The approach by Mahoney et al. [4] extends Harel's statecharts to create reusable orthogonal abstract statecharts. In order to be able to take advantage of existing CASE tools, their methodology uses UML semantics without adding any major extensions. The approach performs implicit weaving of statecharts based on orthogonality and event propagation. This makes it possible to adapt existing behaviour by adding aspects orthogonally, thus extending the model without impacting any of the other orthogonal regions. The approach also defines design guidelines that, when followed, enable traceability of crosscutting requirements from the design to code.

The main drawback of the approach that was noticed by the authors was the tight coupling between the core and the aspect statechart due to the explicit event propagation performed by the developer. To avoid such coupling, the authors introduced the concept of event reinterpretation, i.e., high-level declarations allowing an event in one statechart to be treated as a completely different event in another statechart.

A Java framework was implemented as a proof of concept that permits the translation of a statechart design into skeleton code for a class. However, the authors do not provide an integrated and concrete model view where aspects would already be woven into base classes.

Zhang et al. [27] propose the *High-Level Aspects for UML State Machines (HiLA)* approach, in which they significantly extend UML state machines with aspect-oriented modelling techniques. They use state machines to specify behaviour of base machines and aspect machines, which can be parameterized using UML template parameters similar to what is done during CORE-RAM customization. They provide several asymmetric pointcut-advice composition mechanisms that enable aspects to disallow and restrict transitions, describe mutual exclusion between two states in orthogonal regions and coordinate multiple state machines. This approach, while powerful for specifying detailed behavioural designs, is not adequate for our needs because of the complex composition semantics of the different composition operators.

## 8   Conclusion

In concern-driven software development, concerns are modelled separately, and model composition is used to create complex models in which these concerns are tightly coupled. In such a context, specifying the composition of the models is a non-trivial task, in particular when it comes to specifying the composition of behavioural models.

In this paper, we provided insight on the benefits that modelling of invocation protocols can have when used in combination with behavioural specifications expressed using sequence diagrams. Concretely, we showed how we applied this technique to augment the CORE approach, which expresses the structure of software design concerns within structural views based on class diagrams and the behaviour of software design concerns using sequence diagrams, with additional state views that describe invocation protocols. We detailed why Protocol Modelling, a compositional modelling approach based on state diagrams, is an ideal notation to specify such a protocol view, and show how we added support for protocol modelling to the CORE metamodel and the TouchCORE tool [1]. We explained that the new state views can be used to assist both the concern designer as well as the concern user in the model composition specification task. We outlined how the protocol view can be exploited to verify the correctness of compositions.

To demonstrate the effectiveness of our approach and to analyze its strengths and limits, we started the concern-oriented design of the AspectOPTIMA case study. The paper partially presented some of the features of the *Transaction* concern. The complete models of the *Transaction* concern that includes *ExecutionContext*, *OutcomeAware*, *Tracing*, *Checkpointing* and *Recovering* can be downloaded together with our *TouchCORE* tool [1]. In the near future, we are planning to complete the design of the AspectOPTIMA case study to include the remaining features needed for basic transaction support with optimistic and pessimistic concurrency control: *Nested*, *2-Phase-Locking*, *Deferring* and *Validating*. Finally, to fully support *Open Multithreaded Transactions* [8], we also need to add *Collaborative*, *EntrySynchronizing*, *ExistSynchronizing*, *SpawnSupporting*, *Closable* and *OutcomeVoting*.

# References

1. TouchCORE Tool. http://touchcore.cs.mcgill.ca
2. Al Abed, W., Bonnet, V., Schöttle, M., Yildirim, E., Alam, O., Kienzle, J.: TouchRAM: a multitouch-enabled tool for aspect-oriented software design. In: Czarnecki, K., Hedin, G. (eds.) SLE 2012. LNCS, vol. 7745, pp. 275–285. Springer, Heidelberg (2013)
3. Alam, O., Kienzle, J., Mussbacher, G.: Concern-oriented software design. In: Moreira, A., Schätz, B., Gray, J., Vallecillo, A., Clarke, P. (eds.) MODELS 2013. LNCS, vol. 8107, pp. 604–621. Springer, Heidelberg (2013)
4. Elrad, T., Bader, A., Mahoney, M., Aldawud, O.: Using aspects to abstract and modularize statecharts. In: 5th Aspect-Oriented Modeling Workshop in Conjunction with UML 2004 (2004)
5. Hoare, C.: Communicating Sequential Processes. Prentice-Hall International, London (1985)
6. International Telecommunication Union (ITU-T). Recommendation Z.151 (10/12): User Requirements Notation (URN) - Language Definition, October 2012
7. Kang, K., Cohen, S., Hess, J., Novak, W., Peterson, S.: Feature-oriented domain analysis (FODA) feasibility study. Tech. Rep. CMU/SEI-90-TR-21, Software Engineering Institute, CMU (1990)

8. Kienzle, J.: Open Multithreaded Transactions – A Transaction Model for Concurrent Object-Oriented Programming. Kluwer Academic Publishers, Dordrecht (2003)
9. Kienzle, J., Al Abed, W., Klein, J.: Aspect-oriented multi-view modeling. In: Proceedings of the 8th International Conference on Aspect-Oriented Software Development - AOSD 2009, 1–6 March 2009, pp. 87–98. ACM Press, March 2009
10. Kienzle, J., Duala-Ekoko, E., Gélineau, S.: AspectOPTIMA: A case study on aspect dependencies and interactions. In: Rashid, A., Ossher, H. (eds.) Transactions on AOSD V. LNCS, vol. 5490, pp. 187–234. Springer, Heidelberg (2009)
11. Kienzle, J., Gélineau, S.: AO challenge: implementing the ACID properties for transactional objects. In: Proceedings of the 5th International Conference on Aspect-Oriented Software Development - AOSD 2006, 20–24 March 2006. ACM Press, pp. 202–213, March 2006
12. Klein, J., Kienzle, J.: Reusable aspect models. In: 11th Aspect-Oriented Modeling Workshop, Nashville, TN, USA, 30 September 2007, September 2007
13. McNeile, A., Roubtsova, E.: Composition semantics for executable and evolvable behavioral modeling in MDA. In: BM-MDA 2009 Proceedings of the 1st Workshop on Behaviour Modelling in Model-Driven Architecture, pp. 1–8 (2009)
14. McNeile, A., Roubtsova, E.: Aspect-oriented development using protocol modeling. In: Katz, S., Mezini, M., Kienzle, J. (eds.) Transactions on Aspect-Oriented Software Development VII. LNCS, vol. 6210, pp. 115–150. Springer, Heidelberg (2010)
15. McNeile, A., Simons, N.: Protocol modelling: a modelling approach that supports reusable behavioural abstractions. Softw. Syst. Model. 5(1), 91–107 (2006)
16. Miller, G.: The magical number seven, plus or minus two: some limits on our capacity for processing information. Psycholog. Rev. 63(2), 81 (1956)
17. Object Management Group. Unified Modeling Language: Superstructure (v 2.4.1), December 2011
18. Rashid, A., Ossher, H. (eds.): Transactions on Aspect-Oriented Development (TAOSD VI), vol. 5490. Springer, Heidelberg (2009). Special Issue on Dependencies and Interactions with Aspects
19. Rossi, M., Brinkkemper, S.: Complexity metrics for systems development methods and techniques. Inf. Syst. 21(2), 209–227 (1996)
20. Rumpe, B.: Towards model and language composition. In: Proceedings of the First Workshop on the Globalization of Domain Specific Languages, GlobalDSL 2013, pp. 4–7. ACM, New York (2013)
21. Schmidt, D.C.: Model-driven engineering. IEEE Comput. 39, 41–47 (2006)
22. Schöttle, M.: Aspect-Oriented Behavior Modeling in Practice. M.Sc. Thesis, Department of Computer Science, Karlsruhe University of Applied Sciences, September 2012
23. Schöttle, M., Kienzle, J.: On the challenges of composing multi-view models. In: The GEMOC 2013 Workshop Co-located with the 16th International Conference on Model Driven Engineering Languages and Systems (MODELS 2013), October 2013
24. Sweller, J.: Cognitive load during problem solving: effects on learning. Cogn. Sci. 12(2), 257–285 (1988)
25. Whittle, J.: The truth about model-driven development in industry - and why researchers should care (2012). http://www.slideshare.net/jonathw/whittle-modeling-wizards-2012/

26. Whittle, J., Hutchinson, J., Rouncefield, M., Burden, H., Heldal, R.: Industrial adoption of model-driven engineering: are the tools really the problem? In: Moreira, A., Schätz, B., Gray, J., Vallecillo, A., Clarke, P. (eds.) MODELS 2013. LNCS, vol. 8107, pp. 1–17. Springer, Heidelberg (2013)
27. Zhang, G., Hölzl, M.: HiLA: high-level aspects for UML state machines. In: Ghosh, S. (ed.) MODELS 2009. LNCS, vol. 6002, pp. 104–118. Springer, Heidelberg (2010)

# Author Index

Printed in the United States
By Bookmasters